驻华大使眼中的中国经济

THE CHINESE ECONOMY IN THE EYES OF FOREIGN AMBASSADORS

林建华 主编

北京大学出版社
PEKING UNIVERSITY PRESS

图书在版编目（CIP）数据

驻华大使眼中的中国经济/林建华主编.—北京：北京大学出版社，2007.4

ISBN 978-7-301-12006-4

Ⅰ.驻…　Ⅱ.林…　Ⅲ.经济-中国-文集　Ⅳ.F12-53

中国版本图书馆CIP数据核字(2007)第044075号

书　　名：驻华大使眼中的中国经济
著作责任者：林建华　主编
策 划 编 辑：陈　莉
责 任 编 辑：陈　莉
标 准 书 号：ISBN 978-7-301-12006-4/F·1579
出 版 发 行：北京大学出版社
地　　址：北京市海淀区成府路205号　100871
网　　址：http://www.pup.cn
电　　话：邮购部 62752015　发行部 62750672　编辑部 62752926
出版部 62754962
电 子 邮 箱：em@pup.pku.edu.cn
印　刷　者：北京汇林印务有限公司
经　销　者：新华书店
650毫米×980毫米　16开本　15.75印张　插页14　196千字
2007年4月第1版　2008年5月第2次印刷
定　　价：38.00元

美国驻华大使雷德先生演讲现场

北京大学经济学院副院长孙祁祥教授向美国驻华大使雷德先生颁发纪念册

美国驻华大使雷德先生在北京大学签名留念

美国驻华大使雷德先生与北京大学经济学院部分教师合影

德国驻华大使史丹泽博士演讲现场

德国驻华大使史丹泽博士与北京大学经济学院部分教师合影

北京大学经济学院副院长孙祁祥教授向德国驻华大使史丹泽博士赠送北京大学经济学院纪念鼎

德国驻华大使史丹泽博士与北京大学领导、北京大学经济学院领导会晤

北京大学经济学院副院长孙祁祥教授向时任瑞典驻华大使
雍博瑞博士（2006 年 10 月离任）颁发纪念册

时任瑞典驻华大使雍博瑞博士（2006 年 10 月离任）与北京大学经济学院
部分教师合影

加拿大驻华大使罗岚先生演讲现场

北京大学经济学院副院长孙祁祥教授向加拿大驻华大使罗岚先生赠送北京大学经济学院纪念鼎

加拿大驻华大使罗岚先生（左二）、北京大学副校长吴志攀教授（左一）、北京大学经济学院副院长孙祁祥教授（右一）的合影

加拿大驻华大使罗岚先生与北京大学经济学院部分教师合影

北京大学经济学院副院长孙祁祥教授向时任英国驻华大使
韩魁发爵士(2006 年 1 月离任)颁发纪念册

时任英国驻华大使韩魁发爵士(2006 年 1 月离任)与北京大学经济学院
部分教师合影

时任英国驻华大使韩魁发爵士(2006 年 1 月离任)在纪念册上签名留言

时任英国驻华大使韩魁发爵士(2006 年 1 月离任，左三)、北京大学副校长吴志攀教授(右三)、北京大学经济学院副院长孙祁祥教授(左二)等的合影

北京大学经济学院副院长孙祁祥教授向澳大利亚驻华大使
唐茂思博士赠送礼品

澳大利亚驻华大使唐茂思博士与北京大学经济学院部分教师合影

澳大利亚驻华大使唐茂思博士（左二）、北京大学国际合作部李岩松部长（右一）、北京大学经济学院副院长孙祁祥教授（左一）的合影

瑞士驻华大使马提内利先生及使馆人员与北京大学经济学院部分教师合影

北京大学经济学院副院长孙祁祥教授向瑞士驻华大使马提内利先生颁发纪念册

瑞士驻华大使马提内利先生（左二）、瑞士驻华大使馆文化教育处副主任颜力维先生（右一）、北京大学副校长林建华教授（右二）、北京大学经济学院副院长孙祁祥教授（左一）的合影

北京大学经济学院副院长孙祁祥教授向以色列驻华大使海逸达博士颁发纪念册

北京大学副校长吴志攀教授向以色列驻华大使海逸达博士赠送礼品

北京大学副校长吴志攀教授(左三)接见以色列驻华大使海逸达博士(右三)

以色列驻华大使海逸达博士与北京大学经济学院部分教师合影

编　委　会

序

改革开放以来,中国经济增长取得了举世瞩目的成就。国家统计局的数据表明,1979 年至 2004 年间中国的 GDP 年均增长率为 9.6%, 2005 年 GDP 增加率为 10.2%, 总量突破 18 万亿元。2006 年上半年国内生产总值同比增长 10.9%, 总体经济发展态势良好。随着国际化进程的加快,国际合作日益加强,中国现在是美国的第三大贸易伙伴国,欧盟的第二大贸易伙伴国。可以说,中国已经成为世界经济舞台上一支重要的力量,在国际经济事务中扮演着越来越重要的角色。正如美国驻华大使雷德先生说的,"去年春天(指 2004 年春——笔者注)当温家宝总理指出中国经济过热,政府将采取措施使经济发展放缓时,世界各地的工业原料价格几乎立即下跌。这就是影响力的明证"。

但是我们也应当看到,中国令人鼓舞的经济增长数字背后,也面临着诸多问题:对资源的过度开发,对环境的破坏,社会保障体系不健全,高经济增长与高失业率并存,医疗、教育制度的改革引发的不确定性增加以及人口问题、农村问题等,都是困扰中国经济长期增长的问题。如何促进经济社会协调发展,建立一个可持续发展的和谐社会,不仅是中国政界与学界考虑的问题,也引起了外国政界与学界的广泛关注。

正是为了更好地研究探讨中国经济发展的规律,同时借鉴国外的先进经验,北京大学经济学院和北京大学国际合作部共同举办了"外国驻华大使眼中的中国经济"系列讲座,邀请了多位外国驻华大使到北大纵论中国经济。这个活动旨在从外国政要的视角，阐述中国的经济变化，并结合各国的经验，给中国政策上的建议。同时，像经济学院其他的系列讲座（如"财经高管论坛"或"经济学讲坛"）一样，作为北京大学经济学院教学科研活动重要的辅助手段，该活动对开阔师生的视野，学习用国际化的视角分析、解决中国的经济问题，也具有十分重要的意义。

十分感谢八位驻华大使能够接受邀请，前来北大给我们师生开设讲座。他们依次是美国驻华大使雷德先生（Mr. Clark Randt, Jr.）、德国驻华大使史丹泽博士（Dr. Volker Stanzel）、瑞典驻华大使雍博瑞博士（Dr. Börje Ljunggren），加拿大驻华大使罗岚先生（Mr. Robert Wright），英国驻华大使韩魁发爵士（Sir Christopher Hum），澳大利亚驻华大使唐茂思博士（Dr. Alan Thomas），瑞士驻华大使马提内利先生（Mr. Dante Martinelli）和以色列驻华大使海逸达博士（Dr. Yehoyada Haim）。他们思想的火花，智慧的语言，赢得了北大师生的掌声和尊重。八场精彩演讲构成一组华彩乐章，带来的不仅是一场精神的盛宴，更引发老师和学生深入的思考。请允许我在这里选取一些精彩片断，以飨读者：

"最近，一个著名的美国投资银行家在纽约介绍我的时候说：在我们一生中经历的最重要的事情就是中国的崛起。"——美国驻华大使雷德先生

"（中国经济）迅猛的增长能否继续？德国的工业在这前所未有的激烈竞争环境中还能保持原有的地位吗？"——德国驻华大使史丹泽博士

"社会福利不需要以牺牲经济增长为代价，统计数据也说明了这一点。但我们必须确保所实施的计划是有效率的计划，而不会浪费资源。"——瑞典驻华大使雍博瑞博士

"在过去的五年里，我们两国的双边贸易翻了一番，两国领导人还提出了新的目标，要在2010年使加中贸易额再翻一番。"——加

拿大驻华大使罗岚先生

“伦敦经济学院对与中国建立合作关系的兴趣反映了英国乃至世界的趋势。基本上所有的部门,包括政府、公司和学术机构都认识到他们必须有一个中国策略。”——英国驻华大使韩魁发爵士

“澳大利亚眼中的中国是一个对能源和资源有强劲需求的国家,她推动了世界商品价格,如石油和铁矿石的价格。这种世界价格的增长给澳大利亚一部分地区带来了繁荣。”——澳大利亚驻华大使唐茂思博士

“中国是瑞士在亚洲最大的贸易伙伴。我们也一直在努力加深中瑞在政治、经济、科学、教育、文化和环境等方面的合作关系。”——瑞士驻华大使马提内利先生

“以色列是世界上拥有工程师比率最高的国家,在世界上人均大学程度和学术论文发表的比率也都是最高的。”——以色列驻华大使海逸达博士

我还想借此机会感谢我的同事们。他们是北京大学前副校长郝平教授、副校长吴志攀教授、副校长林建华教授、校长助理兼北京大学国际合作部部长李岩松老师、国际合作部夏红卫副部长、北京大学经济学院刘伟院长、北京大学经济学院副院长孙祁祥教授,他们为这个系列活动的举办和本书的出版做了很多艰苦而细致的工作。感谢他们卓有成效的工作。

谨将此书献给所有为促进中国的国际合作而努力工作的人们!

北京大学校长 许智宏

2006年9月12日于北大

Preface

Since the start of the economic reform, China has made some remarkable achievements in economic development. According to the National Bureau of Statistics of China, during 1979—2004, Chinese gross domestic product (GDP) grew at an average rate of 9.6% annually. In 2005, the GDP growth rate reached 10.2% and the total volume exceeded 18 trillion Chinese RMB. In the first half of 2006, Chinese GDP showed an increase of 10.9% and the overall economic condition was strong and healthy. With increasing extent of globalization, the international economic cooperation between China and foreign countries saw some significant development. Currently, China is the third largest trading partner of the United States and the second largest trading partner of European Union. China has become a significant power in the world economic arena and is playing an increasingly important role in international affairs.

However, we shall also recognize that behind the promising figures of economic growth, China still faces many problems. For example, the over exploitation of the environment and resources, the incomplete social security system, the coexistence of high economic growth and high unemployment, the uncertainties caused by the reforms of health care and education systems, a population that is rapidly aging and the vast rural areas whose development still lags behind. All these problems pose risks to the Chinese economic development in the long run. The question of how to maintain balanced economic and social development and to establish a sustainable harmonious society has drawn wide attention among academia and policy makers both in China and abroad.

In order to better understand Chinese economic development and to learn from other countries' experiences, the School of Economics and the Office of International Relations of Peking University jointly sponsored the lecture series entitled "Chinese Economy in the Eyes of Foreign Ambassadors". This lecture series was intended to give the audience an opportunity to interact with foreign ambassadors who expressed their opinions on Chinese economy from the perspective of foreign politicians and provide suggestions to the Chinese policy makers. In addition, like other lecture series hosted by the School of Economics, for instance, "Chinese Economy from the Perspective of Business Elites" and "Economics Forum", the Ambassador lectures are an important supplement to the teaching and research activities of the School of Economics. It widens the scope of the students and the faculty, who should analyze and solve Chinese economic problems from an international perspective.

I'd like to express my deep gratitude to the eight ambassadors who have accepted our invitation and gave lectures in Peking University. They are: Mr. Clark Randt, Jr. (Ambassador of the United States), Dr. Volker Stanzel (Ambassador of Germany), Dr. Börje Ljunggren (Ambassador of Sweden), Mr. Robert Wright (Ambassador of Canada), Sir Christopher Hum (Ambassador of United Kingdom), Dr. Alan Thomas (Ambassador of Australia), Mr. Dante Martinelli (Ambassador of Switzerland), and Dr. Yehoyada Haim (Ambassador of Israel). Their thoughtful speech wan applauses and respect from the students and faculty of Peking University and led us to further contemplate various issues of Chinese development. Here please allow me to quote some of the highlights of the ambassadors' speeches.

"A leading American investment banker recently introduced me to an audience in New York by saying the single most important event in our lifetime is the rise of China." —Mr. Clark Randt, Jr., American Ambassador to China.

"Will the dramatic growth continue? Will German businesses continue to be able to hold its own in the environment of ever-fiercer competition?"

—Dr. Volker Stanzel, German Ambassador to China.

"It is perfectly possible to have social programs committed to welfare which sustains growth. It is not at the expense of growth. That social programs would harm growth is not correct according to data."—Dr. Börje Ljunggren, Swedish Ambassador to China.

"While bilateral trade between our countries has doubled over the last 5 years, our leaders have challenged us to double Canada-China trade again by 2010."—Mr. Robert Wright, Canadian Ambassador to China.

"The LSE's interest in developing partnerships with China is a reflection of what is happening not just in Britain, but worldwide. Virtually all sectors, governments, companies and academic institutions feel they must have a China strategy."—Sir Christopher Hum, British Ambassador to China.

"Australians see China as a country where growing demand for energy and resources is pushing up world commodity prices such as oil and iron ore. The increase in world prices is creating a boom in some parts of Australia."—Dr. Alan Thomas, Australian Ambassador to China.

"China is our first trading partner in Asia but we are constantly depending this relationship at the political, economic, scientific, educational, cultural and environmental levels."—Mr. Dante Martinelli, Swiss Ambassador to China.

"Israel has the most engineers per capita in the world. The average rate of high education and academic publications per capita of Israel also top the world."—Dr. Yehoyada Haim, Israeli Ambassador to China.

Finally, I'd like to thank all my colleagues, whose hard work has made the lecture series and the publication of this book possible. Especially I will mention the following names: Professor Hao Ping, former Vice President of Peking University, Professor Wu Zhipan and Professor Lin Jianhua, Vice President of Peking University, Mr. Li Yansong, Director of the Office of International Relations, Mr. Xia Weihong, Vice President of the Office of International Relations, Ms. Bai Yan, Director of the Office of Foreign Experts, Professor Liu Wei, Dean of the School of Economics, Professor Sun Qixiang, Associate Dean of the School of Economics.

This book is dedicated to everyone who works diligently for the cause of Chinese international cooperation.

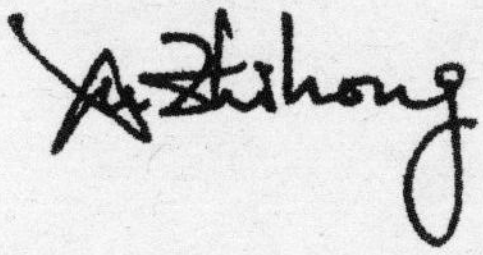

Zhihong Xu
President, Peking University
Fellow, Chinese Academy of Sciences
Sept. 12, 2006 in Peking University

目录

目录

Contents

Contents

美国驻华大使

雷德先生 (Mr. Clark Randt, Jr.)

雷德 (Mr. Clark Randt, Jr.)

雷德先生毕业于耶鲁大学，并获得密歇根大学法学博士学位。他也曾就读于哈佛大学法学院，并获得东亚法律旅行研究奖学金，赴中国进行过研究。雷德先生曾任香港美国商会的理事和第一副会长。他还是美国律师协会、美国国际法协会和香港法律协会等组织的成员。1968—1972年间，雷德先生在美国空军的安全部门任职，他还担任过美中贸易国家委员会中国事务代表 (1974) 以及美国使馆一等秘书和商务专员 (1982—1984)。雷德先生于2001年被任命为美国驻华大使。

Mr. Randt graduated from Yale University and received his Juris Doctor from the University of Michigan. He also attended the Harvard Law School where he was awarded the East Asia Legal Studies Traveling Fellowship to China. Mr. Randt is also a former Governor and First Vice President of the American Chamber of Commerce in Hong Kong. He is a member of the American Bar Association, the American Society of International Law, and the Hong Kong Law Society. From 1968 to 1972, Mr. Randt served in the United States Air Force Security Service. In 1974, he worked as the China representative of the National Council for United States-China Trade. From 1982 through 1984, he served as First Secretary and Commercial Attach at the US Embassy. Mr. Randt was appointed as the US Ambassador to China in 2001.

发展的中国需要更开放的姿态

美国驻华大使　雷德先生(Mr. Clark Randt, Jr.)

2005年4月27日　北京大学

演讲全文

非常感谢你们热情的邀请。我想在座各位的英文都比我的中文要好得多,我就不用我糟糕的中文演讲了。非常感谢你们邀请我来到颇具声望的北京大学经济学院。

作为一个律师和这么多经济学家在一起,我当然觉得诚惶诚恐。这次接受邀请在此演讲,我有些紧张。我必须承认,在此之前我还从来没有被谁邀请谈论过经济问题。我很荣幸,但你们必须容忍我,因为这是我初次涉足经济学这个复杂的领域。然而作为美国大使,我明白经济在两国关系中的重要地位,我们在这方面确有一些观点。我很荣幸我被安排在这个系列讲座的第一场,当然希望这不会是最后一场。

在美国有许多关于律师的笑话,我并不喜欢它们。我们也有一些关于经济学家的笑话。据说经只有济学家和天气预报员是可以既赚钱而又从来不必正确的职业。我们也知道有关经济学家的矛盾:当所有经济学理论都无法解释问题的时候,经济学家们仍需照常工作。

中国文明是世界上最古老的延续至今的文明,中国人有理由为之而骄傲。而中国经济,如同几周来在北京开始绽放的花朵,则在世界舞台上刚刚崭露头角。全世界的人们都因中国经济的发展而震惊。

我们知道经济增长是国内局势稳定的基础,并将随着时间的推移,转化为一国的实力。最近,一个著名的美国投资银行家在纽约介绍我的时候说:在我们一生中经历的最重要的事情就是中国的崛起。日本经济在1950到1971年间以平均8.6%的年增长率增长。而在过去25年,中国经济的平均增长率是9.3%。在不到20年的时间里,世界1/5的人口从世界经济体系之外积极地参与了进来,并且有着与日俱增的影响力。去年春天当温家宝总理指出中国经济过热,政府将采取措施使经济发展放缓时,世界各地的工业原料价格几乎立即下跌。这就是影响力的明证。

中国经济的迅速崛起意味着中国和其他国家都面临着新的挑战。中国国内和与别国间的经济竞争增加了,中国人和在华进行贸易与投资的人的商业机会也增多了。这使得中国人均GDP和1980年相比是那时的4倍。一个新的中产阶级在中国出现,并且其规模在未来的20年内将成为世界上最大的。成千上万的人们从绝对贫困中解脱了出来。在过去20年里,整个发展中世界里的贫困人口减少中有接近75%发生在中国。这是引人注目和值得赞美的成就,中国可以为之骄傲。这些成就的实现,有赖于中国领导人的实事求是和勇于改革。从1979年起,中国领导人有意识地做了一些大胆的决定使中国向市场经济转型,提高效率,增强竞争,从而极大地提高了生产力和收入水平。中国在改革国内市场的同时还引进外资。目前中国是世界第三大贸易国,2004年是全球第二大外国直接投资吸收者,紧随美国之后。此外,中国的购买力让中国成为许多原材料

的世界价格的制定者，给原材料出口方带来了巨额利润，同时也给那些原材料进口方带来了通货膨胀。中国已经无可争议地成为世界经济舞台的一个主要角色。

对中国的出口不仅对韩国、日本、澳大利亚和东南亚十分重要，对欧洲、拉丁美洲的重要性也日益上升，当然也包括美国。目前中国是美国第五大出口市场，同时中国也成为世界工厂。中国国内市场已经成为吸引贸易和投资的有力引擎。譬如在汽车业，1985 年仅有 19 000 台私家车在中国道路上行驶，而 2003 年这一数字已经达到了大约一千万。目前大约 2/3 的外国在华直接投资将资金用于于出口产品的生产，而另外 1/3 致力于满足中国国内需求。我们预测，这些比例将很快逆转。世界所有的投资者和政府都在关注中国，关注中国政府所选择的经济政策。

中国已经持续了 25 年的爆炸式经济增长，目前看来还会继续，但其中不乏风险。你们的领导人很清楚地看到当改革跟不上经济增长的脚步时所出现的不平衡。从 20 世纪晚期开始，世界经济出现了两大转变：第一是发展中国家从农业经济转向现代的工业、服务业经济；第二个是计划经济的国家转向市场经济。在中国，这两个转变在同时发生。中国经济的转型就其广度和复杂程度而言都是无可比拟的。温家宝总理 2003 年 12 月访美时与布什总统在白宫午餐会上提到，任何问题，无论多么微不足道，只要乘以 13 亿，就变成了一个很大的问题。因此，有效地运用各种市场工具对中国经济和中国人民来说显得尤为重要。

在座的都很了解当前中国经济面临的挑战。国企改革——国有企业产值占 GDP 比重不断下降，但却仍继续消耗大量的宝贵的资金以维持经营；银行系统改革——中国的银行拥有大量坏账，至少占其总资产的 20%，有可能还要多得多，而目前这些银行仍然由于缺乏精确判断新贷款风险的能力从而无法减少新的坏账；农业改革——中国农业机械化进程刚刚起步，农业中可能有多达 2 亿的就业不足人口；应对不断加剧的贫富分化所带来的社会问题，尤其是东部沿海富裕省份和内陆及东北一般比较贫困的省份之间的差距。单单考虑应届毕业生以及国企下岗职工和农村失业人口，中国每年就需要创造2400万个工作机会。另一个即将到来的挑战是中国还必须为其社会保障体系融资，这个体系所面对的是全球老龄化最快的人群之一。这将是一项长期的挑战，并牵涉中国经济发展的各方面前景。我们估计中国的13亿人口中，有4.36亿已经处于55至75岁之间。目前，中国每6个劳动人口负担一个60岁或以上的人。由于独生子女政策的影响和目前人口变化的趋势，到2040年将只有2个劳动人口负担一个非劳动人口的生活。而在2040年将达到60岁的人现在都已经出生了。中国还没有养老金制度和一个适当的社会保障网来应对这个问题，这需要中国以最大的效率来利用人力资源和资金，并且不断地引进和有效地利用外资，运用一个有效的市场机制来达成这些目标。

目前中国经济的发展取决于改革、扩大市场、完善法律。法规和保护私有财产对经济活动至关重要。要继续健康的可持续的发展，继续改革，加强经济法规的执行将是至关重要的。中国积极参与全球体系的决定令中国获益良多，已经成为一个重要角色和主要外资流入国。作为全球贸易体系中富有影响力的成员，中国必须承担相应的责任。这些责任是什么呢？对中国来说，外国投资者是非常重要的资源，贡献了资金、技术和管理专长。这些贡献已经帮助中国取得了经济的快速增长。中国出口产品中超过一半是由在华外资企业生产的。2004年，按累计投资计算，美国在中国的投资位居第二，紧随香港地区之后。但如大家所知的，香港地区的投资额由于存在所谓的中国回流投资而被夸大了。

虽然在这里存在如此之多的机会，许多美国公司仍然不愿意在中国投资，或者说不愿意把他们最好的技术带到中国来。其中最大的原因就是担心在中国缺乏对知识产权的保护。在一般的监管透

明度和法制问题之外，中国对知识产权的保护对几乎所有的美国公司来说都是十分关键的。侵犯知识产权的具有破坏性的影响阻碍了进一步的外国直接投资，尤其是那些高价值产业内的投资。而这些产业正是中国希望在下一步发展的。保护知识产权也非常符合中国企业的利益，因为他们正试图生产技术上更为复杂的产品或在国际市场上建立中国品牌的知名度和忠诚度。

自加入世贸组织以来，中国中央政府在这方面所实行的司法改革无疑是鼓舞人心的。但是还需要进一步努力，尤其是在执法方面。不力的执法和过轻的惩罚令侵犯知识产权的行为十分猖獗。很遗憾地告诉大家，2003 年美国海关在美国边界缴获的假冒产品中有 66% 来自中国。在这种情况下，产品的安全性问题也日益引起重视，比如假冒药品和汽车零部件等。这些趋势将会损害中国合法商品的国际形象。

正如我前面说的，中国是美国第三大贸易伙伴。从 2001 年起，美国对中国的出口增长了不止一倍。但是，中国对美国的出口增长得更快。2004 年中国对美国双边贸易的顺差高达 1 620 亿美元。今年第一季度，这一数字上升得更快了。这一巨大而看起来持久的贸易不平衡在美国国内引发了激烈的指责，认为在中国没有一个公平的竞争平台。美国国内普遍的看法是中国没有遵守游戏规则。美国人不仅仅想要自由贸易，也想要公平贸易。温总理 2003 年 12 月在哈佛大学的演讲中承认两国贸易不平衡的问题必须得到处理。他提出了一个我认为理想的方案——扩大美国对中国的出口而不是削减中国对美国的出口。继续存在的贸易壁垒还在限制美国货物和服务向中国的出口，而中国所有出口的 30% 是流向美国市场的。

在目前人民币盯住美元的情况下，只要中美之间的贸易不平衡还在继续增长，那么在美国国内就会有人指责中国政府以不公平的方式使中国出口产品的价格低于其在基于市场的灵活汇率机制下的情况，而抬高美国出口产品的价格。换句话说，当前的盯住汇率制度是对中国出口的补贴。随着时间的推移，这样的体制将给中国国内经济的宏观调控带来不利影响，产生通胀压力。在过去的二十多年里，中国学到的重要教训就是中国不应该害怕竞争，而是应该欢迎竞争。在中国，竞争促进了效率，实现了增长。我们相信中国应该加快改革，扩大开放，这是符合中国自身利益的。

中国的经济就如同一辆自行车，必须要按一定的速度前进才能不倾倒。所以在改革过程中必须保持增长步伐，这就需要有足够的资金，并且要有效率地使用这些资金。就像骑自行车一样，中国经济需要一系列细致的调整来继续前进。中国不能仅仅依赖行政措施。这些措施往往是临时性的而且效率不高。中国应当越来越多地应用整套基于市场的宏观经济调节政策，包括利率和汇率。中国令其经济对这些市场工具的适应程度越高，中国在未来经济危机中面临的风险就越小。

已故的邓小平鼓励他的同事"摸着石头过河"。可以理解这个伟大改革的守护者决定下一步行动的时候的谨慎。然而，邓小平更是高瞻远瞩的。当其他人犹豫的时候，他敢于冒险，勇敢地继续改革经济。正如经济需要持续增长，中国的改革开放也需要继续下去以完成向一个现代化的世界级的经济体转变。如果你在河流中停留得太久，就很可能失去动力而被冲走。中国经济可持续增长所面临的挑战确实存在着。它们很复杂也很巨大。但是也有工具和策略来成功面对这些挑战。其中最重要的之一就是运用市场的力量来为你们、为中国经济和中国人民服务。另一点值得注意的是在互惠互利的基础上让贸易与投资伙伴参与进来。这将造就一个持续稳定增长的强大而繁荣的中国，一个为世界经济的健康发展作出贡献的完全的伙伴！谢谢！

现场对话

听众:欢迎您来到我们的大学并感谢你的精彩演讲。如您所知,中美正在就版权问题进行谈判。您能讲一下最近的进展么?谢谢。

雷德:版权是知识产权中的一个领域,我们对此感兴趣并一直在讨论。至于讨论的细节,我并不知情。但我知道讨论在进行中。这是我们关于知识产权问题开展的广泛合作的一部分。在知识产权保护的概念下包含许多非常不同的方面。譬如说,我们有版权。如果你写书并希望你的书能受到版权保护,那么你就会对其感兴趣。版权也保护了电影和其他一些产品。另外还有对机械设备的专利权保护。那是完全不同的一套体系和法律。保护药品和软件的法律也不相同。因此我们同时进行着好几个不同的对话。我们的对话确实在继续。我们与中国就知识产权问题的接触是在一个叫做联合商贸委员会(JCCT)的广泛框架下进行的。在该委员会中,中方目前由吴仪副总理担任主席,美方主席由我们的商务部长和贸易代表担任。这个夏天他们很可能还将会面。在JCCT的框架下有一个负责知识产权问题的工作小组,由具不同专长的专家组成。

听众:我是经济学院大二的学生。众所周知,人民币汇率在世界经济中起着越来越重要的作用。美中贸易也在过去二十几年里给双方都带来了许多好处。最近一个美国国会议员提议如果人民币不在未来的六个月内升值的话,将对中国出口商品征收高额关税。您能谈谈您的看法么?谢谢。

雷德:我对经济学的了解可能不多,但我明白作为一个政府官员,谈论汇率是一件危险的事情。我理解你的意思。美国政府的立场并不是认为人民币被低估了或是被高估了,而是无论币值的高低,汇率都应该由市场来决定。毫无疑问,在华盛顿这正成为一件大事。我在我北京的办公室里都能感觉到华盛顿传来的热浪。我能感受到不断增长的压力。

你说的没错,在美国国会里有两项这样的提案。其中一个要求对所有中国商品征收27%的关税,另外一个要求通过其他手段来惩罚中国出口商品。这两个提案在国会里被激烈地讨论,并且不幸的是还得到了很多支持。我认为美国政府很愿意和中国政府合作来解决这个问题,而不是由国会使用这种立法的方案从我们手中取得主动权。我们的中国朋友们必须和我们合作。有些国会议员常来北京看我。他们说听说中国正在走向灵活的基于市场的汇率制度。可是在华盛顿,人们的想法是,“早在一年半以前他们就这样说了!”正如你们所知的,对于像中国这样一个拥有五千年历史的国家来说,耐心也许意味着十年、一百年甚至更多。但对于美国来说,耐心只是几个月的事情。我想恐怕关于人民币升值的压力正在上升。我们督促我们的中国朋友和我们合作,一起来应对这种期望。我们应该看到一些结果和实实在在的行动以证明中国正朝着正确的方向前进。谢谢。

听众:我是国际关系学院的学生。您强调中国是美国最重要的伙伴之一,但两国之间仍然在政治和经济方面存在一些误解。为了构建一个更好的未来,尤其是对年轻一代来说,美国政府是否计划提供更多的学生交流机会以增强相互理解呢?谢谢。

雷德:你应该在外交学院!我就像听到了一个签证问题,非常外交化的措辞。我经常听到类似的问题。我认识直接负责签证事宜的女士。不知你们当中是否有人见过她。她是美国助理国务部长,负责包括签证在内的所有领事馆服务。她前一阵子来北大做过演讲。我们认为这些交流符合我们的国家利益。

你们可以理解这些交流必须放在美国国家安全的背景下来考虑。确实,在“9·11”之后我们增加了一些手续。换句话说,需要多

一些文件或其他的一些东西。实际上,如果你是一个工程师或者科学家,那么为获得签证将会多花很多时间。但如果你是经济学家,那么你就没有什么问题,不必经历这些。如果你是工程师,具有技术背景,在"9·11"之后我们有了一些特殊的要求。我们必须把这些申请发回华盛顿,然后华盛顿再发回给我们说这个人没有问题。这被称作安全顾问意见。但这只是针对那一类人。现在回复意见平均会在三周内出来。有些人并没想到会花三周那么久。在全世界我们有 9 000 多份这样的申请,但除了 43 份以外其余全部都获得了批准。所以最后被拒绝的可能性是很小的。对经济学家来说,区别只在于多一些书面材料,预约时间稍微变长些而已。

对于学生,我们实际上"欺骗"了我们的预约系统,因为我们知道让学生等到学校开学才拿到签证不是一件好事。如果申请的是学生签证,我们会尽量安排更早的面试好让学生能够按时出发而不至于迟到。事实上,当我告诉人们在"9·11"前后拒签的比例一点都没有变的时候人们通常都很惊讶。唯一的区别是签证的处理时间变长了。由于时间被拖长而有些人放弃了希望。我们理解这是一个问题。请你们来申请,但就是请来得早一些。我们欢迎你们。我们并不试图把你们拒之门外。我收到过美国很多著名大学校长的愤怒的信件,以为我试图把他们的中国学生拦在了外面。事实并非如此,我们的大门的的确确仍旧是敞开的。

实际上目前我们还向中国政府提出了一个提议。有个问题是一些中国学生会在假期回国,然后可能就回不去了。我们了解这个情况并且认为这不是一件好事。我们曾向中国政府提议,给予那些学生一年内多次入境的签证。目前外交部正在积极为你们工作。我们相信,在不久的将来会有一个有利解决方案。再说一次,我们欢迎你们并且期待着你们的申请。

听众:下午好,大使先生。欢迎您来到北大。我是经济学院大二的学生。我想问一些关于美中贸易摩擦的问题。我最近从报纸上得知,美国政府提出很多针对中国的贸易问题,并要决定是否重新对中国纺织品实行配额制来保护美国国内纺织和制衣行业。另一方面,美国也有很多投资者在中国获益。那么,这种保护主义政策是否对在华投资有负面影响?美国政府又是如何平衡美国投资者在中国和美国国内所获得的利润呢?我们能把这些贸易摩擦转变为双赢的局面么?我们如何做到这一点?

雷德:我们也认为贸易确实是双赢的。至于纺织品的问题,对这个问题的恰当理解是,当中国签署入世协议时,我们担心的事情之一是在取消配额之后,中国纺织品会如海啸一般席卷美国。因此,面对如潮水般的中国进口商品,我们需要所谓的“巨浪保护”措施来保护我们的产业。中国当时也同意了这样的安排。确实,当2005年1月1日配额取消的时候,棉衬衣的进口数量由2004年1月的61.9万件增加到了大约1 800万件,增长超过1 000%。好消息是,“巨浪保护”措施仅仅持续12个月,而不是永久的。当这些安全保护措施被使用时,我们首先会调查美国产业是否受损。在此期间从中国进口的所有种类的纺织品仍将增长7.5%,保护措施只会持续一年。实际上,一些原来的措施即将被取消或者已经被取消。所以,这只是一项临时的措施,以保证美国国内这些受到伤害的产业的失业劳动力能够被重新安置。事实上,在调查期间对中国出口商来说,最糟糕的情况也是有限的。你们已经出口了1 800万件衬衫,另外还可以增长7.5%。虽然这听起来可怕,但它实际上并不那么可怕。这只是我们应对困难的过渡时期的一种方式。我们会度过这一时期。

你问到在这里的投资者,包括纺织品工厂和进口商的利益,这很有意思。在美国,政治体系是这样运行的。他们应该像我们的纺织品制造商一样努力地在国会展开游说活动以达到恰当的平衡。一个好消息是,我们两国的元首是好朋友,并且对什么是真正重要

的问题有良好的理解。这一点在他们去年在圣地亚哥举行的亚太经合组织会议上的面谈中得到了确认。5 月 9 日他们将在莫斯科会面。那天是二战结束纪念日。我们两国的元首都清楚,美中共同利益如此巨大而重要,以至于尽管我们有这些分歧,我们仍然可以处理这些分歧,而贸易正是这些领域之一。中国越成功,就越可能遇到更多的贸易问题。这是正常的,不可避免的。我们会和你们的官员一起来处理这些状况。因为这对双方国内的政治和社会都有影响,所以我们必须通过合作来达到目的。我们坚信自由贸易会给中国带来好处。中国能够竞争并且会在竞争中表现很好。一个灵活的以市场为导向的汇率机制也会令中国受益,因为它能够为你们提供更多的用以调节国内经济的工具。因此双赢会实现的!

听众:我是经济学院的教授。我曾经在贵国学习过。感谢您今天下午关于中国经济的演讲。您谈到了中国正经历着两大转变。一个是中国正从农业经济向服务业经济转变,另一个是从计划经济向市场经济转变。我的问题是,虽然我们改革了很多东西,也取得了很多成就,为什么中国经济还没有被视为市场经济呢?中国经济还应该在哪些方面努力从而加快这个转变的进程?您能提供您的建议吗?我的第二个问题是,您刚才说中国经济像一辆自行车,那么您认为我们是太快了还是太慢了呢?谢谢。

雷德:非常感谢您的问题。当我知道一位教授向我提问的时候我自然感到有些担心。我知道我会有麻烦。有关市场经济,获得世界承认中国为市场经济是中国政府的目标。澳大利亚最近承认了中国是市场经济,许多其他国家也承认了这一点。在美国,这是律师们会欣赏的事情之一。你说到一个具有普通含义的词汇,但它同时也是一个专门术语。在美国市场经济一词有特殊的定义。当谈到市场经济时,我们不是如一般人那样仅仅认为在中国有很多市场机制生效的地方。当然肯定有,但具体要看是在哪个行业。毫无疑问,有些行业已经完全由市场驱动了。但是,在美国,市场经济地位是一个专门术语,因为它涉及立法,与贸易方面的法律有关。在此情况下中国将会得到不同的但并不见得是更好的待遇。实际上这是更好还是更坏还有待商榷。在美国这个术语是十分技术性的。我们的商务部负责这件事并确定具体的准则以判断市场经济是什么样的以及一个国家应该具有什么样的条件才能被认为是市场经济。如同版权问题,这个问题涉及很多细节。在JCCT下,吴仪副总理和薄熙来部长也提出了关于市场经济地位的问题。实际上我们有一个工作组来研究中国具体要做些什么。如果你对此有兴趣,我们可以派一个我的同事来和你探讨这个问题,一个比我更聪明的人。我很幸运有很多优秀的人为我工作。如果我遇到很难的问题但无法回答的时候,我就会去向他们求助。

关于你的第二个问题,事实上,那需要一个比我的经济学背景多得多的人来回答。我只知道,在中国官员中似乎有一个共识:考虑到失业率问题,保持至少7%的增长率是必需的。这似乎是一条底线。但这仅仅是我作为一个门外汉的观点,仅此而已。谢谢。

Developing China Needs a More Open Gesture

Mr. Clark Randt, Jr., American Ambassador to China

April 27, 2005 in Peking University

Speech

Thank you very much for the kind invitation, I'm afraid everybody here's English is much better than my Chinese, so I won't attack your ears with my poor Chinese today. Thank you very much for inviting me to the prestigious Peking University School of Economics.

As a lawyer, of course, I'm humbled to be with so many economists. Not without trepidation, I accept the invitation to speak here. I have to confess that no one else has ever asked me to speak about economics before. I'm very pleased but you have to bear with me because this is my maiden voyage to this complex area of economics. But certainly as US Ambassador, the economy is very much an important part of our relationship, and we definitely have some views on this matter. But I'm honored to speak at the first in this lecture series and I certainly hope it won't be the last.

In my country there are a lot of jokes about lawyers, but I don't like those. We do, however, have a few jokes about economists. In America, it's said that economists and weather forecasters are the only people who can make a good living without ever being right. We also know the paradox about economists. During periods when none of the economic theories are working, all of the economists are.

Chinese people are rightly proud that China boasts the oldest continual civilization in the world. Much like the flowers that just began blooming in the past couple of weeks here in Beijing, in economic terms, China has really just blossomed on the modern global economic scene. All around the world, people are now transfixed by the economic development in China.

We all understand that economic growth underpins domestic stability and translates over time into national power. A leading American investment banker recently introduced me to an audience in New York by saying the single most important event in our lifetime is the rise of China. Japan's economy, for instance, for the 25 years period from 1950 to 1971 grew at an average annual rate of 8.6%. For the last 25 years, China's economy has grown at the average growth rate of 9.3%. Within the space of two decades, a fifth of the world's population has been brought from completely outside the world economic system to active participation and increasing influence within it. When Premier Wen Jiabao said last spring that China's economy was overheating, and as a result, the government would take measures to slow it down, prices of industrial commodities around the world almost immediately began to fall. This is clear evidence of influence.

China's rapid rise in the world economy has meant new challenges for the Chinese people and for countries around the world. Economic competition has increased, both inside China and between China and other countries; economic opportunities have expanded for both Chinese and those investing in China and trading with China. The process has resulted in Chinese per capita GDP more than quadrupling since 1980, creating a new middle class that could, in two more decades, become the largest in the world. Hundreds of millions of people have been lifted out of absolute poverty; nearly 75% of the reduction in the developing world poverty over the past

two decades has occurred in China. These are remarkable and laudatory accomplishments of which China can be proud. These changes have been possible because Chinese leaders saw truth from facts and consciously made bold decisions to transform Chinese economy in a market economy, raising efficiency and increasing competition and dramatically increasing productivity and incomes. Internal market reforms have been accompanied by a gradual opening to trade investment from abroad. From a standing start in 1979, China is now the third largest trading country in the world, and in 2004 was the second largest recipient of foreign direct investment, trailing only the United States. In addition, Chinese global purchasing power permits China to be a global price setter for many raw commodities, bringing windfall profits to commodity exporters and inflation to commodity importers around the globe. China is inescapably a major player on the world economic scene.

Exports to China are the driving force for the economy of Korea, Japan, Australia, Southeast Asia and are increasingly important for Europe, Latin America, and of course, the United States. China is now the United States' fifth largest export market and China has already made itself the world's factory. And the Chinese domestic market has become a powerful motor for attracting trade and investment. In the automobile industry for instance, in 1985, there were approximately 19 000 privately-own passenger vehicles on China's roads; in 2003, there were approximately 10 million. Today, around two thirds of the foreign direct investment in China funds the production of the goods for exports with one third producing for the domestic market. Those ratios, we predict, will soon be reversed. All investors and all governments are now watching China and the economic policies chosen by the Chinese government.

China's 25 years of economic explosion appears set to continue, but not without risks. Your leadership clearly is aware of the imbalances created, when reforms do not keep pace with prolonged economic growth. There have been two great economic transitions occurring around the world since the late 20th century. The first is that of developing countries, moving from rural, agricultural economies to modern industrial and service economies. The second is that of countries moving from centrally planned economies to market oriented ones. In China, these two great shifts are taking place simultaneously. The economic changes in China are unparalleled in scope and arguably in complexity. Premier Wen Jiabao told President Bush at lunch in the White House when he visited United States in December 2003, that any problem, no matter how small, becomes a huge problem when you multiply it by 1.3 billion. Because of this, it is important that the Chinese use all the tools of the market to benefit the economy and its people.

You are all aware of the many economic challenges currently confronting China: reforming the state-owned enterprise sector, which produces an ever smaller portion of the GDP, but continues to consume a large proportion of valuable capital resources to stay afloat; reforming the banking system, weighed down by non-performing loans amounting to at least 20% of total banking assets and possibly much more, while still being incapable of accurately pricing the risks of the new loans to minimize new bad debts; reforming the agricultural sector that has scarcely begun the mechanization process and may contain as many as 200 million under employed workers; dealing with the social consequences of the growing divide between rich and poor, and in particular, between the rich coastal provinces and generally still impoverished provinces in the interior and in the northeast; having to create some 24 million new jobs a year just to accommodate the new school graduates and the workers displaced by state-owned enterprises and agricultural reforms; and looming on the horizon, funding the social security requirements of one of the most rapidly aging population in the world. This may be a longer-range challenge, but it is one that increasingly looms over all of China's economic prospects. Today we estimate 436 million of China's 1.3 billion people are already between the ages of 55 and 75. Currently, you have six working-age adults for every person age 60 or over. By 2040, according to current demographic trends, as influenced by the one-child policy, there will only be two people to support each non-working person. And of course, all of those who will be age 60 or more in 2040 are already born. There is currently no pension system or social security network in China adequately equipped to

deal with this situation. To meet these challenges, China needs to make the most efficient use of human and financial capital, and continue attracting and efficiently using foreign capital investment. An efficiently functioning market system will achieve these goals.

China's economic development today depends on reforms, expanding the reach of the market and improving the laws. Regulations and private property protections are essential to economic activities. To continue healthy, sustainable development, continuing to reform and improve the enforcement of economic regulations will be crucial. China has clearly benefited from its decision of active participation in the global system, becoming a leading power and recipient of foreign investment. As an influential member of the global trading system, China must accept the responsibility that comes with such status. What are some of these responsibilities? For China, foreign investors are a vital resource, contributing capital, technology and management expertise. These contributions have helped China achieve its rapid expansion. Over half of China's exports were produced by foreign invested enterprises. Through 2004, United States ranked the second most important accumulative foreign investor in China, following only Hong Kong, whose statistics, as you all know, have swelled by the so-called Chinese round-trip investment.

But despite of the opportunities here, many US firms are still unwilling to invest in China or, I should say, not willing to bring their best technology to China. The biggest single reason for this is the concern of the lack of intellectual property right protection in China. In addition to matters relating generally to regulatory transparency and the rule of law, protection of intellectual property rights in China is a crucial issue for nearly all United States enterprises. The destructive effects of IPR violation discourages additional foreign direct investment, especially in the higher-value industries that China hopes to develop next. Chinese companies also have a strong interest in IPR protection, as they develop and manufacture more technologically sophisticated products, or try to develop brand loyalty in the marketplace internationally.

Legal reforms undertaken by the Chinese central government since accession to WTO, in this regard, are encouraging. However, more work needs to be done, particularly at the enforcement level. Poor enforcement, combined with weak punishment, allows for rampant IPR violations. I am sorry to report that in 2003, 66% of all counterfeit goods seized at United States borders by the United States Customs Service came from China. In this context, product safety is an increasing concern. For instance, in the case of counterfeit pharmaceuticals and automotive parts, this trend can only damage the world's perception of the legitimate Chinese goods.

As I said, China now is the United States' third largest trading partner. Exports of US products to China have more than doubled since 2001. Exports of Chinese goods to the United States have grown much faster, so fast that in 2004 China had a bilateral trade surplus of US $162 billion with the United States. And this deficit figure is growing even faster in the first quarter of this year. This huge and seemingly sustained imbalance is arousing heated charges in the United States that in China there isn't a level playing field. And it is widely perceived in the United States that China is not playing by the rules. Americans want not only free trade, but also fair trade. Premier Wen in his speech at Harvard University in 2003 recognized that the problem of growing trade imbalance between our two countries must be addressed. He advocated what I believe to be the ideal solution, expanding United States' exports to China rather than cutting back China's exports to the United States. Remaining trade barriers are still restricting the sales of American goods and services in China. At the same time, over 30% of China's current exports go to the United States.

With the RMB value pegged to the value of US dollar, as long as the trade imbalance continues to grow, there will be charges in the United States that Chinese government is unfairly making Chinese exports cheaper and US exports more expensive than they would be with a flexible market-based exchange rate mechanism. In other words, the peg system works as a subsidy to Chinese exports. Over time, the current system will have a

dilatory effect on China's domestic economy, impeding the use of proper economic controls, and stimulating inflationary pressure. One important lesson in the past two decades is China should not fear competition. It should welcome it. In China, competition has improved efficiency and created growth. We believe China should move quickly to open its markets further because it's in China's own interests to do so.

China's economy is much like a bicycle that must be kept moving forward fast enough so it doesn't fall. Therefore, it is essential that during the reform growth rate be maintained and that means there must be sufficient capital, and the capital must be efficiently used. Like a bicycle, the economy must be guided by a series of delicate adjustments as it moves forward. China should not just rely on administrative measures. They are usually inefficient and temporary in nature. China should increasingly use the entire range of market-based macroeconomic adjustment policies, including interest rate and exchange rates. The more China adapts its economy to these tools, the less risk China will face in an economic crisis.

The late Deng Xiaoping urged his colleagues to cross the river by feeling the stones. It's understandable that the custodian of such a great reform should use caution deciding upon what step to take. At the same time, however, Deng Xiaoping was a visionary, who took measured risk and moved boldly to reform the economy when others hesitated. Just as economic growth must keep moving forward, so the reform and opening process must move forward to complete China's transition to a modern world-class economy. If you slow down too long in the middle of the river, you might lose your momentum and get swept away. The challenges to China's sustainable economic growth are certainly real. They are complex. They are of great magnitude. But there are also tools and strategies available to successfully meet these challenges. One of the most important of these is to put the power of the market to work for you, for the Chinese economy and for the Chinese people. Another is to fully engage trade and investment partners on a mutually beneficial basis, following the rules and practices of the global system. That will make for a steadily growing, strong and prosperous China, a China that is a full contributing partner to the health of the world economy. Thank you very much.

Q & A

Audience: Welcome you to our university and thank you for your wonderful speech. My question is, as you know, China and America are negotiating the copyright issue, and I'd like to know how it is going on recently.

Randt: Copyright is one of the areas of IPR, which we are interested in and we have been discussing. As to the details of the discussion, I have to confess that I am not aware. I know the discussion is ongoing and it is part of our broad IPR engagement. IPR covers a lot of very different kinds of protections under the concept of intellectual property right protection. For instance, we have copyright. This is going to be interesting for you if you write books and want your books copyrighted. Copyrights help protect movies and other things. There are patent protections for mechanical devices. That's a whole different regulatory regime, different laws. Pharmaceuticals have different laws from software. So there are many separate talks going on at the same time. Our talks do continue. The framework broadly for our engagement with China on IPR issue is called Joint Commission on Commerce and Trade. That's chaired by Vice Premier Wu Yi now and on the US side, by our Secretary of Commerce and US Trade Representative. They will be meeting probably this summer again. Under JCCT, there is a working group that handles IPR issues with experts of different specialties.

Audience: I am a sophomore from the School of Economics. We all know that the exchange rate of RMB plays a more important role in the world economy. And also the trade between US and China in the past 20 years has benefited both countries a lot. Recently a senator of US has propounded that a high tariff should be imposed on the exports of China if RMB does not appreciate within the next six months. What's your opinion on this? Thank you.

Randt: I may not know much about economics, but I know that for a government official to talk about exchange rate is a dangerous thing. I understand what you are saying. The United States' position is not that the RMB is undervalued or overvalued, but is that the market should set the value, whatever value is appropriate. There is no question that this is becoming a big issue in Washington. I can feel the heat from Washington here in my office in Beijing. I can feel the pressure building up.

You are quite correct that there are two bills in the Congress. One imposes across-the-board 27% tariff on all Chinese goods and another asks to punish Chinese exports through other mechanisms. These are being pursued vigorously in our Congress and have much popular support, unfortunately. I can say that US government would much rather work with the Chinese government to manage this situation than to have the Congress take it from our hands by using this sort of legislative solution. Our Chinese friends have to work with us. I have Members of Congress coming to visit me quite often here in Beijing. They say that we've heard China is moving towards a flexible market-driven exchange rate mechanism. The view in Washington is that, "Oh, that's what they said a year and a half ago." As you all know, for a country with five thousand years of history, patience in China means ten or a hundred years or something. But patience in the US means a couple of months. I am afraid the pressure is building up and we urge our Chinese friends to cooperate and help us manage the expectation. We should see some results and show some concrete action that shows China is moving to the right direction. Thank you.

Audience: I am a student from the School of International Studies. You have emphasized that China is one of America's most important partners. But we still find some misunderstandings between these two countries in the areas of politics and economy. In order to build a better future, especially for the younger generation, does your government have any plan to offer more opportunities for the students to exchange and to understand each other? Thank you.

Randt: You should be in the Foreign Affairs School. I thought I just got a visa question, very diplomatically framed. I get those all the time. I know the woman who is directly in charge of this. I don't know if any of you see her. She is the Assistant Secretary of State and she is in charge of all consulate services including visas. She came to Beida herself to give a speech. We think these exchanges are very much in our national interest.

You can understand that has to be set against to our interest of homeland security and safety in the United States. In truth, since 9-11 there are more procedures. In other words, there are more papers, there are more this, there are more that. Actually, it can take significantly more time if you are an engineer or a scientist. If you are an economist, you are ok. You don't have to suffer this. But if you are an engineer with the technical background, there are some special requirements since 9-11. We have to send that application to Washington and Washington will get back to us and say that this person is ok. Those are called security advisory opinions. But that only applies to that class of people. Now the answers come back within an average of three weeks. For some people, three weeks is not what they expect to have. We had over 9 000 requests of that kind all over the world and all but 43 have been approved. So it's very rare to the end of the day that you get turned down. For economist, it's just a matter of some paperwork and a little longer time to get an appointment.

For students actually, we cheat the appointment system because it is not very nice for you to wait until after school starts. If the application is for a student visa, we try to make sure the interview is sooner rather than later so that you will be on your way and won't be late for school. In fact, people are quite surprised when I tell them that the percentage of refusals since 9-11 is exactly the same as it was before 9-11. The difference is that it just takes longer. And because it takes longer, some people give up hope. We understand that is a problem. Please come, please just come earlier. We do welcome you. We are not trying to keep you out. I get hate mails from the presidents of all the distinguished universities in the United States who are missing their Chinese students, thinking I am trying to hold them back. That's not true. We are not. The door definitely

is still open.

In fact, we have a proposal before the Chinese government now. One of the problems we have is that students would come back on holidays and couldn't go back. We are aware of that. We don't think that's very nice either. We have proposed to the Chinese government that we give the students visas that are year-long multiple entry. I think the Ministry of Foreign Affairs is working hard on your behalf. I think very soon there will be a favorable solution. Again, we welcome you and look forward to your applications.

Audience: Good afternoon, Mr. Ambassador. Welcome to Beida. I am a sophomore student from the School of Economics. I have some questions about the trade friction between US and China. I recently read the newspaper that US government has brought many trade cases against China, and to determine whether quotas should be re-imposed to protect the textile and clothing manufacturer in US. On the other hand, many US investors benefit here in China. Will this kind of trade protectionism have bad effect on the investment in China? How does the US government balance the profits earned by US investors in China and those in US. Can we turn this kind of trade friction into a win-win game? And how can we do this?

Randt: Trade is a Win-Win game, we think so too. Concerning the question of textile, to understand this properly, when China signed the accession agreement to WTO, one of the things we were worried about is when the textile quota came off, there would be a tsunami of Chinese textiles engulfing the United States. So we need the so-called surge protection to protect the industry from this surge of Chinese imports and China agreed to that. Indeed, when the textile quotas were taken away in January the 1st this year, the import for cotton shirts increased from 619 000 units in January a year before to 18 million or something this year, which is over 1 000% increase. The good news is that the surge protection only lasts for 12 months. It does not last forever. When these safeguard measures apply, first there is an investigation, whether it's hurting the US industry. During that time, Chinese imports of any given textile category will be held to an increase of 7.5%. It only lasts a year. In fact, some of the original ones are about to come off or have come off. So it's a temporary measure so the workers who are displaced in the industry that are injured by this can reallocate in the US. In fact, the worst that can happen to Chinese exporters, while the investigation is going on, are limited. You have the 18 million units of cotton shirts, plus a 7.5% increase. It sounds terrible, but in fact the way it works is not terrible. It's just a way of managing this transitional period that is difficult. We will get over that.

It's an interesting question that you asked what about the interests of foreign investors here, textile factories and importers. In the US, that's how the political system works. They should be lobbying in Congress as hard as our textile manufacturers to achieve the proper balance. The good news is our presidents are good friends and have a good understanding of what's really important. This was confirmed when they met face to face last year in Santiago at APEC. They will be meeting on May the 9th in Moscow, which is the anniversary for World War Ⅱ. Our presidents understand that the common interests between the US and China are so great and so important that, while we have these differences, we can manage these differences, and trade is one of those areas. The more successful China is, the more trade problems you are going to have. That's only natural, inevitable. We will work together with your officials to manage this. It takes two to manage this because there are political and social implications on both sides. We are quite convinced that free trade will benefit China. It can compete and will compete very well, and a flexible market-driven exchange rate will be beneficial to China because it will give you more tools to use on domestic economy as well. So, Win-Win!

Audience: I am a professor in the School of Economics. I have studied in your country. I appreciated what you have said this afternoon about Chinese economy. You mentioned that China is experiencing two great transitions. One is that China is being transformed from an agriculture economy to a service economy, and the other is from a planned economy to a market economy. My question is, although we have reformed a lot and have

achieved a lot, why the Chinese economy is still not regarded as a market economy. In what aspects the Chinese government should do to make the transition to market economy quicker? Could you provide your suggestions? My second question is you just said that Chinese economy was like a bicycle—then do you think we are too fast or too slow? Thanks.

Randt: Thank you very much. I was properly worried when I heard that I got a question from a professor. I knew I was in trouble. With respect to the market economy, it's very much the goal of the Chinese government to be recognized around the world as a market economy. Australia just recently recognized China as a market economy and many other countries did too. With respect to the US, it's actually one of the things lawyers will appreciate. You take a term that has a common meaning and it becomes a term of art. There are special definitions in the US for market economy. When we talk about market economy, it's not just the general laymen's view that there are a lot market mechanisms working in China, which there surely are, depending on which industry it is. Some are completely driven by market, undoubtedly. But the status of market economy is a term of art in the US because it refers to legislation, and it deals with trade laws. China will be treated differently, not necessarily better. Actually whether it's better or worse is subject to debate. This term is used technically in the US. Our Department of Commerce is in charge of this and making the decisions on the specific regulations that detail what a market economy is, what a country has to have to be a market economy. They are very detailed, like the issue of copyright. Under the JCCT, market economy status was an issue raised by Vice Premier Wu and Minster Bo. Between our two governments, we actually have a working group to ask exactly about what China has to do. I don't know the whole list of things. If you are interested, we can send one of my officers, someone smarter than I. I am very lucky because I have great people working for me. I get tough questions and if I don't have the answer, I can go and ask our officers.

Concerning your second question, in truth, it requires someone with more economics background that I have for sure. It seems to me there is a consensus among Chinese officials that to stay even as far as unemployment is concerned, 7% growth is essential. That's sort of the baseline. But again, I offered my opinion purely as an amateur and it should be taken as such.

德国驻华大使

史丹泽博士 (Dr. Volker Stanzel)

史丹泽 (Dr. Volker Stanzel)

史丹泽大使在科隆大学获得博士学位，他曾在法兰克福大学攻读日本学、汉学和政治学并赴日本京都大学学习。他1979年进入德国外交部工作，先后任职于德国驻意大利、日本、也门和中国大使馆。史丹泽博士还担任过德国驻华大使馆新闻处处长(1990—1993)，外交部应急中心指挥部主任(1993—1995)，外交部和平利用核能和不扩散处处长(1999—2001)以及外交部第三政治司司长(2002—2004)等。2004年9月，史丹泽博士被任命为德国驻华大使。

Dr. Volker Stanzel studied Japanese and Chinese Studies and Political Science in Frankfurt University, then he studied in Kyoto University and received his PhD from Cologne University. He joined the Foreign Service of the Federal Republic of Germany in 1979 and has worked at the German Embassies in Rome, Tokyo, Aden and Peking. Dr. Volker Stanzel has headed the Press and Information Department at the German Embassy in Peking (1990—1993), the Operation Centre at the Foreign Office in Bonn (1993—1995), the Department for Non-proliferation and Civilian Use of Nuclear Energy at the Foreign Office in Berlin(1999— 2001), and Director-General for Political Affairs(2002—2004). He assumed his new position of German Ambassador to China in September 2004.

发掘潜力　促进合作

德国驻华大使　史丹泽博士(Dr. Volker Stanzel)

2005年6月9日　北京大学

演讲全文

非常感谢孙教授的邀请和介绍,也谢谢你念出我的中文名字。能够来到北大我感到非常荣幸,尤其是在得知我能在这里用英语进行演讲。这非常令人印象深刻——想象一下如果一个中国人在我家乡的大学用中文进行演讲会是怎样。记得我刚刚开始学习汉语时,班上有很多学生学习汉语,但是当他们意识到学习中文的难度之后,就只剩下四五个人了。

现在让我们切入主题。事实上,在来到北京就职之前,作为未来的德国驻华大使,我就曾经需要面对"如何看待中国经济"这个问题。例如,在我离开德国之前几天,大使们与工商业代表举行了一次会议,我被柏林的德国和中国企业界邀请在会议上发表演讲。可想而知当时的我说不出太多东西。事实证明,整个德国都在好奇:中国的城市建筑越来越高,北京和上海的道路上行驶的汽车越来越多、越来越新——这其中当然也包括许多德国生产的汽车。这种景象的背后究竟发生了些什么？伴随着这些好奇的是这样一种担忧：迅猛的增长能否继续？德国的工业在这前所未有的激烈竞争环境中还能保持原有的地位吗？

当然，在之前的那些会议中，我回答不了这些问题。即使是今天，在中国经济这个巨大拼图中，我仍然只是理解了一些小片段而已。你们是经济学的学生，你们的知识储备比我更适合去解释现在正在发生的事情。因此，在我提出自己的观点之后，请告诉我真实的状况。

让我们来看看身边发生了什么。这里的无数的高楼和汽车确确实实存在着。每一栋新的摩天大厦都是一个关于中国未来的宣言。因此我们很容易只看到表面现象。同样，我们的分析也很容易建立在一种对中国经济发展的自豪上。每当我和中国朋友讨论中国在过去的二十多年中改革开放的成就时，我都能感受到这种自豪。中国经历的变化为中德之间的经济合作以及两国之间的政治乃至文化关系提供了坚实的基础。但与此同时，我们要警惕不要迷失在所谓的“中国梦”中。我们所需要的是两国未来的长期成功。这也就是为什么要到中国来的德国商人和政客们都会问我“中国将走向何方？”

现在让我们来看看中国经济成功的一些事实和要素。显然，无论是中国财富的增加和贫穷的减少都得益于二十多年来经济的空前增长。中国的经济增长则得益于国家领导人毫无保留地将经济建设放在首要位置，这集中体现在邓小平那句“致富光荣”的名言。这种实用主义在东西方都行之有效。事实上所有的消费品生产商都将他们的部分甚至全部生产转移到中国，使中国成了所谓的世界工场。尽管在某些领域生产效率还不是很高，但在中国生产对外国公司来说仍然有利可图。同样，中国的企业也从多年来不对等的技术转移中获益匪浅。这种合作是有效并且互利的。中国有利的投资环境带来了大量的就业机会。中国 56% 的出口商品仍然由外资

生产。所有这些事实所基于的基础是显而易见的——中国的工资和社会福利标准很低，并且有些人的工资中并不包含养老金、医疗健康保险等。在这个意义上，确实存在不利于中国以外的劳动力的“社会倾销”。事实上，对中国本国的劳动力也是如此。目前在中国仅有1.6亿的劳动者享有失业救济，1.9亿的劳动者没有医疗健康保险，仅有1.55亿人在养老金计划之中。这些都证明了相对于其他工业社会来说中国仍存在着巨大的缺陷。作为一个外国观察者，这令我想到了这种发展的可持续性，它能够持续多久？同时我也心存疑问：中国强有力的出口表现是否会在像美国、德国这样的发达市场上或在它和亚洲竞争者之间带来一些问题呢？

现在让我用众所周知的纺织品的例子来做进一步解释。中国的产品占据了美国40%的市场份额，在某些部门甚至更高。再加上人民币对美元汇率的影响，美国的制造商失去了竞争力。无论是在美国本土还是国际市场上，他们都在丧失市场份额，进而导致美国就业机会的丧失。你们可能知道，美国一个研究表明在美国有150万人失去了工作。现在并没有相应的关于德国的研究工作，尽管我们在德国也看到了类似的“挤出”效应。这还不包括德国企业在中国设厂造成的德国国内失业。当然，也有可能因为中国的发展使得德国国内产生了其他新的就业机会。这对德国来说，影响是正面的。在我的国家里，对有关这些问题有着激烈讨论。我们没有理由怀疑德国企业陈述的普遍观点：他们在中国设厂和雇用廉价劳动力有利于长期的商业平衡和保持德国就业的安全稳定。我们也不能忘记另一个规则：所有商业交易一定会使涉及的双方——消费者和供给方都获益。全世界的消费者都被中国的低价商品所吸引，零售商同样从中受益。我认为我们的共识在于贸易是经济运转的动力，不断开发出新的商机，因此保护主义永远也不可能成为当前问题的答案。作为一个世界最大出口国的大使我当然会这么说。

第二，现在有一个关于中国在对商品有大量需求的条件下如何融入世界市场的问题。尽管中国的产出仅占世界名义量的4%,它却是继美国之后世界第二大主要能源消耗国以及全球最大的煤炭、钢铁、水泥和其他十种不同金属材料的生产国。20年前,中国是东亚最大的石油出口国,而现在它是世界第三大石油进口国。去年全球石油需求增长的31%来自中国。中国对商品的持续需求刺激着世界的需求量。有张广为人知的图表对石油价格和中国石油进口量作了对比,说明中国的需求左右了世界价格。一方面,由于中国依赖于海外矿产、石油以及运输这些资源的国际航运线而选择实行一种基于务实主义而非意识形态的外交政策;另一方面,那些被挤出市场的经济体会作何反应?更重要的是,这些国家的政府会作何反应?这导致了国际上对中国的崛起是否是和平崛起的问题的讨论。或许这些担忧不会变成大的恐慌,但我们必须承认它们的存在,这意味着中国的改革策略要更积极地考虑如何营造一个可持续的平稳的经济增长环境。

第三个问题是,中国的社会摩擦会演变得多剧烈?它们是否会给中国进一步的经济发展带来冲击?首先,产生主要影响的是国企改革。大量的劳动力成为富余人员,国企提供的大而全的保障体制也在逐渐消失。这对就业市场的影响已经成为一个问题,如果中国确如亚洲发展银行的报告所说的那样拥有9 000万到1.5亿失业人口和30%的农村失业率。现实情况是复杂的。存在大量失业的同时,熟练工人却十分匮乏,公司迫切地寻找工人来完成必要的工作。考虑到1亿至1.2亿的流动人口时,这种失调更为明显。不仅在不同的地区之间存在失衡,不同部门和不同技术水平的工人之间也存在着差距,并且这些差距在不断扩大。在谈到未来改革的需求时我已经提到了社会问题。中国的老龄人口带来了一系列的亟待解决的后果,大量的老年人不得不依靠较少的处于工作年龄的年轻人来照顾。

改革之后,行业的结构已经改变,必须采取新的措施来满足老

龄化社会的需求。养老金体制并非唯一需要完善的。2003年非典的袭击给中国的医疗体制带来了严峻的考验,证明了在医疗保健和健康保险领域需要相当大的改进。对我们来说,考察社会状况的关键词是不公平、不公正和失业的威胁。

第四,经济发展和环境之间的关系。环境问题在德国和其他欧洲国家导致了绿党的创立。拥有13亿人口的中国是世界上最大的经济体之一,并且以最高的增长率刺激着全球经济的增长。但必须清楚指出的是,中国对原材料的巨大需求也给全球环境带来了不可预见的威胁。譬如说如果中国的汽车普及程度和美国一样,那么就不会有足够的钢铁来制造车身,也没有足够的燃料来转动引擎,还会向我们共同的大气层排放过多的二氧化碳。我们已经见证了能源的短缺,许多城市发出了今夏控制用电的预告。不仅仅是北京的街道上经常堵车,铁路系统也严重超负荷运转。

还有更多的例子使问题显得更严重。过去几年的国际讨论指出,不仅石油和其他工业原材料短缺,就是看起来丰富的水资源也告急,更准确地说是饮用水资源。联合国预测今后的战争会基于对水资源的争夺而非其他。近些日子虽然北京的雨水很多,周边地区还出现了暴风雨造成人员伤亡的事件,但北京周边的水库已经接近干涸。我们不得不承认水资源也有失衡的危险。

刚才我们讨论了我们看到的一些问题。我也看到在过去二十多年的改革开放中,我们的财富实现了增长并且得到了管理。对任何外国人,尤其是外国大使来说,试图提出这些问题的解决方案不是十分恰当的。我们所能做的就是提供合作,长期的持续稳定的合作。更具体地,就德国能扮演的角色来说,我认为在现有合作之外,有四个极具潜力的合作领域:能源、交通、环境和投资。可再生能源的应用、智能系统在交通控制中的应用、应用于各种交通工具的新推进技术和新材料(例如可再生材料)是值得考虑的主题,在这些领域德国的公司将大有可为。目前中国2%—3%的能源已经由可再生能源提供。政府希望能将这个数字在2012年提高到10%，而德国公司在这方面有显著的优势。

在去年的国际风能会议上，中国与欧盟签署了价值5亿欧元的风力发电机的协议。去年夏天，德国外交部的官员在山东省参加了世界上最大的太阳能实施计划的开幕庆典，这是一个中德合资的投资计划，在中国已有6 000万平方米的太阳能采集能力，产量相当于中国现有水平的3个核电站或是30亿升的原油的产出，并且可以节约30%—40%的能源。公路、铁路和航空运输能力的提升将变得紧迫。到2020年，中国的铁路网络将要扩张30 000公里，航空运输的速度也会得到普遍提升。在2004年，中国航空乘客总量增长了30%。航空和地面服务都迎来了新的机遇。

不可否认，中国成功地在国际合作和吸引外国直接投资方面起到了重要作用。约一千家德国公司在这里投资了一百多亿美元。但是，国外直接投资的环境还有待进一步提高。一方面，中国政府充分意识到保护知识产权的责任；另一方面我们不得不承认很多外国公司的产品一进入中国市场即被复制，然后低价出售。这并不只是中国一个国家的问题。但如果中国希望在吸引外资的同时能够引进先进的技术，如果中国希望这种技术的输入能够持续下去，那么盗版行为就必须被禁止，至少是被降低到最小的可能。盗版行为必须被当作犯罪行为来处置，政府必须对此严惩不贷。

精明的投资者不会愿意在没有得到合理补偿的前提下冒任何风险，因此我们需要法律制度方面的改进以消除在中国投资的不确定性。外国投资者不仅需要适应中国的文化、中国的生活方式、中国的语言，还需要适应中国不同的解决纠纷的方法，包括商业和贸易纠纷。关于腐败问题有许多讨论。有时当德国公司向当地政府寻求直接的帮助或者申请法律执行时，他们一无所获。两国高层官员的长期对话以及有关法律事务的讨论首先集中在商业和贸易的相关法律问题。这也许是因为这个领域的改进姗姗来迟，但这一步的

迈出能进一步增强经济政策的效力。提高监管和法律执行的透明度也是互惠互利的。在发达经济中,投资收益是双向的。中国在国际舞台上扮演的角色越重要,就越能捕捉到增长的机遇。

在欧洲拥有最大国内生产总值和最大消费者群体的德国无疑是世界上的占据主导地位的经济体之一。它位于欧洲的中部,与几乎所有的主要欧洲经济体相接壤。这种有利的中枢性地理位置使得德国无论是在西欧发达市场还是在中东欧新兴市场上都获得了成功。德国作为全球最大出口国的地位显示出世界各国消费者对德国产品的赞赏。过去5年中,德国的生产力提高了30%以上,大大降低了单位产品的劳动力消耗。此外德国还是世界上最开放的国家之一。交通、电信和能源等关键市场都面向国内外投资者开放。目前已经有超过22000家外国公司在德国开展业务,雇用了210万以上的员工,年收入高达一万亿欧元。但其中罕见中国公司。我相信关注这些领域的中国公司一定可以找到合适的投资机会及合作伙伴,在德国市场上获得成功。

总结起来,如我这样的外国大使如何看待中国经济呢?首先,即使是考虑到之前我所提到的问题,也没有任何理由怀疑中国经济的光明前景。中国可能会经历结构变更,会经历在可以预见的将来更加明显的制度上的压力,或是如1997年、1998年那样的周期性低谷。但是二十多年来中国真实的经济增长率一直维持在8%和15%之间。这也有助于避免社会不稳定。

因此,增长是中国经济自改革开放后二十多年来,特别是在邓小平1992年“南巡”讲话后释放出来的活力的不可避免的结果。对于增长和伴随着增长而来的问题的把握,将是在座各位的任务和责任。你们父母和哥哥姐姐们的努力使得改革开放成为可能,而你们将要让改革开放继续下去。我相信这对在北大接受高等教育的你们来说不难实现。也许将来有一天我的继任者会站在这里为中国经济和德中经济、政治、文化合作描绘更加光明的前景。祝你们成功！谢谢。

现场对话

听众：尊敬的大使先生和孙教授，我是北大经济系的教授。上周我访问了德国，得知最近德国的失业率高达12%。在中国我们同样面临着严峻的失业问题。您对中国的就业政策有什么建议和意见么？谢谢！

史丹泽：谢谢。我想中国和德国的失业问题的原因虽然存在某些类似，但总的来说是非常不同的。我认为，中国的失业问题源于尚未完成的从农业社会向工业社会的转型。这就是为什么农村地区的失业率是全中国最高的。而在德国，导致失业问题的是尚未完成的从工业社会向高科技的现代化全球化社会的转型。

冷战结束后，全球化才真正影响到西欧社会。当然我们那时在国际上已经相当活跃。但是直到前民主德国区域社会主义经济解体并开始转型时，全球化的真正含义才开始变得明确起来。这给德国和其他西欧国家的社会结构带来了压力。一方面这种转型需要一定的时间。同时，人们纷纷被解雇，从而导致了失业的增加。不同于其他西欧国家，德国面临着额外的问题：每年德国政府需要花费800亿美元用于帮助占领土面积1/3的前民主德国区域转型。

为了提升失业人群的生存状况，我们从19世纪末开始就制定了一套被称为“社会保障网”的制度，来帮助人们避免陷入贫困。显然，这套制度经过20世纪50年代初、80年代和90年代早期的不断改进已经适应了工业社会，为工业经济环境下的人们提供了社会保障。现在，我们处于国内外工人相竞争的全球化时代，面临着进一步改进工业社会社保制度的问题。我们的社会保障制度正经历着翻天覆地的变化。我不敢比照德国现在达到的社保水平来给中国

提建议，因为我们的社保制度如上所说需要并处于不断改进中。我们将会拥有一个新的老年保险体制，我们还需要有新的医疗保险和失业救济体制。你现在看到的德国社保体制和5年前的大相径庭，而5年后也肯定远不同于目前的状况。谢谢。

听众：我想问一个关于两国间文化交流的问题。从去年起就有一系列的有关法国文化的活动，包括展览、时装秀和车展等。在法国也有相应的关于中国的展览。我对德国非常感兴趣，而且相信在中国有很多人都想进一步了解德国。你们有类似的关于促进两国文化交流的计划么？谢谢。

史丹泽：谢谢你的问题。让我给出两点回答。首先，德国和中国之间文化交流的水平是非常高的。我们在北京同样有专门的文化机构，并正努力在上海也设立这样的机构。中国也将在今年10月于柏林设立文化机构。两国之间进行着大量的文化交流工作。也许专门在一年内集中展示德国文化并非十分必要，因为我认为只要人们愿意，进一步了解德国是很容易的事情，就像德国人想进一步了解中国也很容易一样。当然，如果有人希望举办文化年的活动，我们随时乐意支持。如果北大希望在德国举办中国年或是在中国举办德国年活动，我们会支持你们的。祝你们好运。

其次，如果我说德中两国间的相互理解和文化交流的水平非常之高的话，这种情况可能不会一直持续下去。相反的情况也是成立的。原因很简单，因为全球化。全球化意味着德国社会在世界上拥有越来越多的合作伙伴。而中国正在走向开放，也将发现日益增多的合作伙伴。对中国而言，存在的危险是过去对中国感兴趣的德国人可能会将兴趣转移到别的国家。反之德国也面临着这样的风险。过去对德国和有关德国的东西感兴趣的中国年轻人可能会把注意力放在他/她之前从未听说过的某个国家上。这对我们双方的大使馆、领事馆和文化机构都是一个特殊的挑战。但我们必须努力保持现有的水准，即使不能够进一步提升的话，来实现两国社会之间更多的交流。我们大使馆现在做的努力远远超出过去，并且仍在寻找有关我们该做什么、如何改进的创见。如果你们谁有好主意的话，欢迎告诉我们。非常感谢。

听众：大使先生，我是经济学院的学生。我们知道您是亚洲事务的专家，尤其是有关中国以及日本的事务。您能就最近中日外交关系降温给出一些评论么？这次降温将怎样影响中国的经济发展？谢谢。

史丹泽：如果我是日本大使的话会发现这是个很尖锐的问题。好的方面是，中日之间的经济关系并没有降温。就在北京那场众人皆知的反日学生游行之后的一天，我碰巧去一家寿司店吃东西。店里都是中国的年轻人，很可能就是前一天刚刚参加游行回来的。因此我想，中日双方在经济上相互的吸引力确实很大，政治因素或者历史敏感问题并不能真正阻碍经济往来。我知道在中国有抵制日货的活动，但我怀疑这样做的必要性，因为中日之间的经济关系并不仅仅局限于中国人购买日本商品。有很多日本商品实际上是在中国生产的，中国生产的商品远销世界多个国家，包括美国、日本等。这是更深一层的经济合作关系。这为双方政治关系和社会联系的改善提供了坚实的基础。至于政治关系，作为一个外国大使来说，我实在不适合作什么评价，尤其是中国的媒体很喜欢将德国和日本的过去做对比。因此在这个问题上我无法置评，请你理解。谢谢。

听众：史丹泽先生您好！我是经院大一的学生。现在中国和德国间互遣留学生越来越多，中国各种层次的学生都有人去德国学习。而中国学生误入德国已经破产的语言学校的事情也时有发生。您觉得应当如何来促进两国之间更加有效的教育信息交流呢？

谢谢。

史丹泽:事实上我必须告诉你教育交流的情况非常好。在德国的中国学生是所有外国留学生中人数最多的,他们通常都能获得很好的成绩。当我们大使馆在网上招聘的时候我也亲身体会到了这一点。有很多在德国学习或工作过的很优秀的中国人,希望能够回来利用自己对德国的了解和德语的专长找一份工作。他们素质之高给我留下了深刻的印象,我甚至担心我可能付不起足够高的薪水。在中国的德国公司也同样不发愁是否能找到曾在德国学习、工作过的优秀员工。我想我们已经上了轨道。

我认为有一件事情需要我们努力的就是要将更多的德国学生带到中国来。据官方数字,现在已经有1 500名德国学生在中国学习。当然,如果算上那些没有受到德国政府资助的自费留学生,这个数字将更高,在中国总共有大约2 000—3 000名德国留学生。这是一个不错的数字,并且在不断增长中。但我们需要更多的德国学生来这里。我的女儿现在就在这里学习中文。这是一个我个人做出的决定。谢谢。

听众:我是经济学院的老师。我注意到欧盟有一个统一的农业政策,将欧盟预算的70%分配给共同农业。美国也有类似的政策。空中客车也向政府要求补贴。最近欧盟和美国都要求中国削减纺织品出口,而纺织品恰恰是一个没有政府补贴的完全竞争行业。我的问题是,欧盟和美国一方面要求中国降低完全竞争行业的出口,一方面又给自己的产业提供补贴,这背后的逻辑是什么?纺织品出口的削减可能会让成千上万的人失业,您怎么看待这个问题?谢谢。

史丹泽:谢谢。事实上你肯定不会认为空中客车是我们农业的一部分。尽管他们的飞机可能很原始,我相信他们会改进的。就空中客车的补贴而言,空中客车和波音是世界上仅有的制造大型飞机的厂家,因而在美国政府和欧盟国家的政府之间也存在着竞争,从而也有补贴上的竞争。考虑到要花费纳税人巨额的财富,没有一个政府会很愿意给某大产业提供补贴。但业界会互相攀比:其他国家给予了补贴,我们也必须这样做。这就是空中客车的情况。

有关农业补贴,我们要看到欧洲的农业发展很不平衡。有些国家,尤其是欧盟新成员的农业还十分不发达,却要和农业高度工业化的国家相竞争。打开地图,你可以看到北部欧洲,包括德国,农业已经实现了高度的现代化;而在南部,包括法国的中部、南部,中欧和南欧的欧盟新成员国,农业并不发达。因此欧盟农业补贴的目的在于寻求成员国农业收入之间的平衡。如果不补贴的话,南欧的农业生产者将会很快被挤出市场而给该国经济造成巨大影响。我也清楚这项补贴政策提高了欧洲农业在世界上的竞争力,人人都清楚长期来说这是不可接受的。但欧洲农业发展的不平衡状况需要相当的时间来改善,因此我们除了继续补贴别无选择。在波兰、捷克或是匈牙利,农业是国民经济的重要组成部分,如果他们不想让30%的劳动力失业的话,就需要对农业进行补贴。因此我认为欧盟扩大之后,农业补贴相比以往将持续更长的时间。这对我们,对纳税人来说都是困难却不得不接受的事实,是我们多年来一直努力寻求改善的状况。在欧盟只有12个或者15个成员国的时候,我们尚且没有取得完全的成功,现在欧盟扩大了,问题就更加困难了。

我们也意识到和国际合作伙伴间一直存在着磋商和谈判。中国并不是唯一一个为此抱怨的国家。美国抱怨的更多。我们和合作伙伴间确实存在着争端,但是在大多数的情况下我们都能够找到一个更为令人满意的妥协的解决方案。而妥协,让双方都能接受的妥协正是国际关系的关键所在。

对纺织业来说,有一个十年的缓冲期。在这十年里,纺织品生产国有足够的机会来应对配额的取消。我们很早之前就明白如果法国南部、印尼和柬埔寨的纺织业不能在2005年1月1日之前做好充

分的准备,他们就将面临巨大的难题。现在我们必须得正视这些国家的政府并没有让自己的纺织业做好准备的现实。中国政府完全有理由说“我们早就告诉你们了,你们也知道要将发生的这一切,为什么不利用好这十年的缓冲期呢?”中国在这一点上完全没有错。然而,问题仍然存在,仍然需要解决,并且不能通过争端的方式来解决,那样会产生国际关系和经济合作中更多的摩擦。

因此这里有三个问题:首先是你谈到的欧洲的问题。这个问题其实相对较小。但这个问题因为一些和欧盟有关但并非其成员国的国家而被放大了,例如我之前提到的印尼,更多地依赖于纺织品的生产。因此我们必须找到一个关于新的缓冲期的妥协办法。这个妥协也应该不会令中国的厂商和工人损失太大,毕竟在 2004 年 12 月 31 日之前他们还受到配额的限制。现在情况已经大大改善了,达成一个临时的妥协不再那么困难。其次,中国和美国之间也存在着问题。这和第三个问题——中国和第三世界的高度依赖纺织品出口的国家,如柬埔寨、孟加拉等国间的问题是相互关联的。因为实际上自 2005 年 1 月 1 日取消配额限制以来,美国的纺织品进口总量并没有显著增加,但是进口结构发生了巨大变化。凭借价格优势,中国将一些小国家挤出了市场。譬如柬埔寨、孟加拉国、墨西哥这样的国家,虽然也享有 10 年的缓冲期,却没能做好充分的准备。我会说这是他们自己的错。但是谁又想这样呢?在柬埔寨、孟加拉和巴基斯坦,上百万的人失去了工作,你们希望看到这个么?当然谁都不想。这样会引起行业内的争端和很多国家的不稳定。所以中国需要做出努力和让步,与这些目前遭受损失的国家分享一点儿优势,以帮助他们进行改革。就在四五天前,我读到了一本书,书中提出了我认为很好的一个解决方案——中国的纺织业的领头羊正在向海外转移部分生产。这样你们就开始了和别国的合作,既帮助了别的国家也对中国纺织企业面临的处境有所改善,能让中国政府在处理和美国之间的争端时处于更为有利的地位。我想这不失为解决之道。

最后,你提到中国的纺织业和农业因为国外农业生产者得到政府补贴而受损。但正如我之前说的,不得不指出外国公司也遭受了中国一种特殊的倾销,所谓的“社会倾销”。因为这里的工资和福利如此之低,以至于中国商品在海外十分具有竞争力。这对德国的消费者来说当然是一件好事,我很高兴我在德国买的中国商品非常便宜,很享受这种社会倾销。所以关于补贴的说法是把双刃剑,情况十分复杂。我们当然不能提议说让中国将工资水平提升到和德国一样,但我们必须寻求一种对双方都有利的平衡。谢谢。

听众:谢谢史丹泽先生给我们带来精彩的演讲,也谢谢孙老师为我们带来这么精彩的项目。我想问问史丹泽先生,您在中国有自己的投资么?如果有,是什么样的投资呢?结果又如何呢,如果我可以问的话。谢谢。

史丹泽:在资本主义社会里关于个人财务的问题是非常隐私的,但我愿意在这里和你分享我的秘密,虽然这是个令人失望的秘密。1993年我离开中国的时候,一个很好的中国朋友告诉我:“邓小平是对的,他主持的改革开放会一直进行下去,中国经济将实现巨大的增长,在中国投资吧!”所以,我回去和我的太太商量这件事情。她说让我们冒一点险吧,于是我们就把薪水的一部分投在了一家香港银行的中国基金里。现在十多年过去了,中国经济确实取得了巨大的成就,我的钱怎么样了呢?前一阵子有个香港的银行家告诉我,你如果能在中国投资十多年而不赔钱,那就是个成功。所以,我们是成功的投资者。

听众:我是经济学院的老师。非常感谢您精彩的演讲。刚才您谈到了中国的经济和中德经济合作,我想进一步了解一下德国的经济状况。根据国际货币基金组织的预测,德国经济将实现2%的增

长率，但德国国内的6家机构却认为增长率只有0.7%。因此我想问问您关于这一点的观点和您做出判断、预测的理由。另外，德国政府正在进行一项名为“2010”的社会福利改革，您对这项改革的计划有什么意见么？它将给德国经济带来什么样的好处？谢谢。

史丹泽：谢谢，从上一个问题你肯定能看出我的个人经济状况了。关于全国经济状况的问题，我也会尽量回答。如前所述，德国面临的是如何更好地融入全球化经济中去的问题，这需要时间。对我们来说，还有继续改革前东德经济的问题。这两个因素影响着德国的经济发展。眼下，德国已经连续三年成为世界上最大的出口国。但同时德国也存在着严重的失业问题。这很容易解释，德国经济的某些部分已经适应了全球化的要求和挑战，但仍有一些部分落在了后面，在世界范围内缺乏竞争力，出现了公司破产和失业。所有进行改革重组但尚未成功的公司都不得不裁员以求生存。这就使得预测德国经济的增长变得困难。实际的情况高度依赖于出口的增长状况，而眼下居高不下的欧元币值对此并无帮助。如果欧元能稍稍贬值的话，出口情况将有更大的改善，尽管我们将面临更高的国内价格和通货膨胀。总的说来，德国经济的增长与全球的发展状况密切相关，因此很难准确地进行预测。

第二个因素是对前东德经济的改革。我们每年投资800亿美元用于这项改革，也取得了很大的成就，但新建立的公司仍然需要在国际市场上，至少是国内市场和欧洲市场上，争得自己的一席之地。在实现这一点之前，这一部分经济的增长很难把握。我想这也解释了不同机构预测的不同。无论如何，我们很满意目前在欧元居高不下的情况下德国的大量出口。如果说最近欧元会有什么动态的话，那就是向下微调，从而为我们的公司带来额外的优势。

第二个问题是关于德国的社会保障制度改革“2010”。就像我在前面说的，我们正处于调整我们的社会保障制度的过程中。这次改革的核心在于便利对失业人口和依靠社会救济度日的人群的管理。譬如说,一个从未工作过的单亲妈妈只能依靠社会救济,而一个曾经工作过的单亲妈妈至少在一定时期内还可以领到失业补贴——我们有两套不同的体制和两群不同的公务员来管理不同的人群。因此我们需要将这些制度合二为一,以便更加便利有效地管理失业救济和社会救济的对象。三年之后,这必将是一个不同的局面。

听众:我是经济学院的老师。我曾经去过德国并且收益良多。我们对东西德的统一很感兴趣,并获得了一个有关从中央计划经济向市场经济转型的小型研究项目的资助,因为我们都需要知道这种改革所应遵循的合理步骤。在研究中我们发现人力资源因素是一个很大的问题。中央计划下国有企业的员工缺乏勤奋以及合作的动力。因此一些德国专家认为东西德合并是一个负担。我想请问,东西德合并对你们这些政策制定者来说真的是一个负担么?你们是否后悔这样的决定?

另外,我认为德国是个非常聪明的民族。这一点可以从大众汽车分散在华投资看出来,它分别在上海和长春合作设厂,在合资公司之间引入竞争。你对这一点怎么看?谢谢。

史丹泽:谢谢你关于分散投资的建议。但是对大众汽车来说,在中国拆分投资是一个负担,因为这样要承担双倍的费用。他们一直在努力试图将在华投资合二为一,那样将更为合理。我想如果把大众的 CEO 请来再讨论这个会更好。

东西德统一并不是如你所说的"吞并"一词那样简单。但是不要忘记,没有人预料到统一会来得如此之快。甚至在统一前的一个月,也没有人想到这件事即将发生。因此当它发生的时候,完完全全是出于东德人民的希望。我们向来就很支持合并,但并没有提出确定的时间表,而任时间流逝。当突然有一天东德人民希望合并的时候,根据我们的原则,我们没有理由反对。如果你看看今天的东

德社会,我们也没有理由为这个决定后悔。转型的过程非常困难,代价也很大,但我们得到了一个统一的德国。我们没有任何理由去后悔。

造成转型过程如此困难的一个原因是,东德的经济实力按照官方数字曾经在世界上排名第十位。我们相信了这个来自东柏林的有水分的数字。因此在统一的过程中,我们没有动用足够的资金和努力来实现东德的转型,因为我们认为东德的大公司只需要很少的资助就能够在市场上立足。事实上他们一家也未能生存下来。我们本该投入了更多的资金和努力。我们因此丧失了宝贵的时间并使大量人失业。如果我们早一点知道我们被误导了的话,情况会不一样。直到今天我们仍然在为此付出代价。谢谢。

Explore the Potential for Cooperation

Dr. Volker Stanzel, German Ambassador to China

June 9, 2005 in Peking University

Speech

Thank you very much, Ms. Sun, for managing to pronounce my Chinese name. Thank you very much for the kind introduction. Thank you very much for the invitation. It's a privilege and a pleasure to be here, all the more because I was told that it was possible to give a lecture in English. It's tremendously impressive if I consider a Chinese person giving a lecture in Chinese at my home university. I remember that at the very beginning of my study, there were many students beginning to study Chinese. But after everybody realized how difficult this language was, I think there were about four or five left.

Now to come to my topic of the Chinese economy as seen through the eyes of foreign ambassadors. Well, even before taking up my post in Beijing, I was actually confronted with the question of how the Chinese economy looked through my eyes as the future German Ambassador to China. For example, at a meeting between our ambassadors and the whole region's German business and industry representatives which took place just a few days before I left, the German-Chinese economic society in Berlin invited me to give a talk. You must have known well that at the time there was very little I would have to say. It shows, however, the immense curiosity which permeates Germany about what actually lies behind the ever higher cityscape and ever in-

creasing number of new cars driven in Beijing and Shanghai, with a lot of those cars being German, of course. The curiosity usually goes with a kind of concern: Will the dramatic growth continue? Will German businesses continue to be able to hold its own in the environment of ever-fiercer competition?

Of course, during those very early meetings, I could not seriously pretend I could reply. Even today I only understand small bits and pieces of a very big puzzle, which is your economy. You are the students from the school of Economics and you are much better equipped to explain what's going on. So after I have made my points, please explain the reality to me.

Now, let me see. There are high buildings, there are many cars. They are really here. Every new skyscraper is a statement about China's future, and it'll be easy to take that at face value. Also, it will be easy to base analysis on the pride which I encounter every time I talk to Chinese friends about this country's economic achievements, achievements over the last two decades of reforming and opening policies. What has been happening here has provided a tremendously solid basis also for German-Chinese economic cooperation, and thus for the improvement of political and cultural relations as well. However, we must take care not to lose ourselves in what has been called the "China Dream". What we want is to provide for the future long-term success of both our countries. Therefore, German businessmen and politicians coming to China are quite right to ask me "How will China go on from here?"

Now let me take a look at some of the facts and some of the elements of China's economic success. Obviously, China owes its increase in wealth and its decrease in poverty to the unparalleled economic growth continuing for more than two decades. This growth owes its dynamism to the unqualified support for the primacy of economic construction given by this country's leaders, which is captured in Deng Xiaoping's famous maxim that to get rich is glorious. This pragmatism has served China as well as the echo it has found in the West. Practically all producers of consumer articles now have moved their productions partially, in some cases wholly, to China. China therefore is called the workshop of the world. Even if the productivity may be somewhat lower in some areas of the industry, the production in China pays off. It is profit yielding for foreign companies. China's enterprises, too, enjoy the result of non-equal technology transfer, which has been successfully pursued over many years. Now this sort of cooperation works and as I said, it is mutually beneficial. The creation of high grade employment in China goes along with the advantageous production environment for foreign investors. 56% of Chinese exports are still based on foreign investment. The cause of these successes is easy to perceive—wages and social standards are lower in China. Costs of employment, pensions, and health provisions are not yet integrated in the wage system. In this sense, there is indeed something that one might call "social dumping", which represents disadvantages for employees outside of China. Actually this also means disadvantages for some employees inside of China. Only 160 million Chinese workers are entitled to unemployment benefits and 190 million don't have health insurance. The fact that only 155 million people are a part of the pension scheme demonstrates the big flaw that exists compared to other industrial societies. That translates directly to production advantages. This leads me, as a foreign observer, to the question of the sustainability of this country's growth. How long can it last? How long can it continue as it is? So first I have to ask, will China's strong export performance create problems in developed markets like US or Germany, or with Asian competitors of China?

Let me explain this using the very famous example of textiles. Chinese products have reached a market share of about 40% in US, and in certain segments it's even higher. With the impact of the exchange rate between the renminbi and the US dollar, US manufacturers are no longer competitive. At home and abroad, they lose the market share to China. The result is the loss of employment in the US. American studies, as you might know, say 1.5 million jobs were lost in US. Now comparable studies for Germany do not exist, even though in Germany we also see a similar process of crowding out

competition. Nor have we answered the question of how many German jobs are lost by building up the production capacities of German companies here in China, or whether other employment of higher skills is, at least temporarily, secured by this effect at home, which will be positive, of course. There is, therefore, an intense discussion of these matters going on also in my country. We have no reason to doubt the general opinion; German companies state that their engagement in China and their shifting lower-paid jobs here serves the long run conservation of business and secures their employment in Germany. However, we should not forget another rule, either. There is no business deal that does not pay off for both sides involved, consumers and supply. Customers all over the world enjoy attractive prices of goods coming from China. The retailing business takes the share of it. I think we all share the perception that trade is the fuel that keeps so many wheels turning, and it always opens up new business opportunities. Therefore, protectionism can never be the realistic answer to contemporary problems. Of course, I say this as the ambassador of the country that ranks number one in the world as exporting nations.

Secondly, there is a question how China integrates into the world with its demand for commodities. Although China accounts for only about 4% of nominal world economic output, it's the second largest consumer of primary energy after the US, and it's the top global producer for coal, steel, cement and ten different kinds of metals. Twenty years ago, China was East Asia's largest oil exporter. Now it's the world's third largest oil importer. Last year, it accounted for 31% of global growth in oil demand. Thus China's seemingly insatiable appetite for commodities is driving global demand. The famous chart that compares oil prices and China's oil imports illustrates how China's hunger drives up prices worldwide. On the one hand, dependence on overseas mines and oil wells and international shipping lines by which those commodities reach China is among the reasons that Beijing has adopted foreign policies driven by pragmatism rather than ideology. On the other hand, how will national economies whose producers are elbowed out of market react? More importantly, how will the governments react? This is behind the question internationally asked ever so often: Whether China's rise can really remain a peaceful rise? Maybe all those fears are superfluous, yet we have to accept that they do exist. That means the strategies of China's transition will have to take them into account proactively in order to secure a sustainable, peaceful environment for its economic growth.

Thirdly, there is the question of how the intense social frictions may become, or, will they have an impact on China's further economic development? To begin with, the transformation process of the state-owned enterprises has had a major effect. For example, a big part of the workforce and the salary workers are made redundant. At the same time, the comprehensive system of social security offered by the state-owned enterprises gradually disappears. Now let's look at the employment effects and the increasing pressure on the job market. If China has 90 to 150 million people without employment and an unemployment rate of about 30% in rural areas, which is what the Asian Development Bank says, then there is a problem. The situation is complex. At the same time, there is a lack of skilled workers and there are regions where companies are eagerly looking around to find people for the jobs that have to be done. This mismatch can also be appraised by considering the 100—120 million migrant workers in China. There seem to be unbalanced situations not only between different regions of the country but also, in an increasing way, between different branches of the industry, and also between different people with different levels of skills. I already mentioned social questions when talking about future needs for reform. China's aging population brings up consequences that prompt urgent solutions. Huge numbers of elderly people have to be looked after by much fewer young people in their active working age.

Due to reforms, the structure of the industry has changed and provisions must be altered in order to tackle the facts of an aging society. Provisions of pensions are not the only field of the social policy requiring adjustment. China's health system came to a test visible for all in the spring of 2003 when SARS hit the nation. It demonstrated that much progress is needed for

medical care and health insurance. For us, the main watchwords, as far as the social situation is concerned, are inequalities, injustices and the threat of unemployment.

Fourthly, the question of the relationship between the environment and economic growth. That is the question that in Germany and in other European nations have led to the foundation of the Green Party. This is one of the biggest economies of the world with 1.3 billion people and about the highest growth rates. But I must say it clearly—it also stands for unforeseeable challenges to the environment worldwide and an enormous demand for raw materials. For example, if the degree of motorization of China would be the same as that in the United States, there would not be enough steel to build the cars, not enough fuel to keep their engines running and too much carbon dioxide emissions into our common atmosphere. We already witness today the shortage of energy production. New cuts in electricity supply in many cities are forecasted this summer. Not only do the streets of Beijing face regular jamming, but the railway network is heavily overloaded.

There're many more examples that seem to signify problems. In international discussions over the last couple of years, it has been pointed out that not only crude oil and raw materials for industrial purpose present a reason for serious struggles, but also the element that seems so abundantly available, namely water, drinking water, will be more precious. The United Nations predicts that future wars may be about water, not territories or influence over others. As it has been raining a lot in Beijing these days, we all have our own umbrellas ready. Just a week ago, storms took human victims in some areas of your country. But the reservoirs around Beijing are nearly empty. We have to state there's a danger of imbalance.

As you've seen as you followed me, we've been highlighting a few problems that we see. I also see that growth in wealth has been maintained during two decades of reforming and opening policies. Thus it will be overly ambitious for any foreigners, especially ambassadors, to pretend to know what solutions might look like. All we can offer is cooperation, long-term cooperation, and sustainable cooperation. To be more specific and to look more at what my country has to offer, I would outline four areas with great potentials for new expansion of our economic ties beyond those that already exist. They are energy, transport, environment and investments. The use of renewable energies, intelligent systems in traffic control, new propulsion techniques for all sorts of transport, and new materials, for instance, renewable materials, are among a wide range of ideas to be considered, where German companies are well situated. Now 2%—3% of China's energy supply already comes from renewable sources. The Chinese government wants to increase this figure to 10% by year 2012. German companies can play a prominent part in this.

During the World Conference on Wind Energy last year, contracts for the production of wind generators worth 500 million Euros were signed. And in the summer of last year, German Foreign Ministry officials attended the opening ceremony of the world's largest construction plant of solar energy collectors in Shandong Province, a Sino-German joint venture with already 60 million square meters of solar collectors all over China. This capacity equals the output of three nuclear power plants of current Chinese standard, or 3 billion liters of oil produced. Furthermore, with the energy production, 30% to 40% savings can be achieved. Extending and upgrading China's transportation infrastructure, road, railway and air, will be an urgent task. By the year 2020, China's railway network should be extended by about 30 000 kilometers, and the average speed will be increased in aviation. The year 2004 saw a total increase in passengers of 30%. Not only aircrafts but also ground installations offer new chances.

This is not to cast a cloud over the China's success in playing a more important role in international cooperation and in attracting more foreign direct investment than any other country in the world. Some 1 000 German companies and German investments of more than US $10 billion are here. But conditions for further FDI growth can be improved. One point, IPR, intellectual property rights, is especially important. The Chinese govern-

ment is well aware of its responsibility for protection of IPR. But we have to state that in many cases foreign companies see their products copied and sold at a much lower price shortly after entering the Chinese market. This is not a problem that just has to be dealt with in China. If China wants to see not only the inflow of investment but also of the technology which would be transferred, if it wants inflows to continue, then product piracy must be stopped or at least reduced to a minimum. It must be treated as a criminal act and the authorities must pursue those who break the laws without exception.

Investors have a sharp eye. They don't like risks unless they pay off. That's why in the legal system I see an area of future progress that may eliminate the uncertainties of investments in China. Foreign investors, business people in general, have not only a problem in understanding and adapting to Chinese culture, Chinese way of life, Chinese language, they must sometimes come to term with a different approach to the settlement of commercial disputes. There's a lot of talk about corruption, in cases where German companies have to face rather odd situations. They try to find straightforward support from local administration and law enforcement, but sometimes in vain. Ongoing official high level dialogues about legal matters between China and Germany first focus on commercial and business law. This is probably due to the fact that improvement in this area is overdue and will help further strengthen economic policies. Transparency of both the regulations and enforcement of law will be mutually advantageous. Investments between advanced economies take place usually on a two-way street. The more China's so-called "global players" take up their international role, the more awareness for the existing opportunity of growth will increase.

Germany is a leading economy with Germany's largest GDP and largest number of consumers among European countries. Germany is located at the heart of Europe, and it shares borders with nearly every major economy in Europe. Its favorable central geographic position provides practical instant access to both the established markets of Western Europe and growing markets in Central and Eastern Europe. Germany is the largest exporter in the world, and that fact demonstrates the widespread appreciation of products made in Germany. Of the past five years, Germany's productivity has risen by more than 30% , and this has led to a decline in unit labor cost. On top of all this, Germany is one of the most accessible economies in the world. The liberalization of key markets like transportation, telecommunications and energy sectors opens the German markets to both foreign and domestic competitors. More than 22 000 foreign companies are already operating in Germany. Among them, so far there are far too few Chinese companies. Foreign companies in Germany employ more than 2. 1 million people, and generate annual revenues of a trillion Euros. Chinese companies focusing on these sectors will certainly find investment opportunities, and will find cooperative counterparts with whom they can make the business a success.

To summarize, how does a foreign ambassador like myself see the Chinese economy? For one thing, I don't see a reason to speak gloomily about China's economic prospects, even in light of the problems I mentioned. There may be structural changes taking place. There may be stresses on the system beginning to show more clearly in the near future. There may be a cyclic downturn after the one or two years of 1997 and 1998. But the real economic growth has stayed in a range of 8% to 15% until the end of the decade. That also helped to avoid social unrest.

So growth is almost the inevitable consequence of the forces unleashed in the Chinese economy more than 20 years ago, even more so in the year of 1992 when Deng Xiaoping launched the Spring Storm. The management of that growth, and of the problems tied to that growth, will actually be your task and your responsibility. Your fathers and mothers, your elder sisters and brothers made reforming and opening possible. You will have to make it last. With the education you receive here in your university, I think it will not be difficult for you to achieve that. In the future, one of my successors as German ambassador, or possibly ambassadress, will stand here and paint an ever brighter picture of the Chinese economy and also of German-Chinese economic, political and cultural cooperation. I wish you all the best of suc-

cess. Thank you very much.

Q & A

Audience: Respected Ambassador and Prof. Sun, I'm a teacher at the School of Economics, Peking University. I visited Germany last week and I learned that Germany's unemployment rate is about 12%. You know, in China we also have serious unemployment problem. Do you have any suggestion and advice for China's employment policies? Thank you.

Volker Stanzel: Thank you very much. I think the reasons for unemployment in China and Germany are similar in a few ways, but also different in many ways. From my point of view, the reason for unemployment here lies mainly in the not yet fully achieved transition from an agricultural to an industrial society. That's why the unemployment in the agricultural sector in China is the highest. In Germany, we have the unemployment due to the uncompleted transition from an industrial society to a high-tech modern globalized society.

Only after the end of cold war basically did globalization really affect West European societies. Of course we're already internationally active. But what globalization really meant only became clear after the communist economies ceased to exist and started to transform as well. That put a lot of pressure upon the structure of German society and many other societies of Western Europe. Unemployment is one of the effects we see as this restructuring process takes its time. In Germany, unlike other Western European industrial societies, we have an additional problem, which is the fact that we have a socialist economy practically in our own society that has to undergo transformation to market economy within our own borders. This means that every year the German government still pays US $80 billion simply to help the transformation of the one third of German territory that used to be GDR. So we have two problems that we're faced with and none of them compares to the problems that China faces.

In order to alleviate the plight that unemployed people face, since the end of 19th century we have developed a very carefully worked-out social system called Social Net, which helps people, catches people so that they don't fall into poverty. That system of social security obviously was adapted to the industrial society as it already existed at the beginning of the 20th century. It was modernized at the beginning of the 1950s, 1980s, and early 1990s. So it provided social security to people in a very different economic and industrial environment. Now we are faced with the problem of adapting this system of social security to the age of globalization when suddenly you have competition between our workers and workers on the other side of the globe. So our system of social security is undergoing some tremendous change. I wouldn't dare propose the stage we've reached now as an example for China, for one of the reasons I already mentioned, and secondly for the reason that our new system of social security is evolving. We will have a different system of old age insurance. We have to have a different system of health insurance. We have to have a different system of unemployment benefits. The system that you find in Germany is very different from what you found five years ago. Thus you can be very sure that five years from now it will be different again. Thank you.

Audience: I have a question about the culture communication between the two countries. As you know, there has been a series of activities about French culture since 2004 such as exhibitions, fashion shows and cars and so on. The same exhibitions about China were held in France. I'm very interested in Germany and I think there are many people in China who want to know more about Germany. So my question is, do you have any plan to improve the culture communications between our two countries? Thanks.

Volker Stanzel: Thank you very much for the question and let me give you two answers. First of all, the level of cultural exchange between Germany and China is extremely high. We also have a culture institute in Beijing. We're

working on a new one in Shanghai. China's going to establish a culture institute in Berlin this year. So we're doing a lot between both countries. And maybe it's not necessary to make extraneous efforts to present German culture during one year because I have an opinion that if people want to know about Germany, it's very easy to do so, just as it's very easy for German people and German students to learn more about Chinese culture. Of course, if someone wants to have a culture year, we're ready to support that. If Beida wants to pick up the initiative to have a year of China in Germany and to have a year of Germany in China, we'll support you. Good luck.

The second part of my answer is, if I say we have an extraordinary high level of mutual understanding, knowledge and culture exchange, I'm afraid, this may not last. Why is it the case? For an easy reason—globalization. Globalization means that German society has an ever increasing number of partners in the world, which want to promote their societies. And Chinese society itself is just about in the period of opening up to the world. It will find itself confronted with our increasing number of partners worldwide. There might be a relative decline in attention paid to our traditional partners. The danger is that Germans who in the past might have been interested in China now may become interested in another country. That's a danger not just for you but also for Germany. Of course, it's the same vice versa. Young Chinese in the past who might have been interested in Germany and German things now might focus their attention on societies which were not even on the screen for them in the past. That translates into a very special challenge for us in our embassy, in our general consulates, in our culture institutes and for your government, people in your culture institutes in Berlin as well. We have to make strong efforts to at least maintain the present level of interest, if not to raise it, to bring about more exchanges between the several societies in both our countries, which then will translate into real culture exchanges. Our embassy now is doing a lot more than in the past. Even so, we're looking around for new ideas of what we do and what we're to promote. So if you or anybody else has some ideas, you're welcome to tell us and we'll try to pursue that. Thank you very much.

Audience: Mr. Ambassador, I'm a student from the School of Economics. We've learned that you've been an expert on Asian issues, especially with Chinese and Japanese issues. So would you please give us some comments on the recent cooling-down of diplomatic relationship between China and Japan? How does this cooling-down affect Chinese economy? Thank you.

Volker Stanzel: Well, if I were the Japanese Ambassador, I think, it's a tough question. The good thing about the situation is that economic relations are not cooling down. The day after the infamous anti-Japanese student demonstrations here in Beijing, I happened to go into a Sushi restaurant and I found the restaurant was full of young Chinese, possibly just returning from the demonstration. Thus I thought, obviously, the economic attraction between both countries is so strong that politics or traditional sentiments do not really stand in the way of economic exchange. I know there has been a call for a boycott of Japanese goods. I don't know if that warning is even necessary because the economic relations between China and Japan are not confined in the area of buying Japanese goods. It is also vice versa. Chinese goods are being bought in Japan and even more Japanese products are produced in China and a lot of factories here export to many other countries, to the US, to Japan. That's a deeper kind of economic cooperation which I think is providing a very solid basis for the improvement of political ties between the societies. As far as the political situation is concerned, as a foreign diplomat, I really should not say too much and especially as Chinese newspapers like to point to Germany's past and Japan's past. So I ask you for your understanding. I really cannot comment. Thank you.

Audience: Respected Dr. Volker Stanzel, I'm a student from the School of Economics at Peking University. I'm a freshman now. We have more students studying in each other's countries and students at all levels go to Germany. However, things like Chinese students going to bankrupt language schools have happened. So what do you think can be done to promote an ef-

ficient education information exchange? Thanks.

Volker Stanzel: Actually I must tell you it was quite good. The number of Chinese students in Germany is the highest number among any group of foreign students in Germany. Usually they do very well on their exams. I see it myself when we put on the internet offers of employment in our embassy. It usually attracts a full range of people who have been studying in Germany and also even been working in Germany who have come back and want to live in China and want to use their knowledge of Germany and German language to look for jobs. I'm always impressed with the extremely high quality of these people, sometimes so high that I have a feeling that I cannot even pay enough. The same is true with our companies here. They have no problem at all in finding highly qualified Chinese employees who have been studying and working in Germany. I think we are on a good path.

The one thing I think we must work on is to bring even more German students to China. There are already 1 500 officially here, and a higher number, of course, without the help of the government, paying for the studies by themselves, people who are not registered with the government. So let's say between 2 000 and 3 000 German students here. It's a good number. It's increasing. But we need more. Actually my daughter is presently studying Chinese here. I personally have made the decision. Thank you.

Audience: I am a lecturer in the School of Economics at Peking University. I observe that the EU has common agriculture policies. 70% of the European budget was devoted to the common agricultural industries. And America has a similar program. Recently I observed Airbus asked for a government subsidy. And recently the EU and US asked China to reduce its clothing and textile export, which is an industry fully based on market competition. There's no government aid in China's clothing and textile industry. So my question is, what's the logic behind that? On the one hand, EU and US subsidize your own agriculture industry, while on the other hand asking China to reduce its clothing and textile export? The reduction of textile exports will cost thousands of poor workers of their jobs. What do you think about this? Thank you.

Volker Stanzel: Thank you very much. You would not say that Airbus is part of our agriculture, actually. Even though their planes might be quite primitive, but I think they're going to improve. Concerning Airbus subsidies, here you have a competition between US government and European government, the competition between Boeing and Airbus, the only companies that produce and sell large-scale planes. So there's competition of subsidies as well. No government, neither the government in Europe nor the government in US is comfortable with subsidizing big industries because it would cost taxpayers a lot of money. On the other hand, the industry always points to the other one. The other one is doing so, so we have to do it ourselves.

That much for Airbus. Now about agriculture subsidies. Agriculture in Europe is very differently developed. Now with new member states, we have a large number of countries in the EU with an agriculture industry not very highly developed. They are competing with countries that have a practically industrialized agriculture sector with very few people but a lot of output being achieved. So if you look at the map of Europe, generally speaking, you may see that on the northern part, including Germany, there is highly modernized agriculture, and in the southern part, including the southern part of France, central France and the Central and Eastern European new member states, we have not as well advanced agriculture. So the subsidies for agriculture in Europe actually are for the purpose of balancing income in the agriculture industries among our member states because otherwise farmers in the southern countries of Europe will be out of business too quickly for the nations' economic stomach. I am aware that this also will have an impact worldwide because European agriculture is made more competitive worldwide as a result of that kind of subsidy. It is intolerable in the long term. Everybody sees that. But with the differentials in development in our European agricultural economies still persisting, still taking years to come to the same level, we have hardly any choice but to continue subsidizing. To underlie my point, I think the subsidies now are going to last much longer than before the enlargement

of the community because the agriculture sectors in Poland, as much as in the Czech Republic and Hungary, for example, are very large sectors of the nations' economies, which need subsidies if they don't want 30% of their workforce out of jobs. That's something we have to live with, which is hard for us, the tax payers, to live with, which we have tried to remedy since many years ago. We have not achieved a complete remedy with twelve member states, not even fifteen member states. It is more difficult this time after the enlargement.

We're also aware of the fact that there're all the time negotiations with our international partners. China is not the only country to complain. The US is complaining even more. So we're in a dispute with other partners. So far, in most cases we have found a satisfactory solution. That's compromise and that's what international relationships are always about. It's finding a compromise that both sides can live with.

About the textile sector, there's a ten year grace period during which producers worldwide had the opportunity to adapt to the lifting of the quotas in the textile sector worldwide. We're all aware that if industries in Southern France, Indonesia, Cambodia did not prepare well for January the 1st, 2005, they would face big problems. And we have to face the reality of these industries that the governments involved did not prepare their industries sufficiently. So now we have a situation. The Chinese government is absolutely right to say, "We told you so, you knew what was coming, and you had 10 years' time. Why didn't you use it?" The Chinese government is absolutely right there. Still, the problem is there and the problem has to be solved. And the problem cannot be dissolved through conflict because that will produce more and more conflicts as we always see in international relations and economic relations.

So what I see are three problems. The first one is about Europe, which is a relatively minor one. It's enhanced by the fact that there're countries associated with the EU, not members of the EU, that depend to a large degree on textile production, such as Indonesia, as I mentioned. So we have to find the compromise. I would say a new grace period, which does not make Chinese producers and workers suffer too much because, after all, they lived with quotas until December 31, 2004. Now the situation is so much better since then. So to find a temporary compromise should not be too difficult. Secondly, there's a problem with the US. That problem is connected to the third problem, namely the problem for smaller countries in the third world that depend to a high degree on textile export, such as Cambodia and Bangladesh. The volume of textile exports to the US is not actually significantly increased due to the lifting of the quotas on January the 1st, 2005, but the structure of textile imports to the US has changed completely as Chinese companies, because of their price advantage, are able to edge out companies from smaller countries such as Cambodia, Bangladesh and Latin American countries. That is the actual problem. Problem two, namely your conflict with the US and problem three, the problem that occurs in smaller continues are connected. Countries such as Cambodia, Bangladesh or Mexico also had this ten years' time, but they did not prepare well. So it's their own fault, you might say. But at the same time, who would want that? People by the millions losing their jobs in Cambodia, Bangladesh or Pakistan? Would you want that? Of course not. It means causing industrial conflicts and instabilities in many countries. So China has to work and take a constructive attitude to give a little bit of the advantages it now enjoys to share with those countries that now suffer in order to help them transform their economies. There's something I read just four or five days ago, which to me shows the way, which is that large Chinese textile producers are now shifting part of their productions out of China into Cambodia. So here you have cooperation and that helps the Cambodians and makes the lives of Chinese companies better here. And it makes the case that the Chinese government has in its disputes with the US so much easier. I think that might be a solution.

Lastly, you allude to the fact that people in China in the agriculture and textile sectors might suffer due to subsidies given to farmers and textile producers in other countries. But let me point to the statement I made in the course

of my presentation before. What we're faced with, what foreign companies are faced with in China, is a specific kind of dumping, social dumping because wages and social securities are so low that prices of Chinese products can be so competitive abroad. That is, of course, to the advantage of me as a German consumer. A Chinese product that I buy in Germany is cheap. I enjoy the benefit of that kind of social dumping. So it's a two edged argument that you're using. The situation is quite complex. Of course, we can not recommend raising wages in China to the levels of Germany. But there has to be some sort of balance, which is to the benefit of both sides. Thanks.

Audience: Thank you very much Dr. Stanzel for giving us such a wonderful lecture. Thank you very much Dr. Sun for giving us such a wonderful program. I want to ask Dr. Stanzel, have you got any investments in China? If yes, what are they? And how about the result, if I may ask? Thank you.

Volker Stanzel: OK. Financial affairs in capitalist countries are usually very personal secrets. But I share my secret with you. It's a depressive secret though. When I left China in 1993, a good Chinese friend told me, "Deng Xiaoping is right, the Spring Storm and the reform policy will continue. We'll see tremendous growth in China. So invest in China." So I talked to my wife. She said let's take a risk. We took a little bit of our salary and we left it with a China fund in a bank in Hong Kong. And fifteen years has gone, and the Chinese economy has grown. What happened to our money? Well, a Hong Kong banker told me the other day, "If you invest in the Chinese economy and in fifteen years you have not made a loss, that is a success." So we're successful.

Audience: I'm a faculty member from the School of Economics, Peking University. Thank you very much for your wonderful speech. Just now you talked much about the Chinese economy and Sino-Germany cooperation. I'd like to know something more about your country's economic situation. The IMF predicts that the economic growth rate in Germany will reach 2%. But there're six German institutes predict that German economic growth rate will be 0.7%. So I'd like to know your opinion about the growth rate in Germany. What's your reason for your judgment and prediction? And the second question is that the German government has carried out a welfare reform plan called "2010" and keeps improving the structure of labor market. I'd like to know your opinion about this agenda. How will the agenda bring benefits to the German economy? Thank you very much.

Volker Stanzel: Thank you. As you just learned from my previous answer, you're able to get information about my personal economy. Now I'll try to answer your first question. The German economy, as I explained sometime ago, is in the phase of transition of adapting to more complicated integration into the global economy, and that takes time. To us, it still has to transform the former socialist economy of Eastern Germany into a modern economy. These are the two factors that influence the economic development in Germany. What we see at present is that no country exports more than Germany does. I think it is the third year in the row that Germany is the country with the highest export volume worldwide. At the same time, we see a high level of unemployment that was mentioned before. It's easy to explain. Some parts of the economy have managed already to adapt to globalization and its demand and challenges. And some parts are lagging behind. And that's where the unemployment comes from. There're companies that are not competitive enough worldwide, companies that go bankrupt. So people are on the street. Or, there are companies that try to restructure and are not yet fully successful. That means the have to lay off people in order to survive. All these factors make it difficult to explain how much growth Germany's economy will enjoy this year or next year. It depends to a very high degree on our export successes. The question is will it continue to succeed with a possible continuously high value of the Euro or will it enjoy more success if the value of the Euro decreases, which, however, will mean higher import prices and higher domestic inflation. So it depends so much on global developments that it's extremely hard to know what we can do precisely this year or next year.

And then the second factor comes in, which is the transformation of the for-

mer Eastern German companies. We've made progress since we have invested so much government money, as I mentioned, US $80 billions per year. But newly founded companies still have to find their places in the world market, or at least in the national market, or the European market. Until then, with each and every of these newly created companies in Eastern Germany, it's also very hard to know. So I think there are good reasons for different predications of the future economy. However, we enjoy this status of being the country with the largest export volume despite the high value of the Euro. If there is any indication recently as to the future value of the Euro, it is to a slightly lower value of the Euro, which will translate into additional benefits for our companies.

The second question was about the social security agenda, 2010, in Germany. As I said before, what we have presently is the phase of adaptation of our total security system. The core of the reform you've been talking about is to facilitate the administration of people who are unemployed, possibly temporarily unemployed, and people who are dependent on social aid. So far we have two different systems. For example, a mother with children who has never been working, if her husband leaves her and she is on her own, depends on social benefits. But if the same mother worked and lost her job, she is entitled to unemployed benefits, for a certain period of time at least. We have two different systems with two different groups of civil servants in whose hands different groups are administered. So the core of the reform is to facilitate the administration of these problems by structuring one system which administers both unemployment and social aid recipients. So if you look at the situations possibly three years from now, it will be different again.

Audience: I'm a faculty member from the School of Economics at Peking University. I have been in your country and benefited a lot from your country. We're interested in the unification of West Germany and East Germany and we have sponsored a small program about transition from a central-command economy to a market economy, for both our economies need to know the logical steps in the transition course. During that time we find the most difficult thing is the human resources in the two countries. Some experts from your part said that to merge with East Germany is a big burden. My question is that, is merging with East Germany a burden for policymakers including you? And do you feel regret?

Also, I think German people are very clever to split investments in China, for example, in the case of Volkswagen's setting up two joint ventures in Shanghai and Changchun. They brought in competition. What's your opinion about this? Thanks.

Volker Stanzel: Thanks for the investment advice. But for Volkswagen, it's a burden to split its investments because of the double costs coming down on the company that they don't enjoy and they've been trying to change it in China, which will be much more rational. We may discuss this if we invite the CEO of Volkswagen here.

Merging with East Germany isn't as easy as the word "eat" you used. Don't forget that nobody anticipated the unification to come about so quickly at that time, not even a month before it happened. So when it happened, it was purely and solely upon the wish of East German people. We always said, ok, the two countries, at a certain point in time we want unification, but did not aim at any specific date or time. We allowed time to pass. When the time came that East German people wanted unification, according to our principle, there's no way to say no. And there's also no reason to regret if you look into East German society today. The transition was extremely difficult. Yes, indeed. It's extremely costly, too. But at the same time, we now know that this is a unified Germany. So there is no reason to regret.

One reason why it turned out to be so difficult is that East Germany was considered one of the strongest economies in the world. At one time it ranked number ten. Of course it was all make believe. Other countries accepted the figures coming from East Berlin, which were absolutely not true. So at the

time of unification, the investments and the transition efforts that the West German government undertook were insufficient because we all thought those big companies in East Germany would need only little aid and would survive in the market, but nothing turned out that way at all. None of the companies was able to survive. Much more investment and many more transition efforts would have been necessary. So we lost a lot of time and people got laid off. If only we knew that in advance. We were misled like everybody else. We're still paying the price actually. Thank you.

瑞典驻华大使

雍博瑞博士 (Dr. Börje Ljunggren)

雍博瑞（Dr. Börje Ljunggren）

雍博瑞大使1942年2月27日生于瑞典南部城市赫尔辛堡。拥有哲学博士学位。瑞典资深外交官，长期从事亚太和国际问题研究，曾任瑞典驻孟加拉、老挝、坦桑尼亚使馆外援负责人、瑞典国际发展署副署长和瑞典驻越南大使等职。1998年参与制定瑞典“亚洲战略”。1999年任瑞典亚太司司长，多次访华。雍博瑞博士于2002年11月至2006年10月担任瑞典驻华及驻蒙古大使。

Dr. Börje Ljunggren was born on Feberary 27th 1942 in south Sweden, Helsingborg. He owns the Doctor degree of Philosophy. As a sophisticated diplomat, he charged affairs about Asia and international relationship and was the Swedish Ambassador to Vietnam. He once headed the Development Cooperation Office (DCO), Swedish Embassy in Bengal, Laos and Tanzania, after which he worked as the Deputy Director General of the Swedish International Development Authority (SIDA).He played an important part in Swedish Asia Strategy Project (1998). Being the head of the Department for Asia and the Pacific(1999), he has visited China many times. Dr. Borje Ljunggren was as the Swedish Ambassador to China and Mongolia during November 2002 to October 2006.

平衡发展　稳步改革

——中国的今天与明天

瑞典驻华大使　雍博瑞博士(Dr. Börje Ljunggren)

2005年9月15日　北京大学

演讲全文

首先,我很高兴、也很荣幸来到北大这样一个国际知名的大学演讲。我想在座的各位北大师生都很优秀。

我要骄傲地说北大和瑞典的大学之间也有合作项目。最近,瑞典五大重点大学之一的斯德哥尔摩大学和北大达成了合作协议。瑞典隆德大学也与北大法学院开展了人权方面的合作项目。我们对这个项目十分满意,它是北大国际法方向硕士学位教育的一部分。今年有30位学生参加了这个项目。就在几分钟前,我们还在讨论瑞典公主于下周二访问北大并与法学院学生进行交流的事情。公主殿下年仅28岁,是瑞典未来的女王。她将来访中国,以增进对中国的了解,并开展一个官方项目。这是她即位准备工作的一部分。我很高兴下周能接待公主殿下。今天我的演讲将首先从五个方面评论中国社会经济方面的发展:首先是经济增长;然后是公平,或者说社会公正；第三是可持续发展；第四是政治变革和民主；第五是环境。之后我将同样从这五个方面来介绍一下瑞典，让大家多了解一些瑞典和瑞典近代的历史。最后，我会以瑞士大使和学者的双重立场就中国的今天和明天得出一些结论。我会讲得非常坦率。

自1978年以来，中国25年的增长是我们所见证过的全球最快的增长。前些日子，我曾听美国著名经济学家 Jaffrey Sachs 说，中国在25年里年均增长9%，其增长率之高、增长期之长，都是人类历史上前所未有的。这是一个特例。当然，中国的增长起点很低。然而，按GDP计算，中国已经是世界第五大经济体，我也肯定中国的排名会继续上升。如果使用购买力平价进行调整，中国经济已经是世界第二大经济体，仅次于美国。我肯定你们都知道购买力平价这个概念。如果在北京理发，你可能只需要支付20元；而如果在瑞典，即使像我这样没什么头发的，也需要支付200元。因此必须使用购买力平价来对比两国经济状况。

更为惊人的是中国对外贸易的增长。1978年，中国出口总额仅为200亿美元。而今年，这一数字将突破7 000亿美元。改革开放前，中国经济是一个非常封闭、内向的经济，对外贸易规模十分有限。去年，中国出口总额占中国GDP的40%。这在任何标准下都是很高的比例。这一比例甚至高于瑞典的出口额占GDP的比例，而瑞典是一个小得多的经济体，与世界经济的融合更加紧密。40%这一比例对大国来说尤其显得高。这样，按进出口总额计算，中国就成了世界第三大贸易国，超过日本而仅次于美国和德国。

中国经济的特点在于，中国大量进口原材料，出口装配后的产品。中国进口的50%以手机等最终产品的形式再流向国外。这种情况下，外国直接投资自然占据了十分重要的地位。过去几年中，中国已经成长为全球最大的外国直接投资接受国。中国每年接受600亿美元的外国直接投资，占全球外国直接投资总额的10%。这也是与改革开放前大相径庭的。改革开放前，中国甚至没有关于外

国投资的法律法规；今天，外国直接投资在中国的地位举足轻重。中国出口产品的50%以上由外国直接投资的企业生产。这同样是一个罕见的数字。此外，中国还惊人地在短时期内实现了技术的飞跃，引进了大量现代技术。一个例子是信息技术：瑞典公司爱立信已经进入中国超过一个世纪。113年前，即1892年，爱立信手机首次出现在中国上海。但是直到1985年，爱立信公司才在中国开设了办事处。那时中国的电话用户总数有2 000万。现在这一数字正在逼近7亿，其中3.6亿为移动电话用户。这就是我所说的技术飞跃。中国在短时期内消化吸收了大量技术。这是我们在全球经济中所见证的部分现象。当然，归根到底这是中国市场经济的发展。我们还不能说中国已经是一个成熟的市场经济，但中国的大部分价格已经是由市场决定的，这是很重要的指标。中国出口总额占GDP的40%标志着中国已经融入世界经济。这一事实意味着中国很多商品的价格都决定于世界市场的价格。因此，中国已经从一个封闭的经济走向了与世界经济互相依存的开放经济。我认为这是具有重大意义的。尤其是三年前中国加入了WTO。今天，中国在世贸组织内起着十分重要的作用。我们希望中国的作为有利于世贸组织的进一步强大。我想为此发展作出贡献也是极为符合中国自身利益的。

这些都是令人印象深刻的数字，但制度建设方面的成果则没有这么令人鼓舞，例如银行系统、监管体系、股票市场等。众所周知，这些领域面临着许多问题。许多人都认为中国经济在短期和中期发展的最大问题就在于金融业以及金融业和国企之间的关系。银行一方面履行着作为银行所应该承担的职责，另一方面又不得不维持国企甚至是亏损国企的经营活动。但这种情况不是一成不变的，我们清楚地看到了银行系统的改革，也看到了国企的改革。四大国有银行中已有三家与外国银行进行了合作，合作对象包括美洲银行、苏格兰银行等，其中一家可能在年底前上市，这是意义重大的事情。中国还进行了货币改革，从盯住美元发展到了一篮子汇率政策，人民币也进行了小幅升值。可以看到中国正在逐步推进改革，这是十分重要的。

中国的法律体系也在不断完善，当然其起点同样很低。最近，我陪同瑞典司法部部长拜访了中国司法部。1958 年至 1978 年间，中国并没有司法部。直到改革开放才设立司法部。当然，今天法制建设对营造一个能支撑经济发展的环境起着至关重要的作用。我认为有几个问题十分关键。长期看来，没有什么比一个灵活、透明、可靠的体制更重要了。股票市场是一个很有趣的例子。过去 8 年里，中国经济年均增长 9%。但今年夏天，股市跌到了 8 年来的最低点。世界上别的国家都没出现过这么高的增长率和这么低迷的股市共存的奇怪现象。当然这反映出人们对股市没有信心，因而不在股市投资而转向其他投资。我认为发展一个能获得人们信任的股票市场和金融体系是十分重要的。其关键词仍然是透明度。我们必须能知道公司内发生了什么事情——公司是盈利还是亏损？是否可靠？因此整个会计系统和公司的年报都很重要。瑞典制定了严格的法律，要求每一个公司都符合透明度的要求，杜绝内部交易等行为。

与此同时，社会层面发生了什么呢？让我们看看全球的贫困状况，全球 60 亿人口中超过 10 亿人每天收入低于 1 美元。这 1 美元是经过购买力平价调整后得到的数字。中国对消除贫困作出了巨大贡献。与改革开放前相比，中国处于这一贫困线下的人口减少了几亿，这是很显著的进步。但是中国仍有大概 1 亿人口处于收入低于 1 美元的贫困线下，有 1.5 亿人每天的消费低于 1 美元。按照中国每天 75 美分的标准来看，中国大概有 3 500 万人处于贫困线下。因此中国仍然有非常贫困的人口和地区。显然，今天中国贫富差距很大，地区之间，尤其是东部城市和内陆城市之间以及城乡之间差距都很大。通常我们用基尼系数来衡量收入的分配。你们知道基

尼系数越低，收入越平均；基尼系数越高，收入差异越大。世界银行的数据显示，中国的基尼系数已经高达0.45，收入差异很大。瑞典的基尼系数大约为0.3，属于世界上收入分配较为平均的国家。巴西的基尼系数约为0.6。我认为中国的收入分配正在变得越来越不平均。当然，从中国存在大量有迁移意愿的农民工这一角度来说，收入的不平均是不可避免的。我们通常引用的数字是中国有1.4亿民工。这是一个很大的数字，要高于世界上多数国家的人口数。仅四川民工就可能高达1 000万，他们在很恶劣的环境下工作，收入低于其工作地区的最低工资，缺乏劳动安全保障，也难以获得医疗保健和教育。但我仍然认为这些劳动力能流动起来是件好事。他们可以获得更多的收入，他们想来北京、广东工作，然后将收入寄回家乡。结果他们储蓄的一部分就被投资于小城镇建设。因此劳动力流动实际上缩小了城乡差距，而不是扩大了这个差距。但这仍是中国所面临的一大社会问题。

收入分配是这一问题的一个方面，另一方面就是所谓的公共服务的可获得性，例如医疗保健和教育。我认为这是政府的主要责任所在。在中国，如果你是甘肃省一个贫穷的农民，当你需要进医院做手术时，只有你自己缴付了手术费后才会得到医治。你需要在医院进行任何医治行为之前缴费。卫生部最近发布的一项调查表示，50%的农村人口无力负担医疗保健，而这发生在一个有社会主义传统的国家里。我认为社会主义社会的本质是公平或者说社会公正。如果人们为了做一个手术而必须深陷债务，甚至决定不去做这个手术的话，我们很难说这是公平的。我知道“和谐社会”这一提法说明中国政府十分重视这个问题。人们也致力于不同的解决方式，例如保险体系和农村合作医疗。我认为这的确是很重要的一个问题。教育问题也很重要，但是扭曲程度相对较轻。大家知道，由于父母无力支持，有些中国的贫穷儿童不能完成学业。我知道政府今年已经增加了预算用于解决贫困失学儿童的问题。我认为这很重要。

机会的公平是关键的。我们不能要求结果的公平。不是所有人都能成为教授,但是生活中起始机会的平等是至关重要的。自然,当我们把收入、医疗、教育、性别这些问题一个一个叠加起来的时候,就可以看到中国所存在的不可否认的不平等性。这个社会必须要是一个包容平等的社会,人人都要能感受到自己是社会发展过程的一部分。

我想讲的第三方面是环境问题。中国的环境如何?我认为中国目前的增长模式不是可持续的增长模式。长期看来,经济增长必须以社会福利的增进为最终目标:适宜居住的城市、良好的环境、新鲜的空气和清洁的水。而这并不是中国目前的状况。中国的城市处于世界上污染最严重的城市之列。水资源十分匮乏,尤其是在华北地区。对此,政府同样提出了五个平衡,人和自然之间的和谐就是其中之一,这非常重要。鼓舞人心的是,中国能处理好这个问题。许多问题能靠科技的发展来解决。从某种角度来说,中国的能源使用相当浪费。中国每1000美元的产出所需耗费的能源是一个发达经济体所需能源的四倍。这非常浪费。结果,自然地,中国排放了大量的二氧化碳和汽车尾气,中国耗费了大量煤资源,并且是世界第二大石油进口国。我认为这是环境问题的关键。当然,油价飙升给每个经济体都带来了能源效率方面的压力,包括中国。但重点是中国必须及时做出决策,以免错过时机。

至于政治方面,我会讲得比较简要。与25年前相比,今天中国人民作为个人享受到了多得多的自由。我想你们都是这一事实的例证。你们整个思维都比几十年前更为自由。但对于像我这种来自于民主传统悠久的国家的观察者来说,政治制度改革仍然是很有意思的一个领域。如果将中国快速的社会变革与政治改革的步伐相比较,政治改革将是一个非常重要的问题。

最后,第五点是国际层面。正如我在开头所说的,中国的外交政策与以往大不相同。1978年至1980年,我曾任驻老挝大使。那时,中

国共产党支持了泰国国内推翻泰国政府的一些运动。中国既有官方的外交政策，也有另一套推动革命的政策。今天，中国的外交政策基于自身的利益，以创造稳定的国际环境为目标，从而实现中国经济的发展，吸引外资、推动贸易增长、引进技术、获得石油和原材料。大家可以看到中国正在海外投资采矿业，如投资于委内瑞拉的石油储备等。因此中国并不仅仅是外国投资的接受者，而同时也向海外进行投资。当然，我认为这是意义重大的。此外，还有中国作为安理会常任理事国对联合国的承诺与支持。现在，正有一个非常重要的峰会在纽约召开。事实上我很自豪地说胡锦涛主席今天正与瑞典首相在纽约进行会谈。联合国体制的改革深度并不够，应该进一步发展。这次峰会没能就核武器控制达成任何一致，核武器在未来甚至可能向恐怖分子扩散。瑞典首相本人对此表示非常失望。

总之，以上是我关于中国的五点看法。让我从同样的角度简要介绍一下瑞典。我想大家都或多或少了解一点瑞典。瑞典地处北欧，气候寒冷。瑞典的冬天比中国的冬天冷且长，但瑞典的夏季和春、秋季都很棒。瑞典只有 900 万人口，虽然它面积很大，是欧洲面积最大的国家之一。瑞典南部的人口密度较高，北方则人口稀少。首都是斯德哥尔摩。我想大家都知道瑞典是世界上较发达国家之一。尽管不是最发达的国家，但就人均 GDP 来说瑞典处于世界的前列，约 30 000 美元。中国的官方数字是人均 1 250 美元，与瑞典的差距很大。但我们应该用购买力平价进行调整，可得出中国目前人均收入为 5 000 美元。这样比较的结果就是 6 至 7 倍的差距，而不是 25 倍。瑞典的现代化进程开始得较晚，为 19 世纪后期。那时我们和日本并列世界上增长最快的经济体。在 20 世纪 70 年代，我们遭遇了经济困难，不得不进行改革。目前瑞典经济运行良好，增长率为欧盟内部第一。不像你们，没有别的国家能如此高速地连续增长这么长的时期，持续 25 年 9% 的增长率几乎是不可能实现的。瑞典的增长率为 3%，就其发达水平来说已经是一个很高的增长率了。

这一数字还能再高一些。瑞典所面临的困境是:一方面我们的经济增长率很高,生产力每年增长6%—7%,另一方面我们的就业机会太少。有时这被称为无就业增长。这是因为瑞典大量投资于科技领域,而当企业的投资需要大量劳动力时,他们就转向中国、印度或东欧这些劳动力价格较低的地方。因此我们看到了资金的外流。但是外国投资也在流入瑞典。我们看到了中国投资,像华为和其他企业在瑞典进行了投资。今天,瑞典约有20家中国公司。瑞典在华公司则达到了250家。爱立信在中国25个省份开展了业务,ABB在中国设立了超过20家工厂。由此可见看出瑞典对开放、贸易和WTO有着强有力的承诺。我们是四、五个按照联合国要求提供GDP的0.7%作为发展援助的国家之一。很多国家,像美国,则贡献的越来越少,甚至低于0.1%。我们在为国际社会作贡献方面历来有着深厚的传统。

在平等、社会公平和收入分配方面,如我所提到的,瑞典的基尼系数是0.3。我们非常注重社会公平。自1932年起,瑞典大部分时间都由社会民主党执政,只有9年例外。对这样一个政府来说,高就业率、公共教育、公共医疗是重点。有时人们认为如果福利过高就会影响经济增长。这不是真实的情况。事实上促进社会福利的计划完全有可能维持经济的增长。社会福利不需要以牺牲经济增长为代价,统计数据也说明了这一点。但我们必须确保所实施的计划是有效率的计划,而不会浪费资源。医疗服务并不是完全免费的,人们仍然需要支付药费等一部分费用。我们认为病人所得到的医疗服务应由他所患疾病的需要来决定,而不是由他的财力来决定。病人不应该因为无力支付医疗费用而遭到拒绝。我们一直都认识到必须拥有高质量的、透明的财政体系。强大的经济是强有力的社会体系的基础。这周日德国将会举行一场选举。他们在这方面做得不是很好,失业率高达12%,还有高额政府赤字。德国经济在改革方面做得不够。瑞典进行经济改革是因为我们在上个世纪90年

代初期就遇到了危机。最显著的是我们对养老金制度进行了改革，我们现在的养老金制度可以持续运营很长时间。不能说这些改革已经完成了。如果谁说改革已经完成，那么他就将陷入困境。

在环境方面，在 20 世纪 60 年代我还是个年轻学生的时候，环境问题就成了瑞典的热点问题。瑞典国内有大量非政府组织致力于揭露污染问题，例如化工厂的污染物渗入地下水层等。这些组织十分活跃。那时我们就建立了首个环境保护机构，类似于中国的国家环境保护总局以及首个相关立法。执政党和非政府组织之间相互回应对方施加的压力。公众和媒体都在引起社会关注方面起了重要作用。现在我们在环保方面有非常严格的立法规定，详细地规定了什么是被允许的。我们也有大量奖惩措施来让公司和家庭实现这些目标。我们的油价很高，因为我们希望借此影响人们的行为，使他们选择公共交通，不要一直使用私家车而搭乘地铁或公共汽车。我自己住在斯德哥尔摩的郊区，从来不开车去上班，而是坐更加便利的地铁上班。这一点很重要，否则瑞典的城市就会像北京一样拥挤。我认为可持续发展是至关重要的。

第四方面是政治和民主。从 1920 年起，瑞典就实施了大家所称的议会民主。男性和女性都有权利参与大选投票。我们每四年举行一次大选。议会中有七个政党。社会民主党是执政党，但在议会中并不占多数，只有 40% 的席位。因此社会民主党与左党、绿党一起联合执政。反对党由其他四个政党组成：一个更为保守的政党、一个中立党、一个自由党和一个基督教民主党。选举的竞争激烈。明年的九月我们就会举行一场大选，这将是一场很有意思的大选。民意调查显示，反对党占领先地位。我们将拭目以待大选的结果。但我是公务员，我的工作不决定于哪个政党执政。我属于职业公务员，招募和提升都基于工作能力。如果大选结果改变了执政党，那么只有包括首相、副首相、政治顾问在内的极少数人会离开政府机构。所有其他人都会留下来继续服务于民主选举出的占议会多数的新一任政府。即使存在大选等变动,政府体系仍然很稳定。我们还有超过100 000个非政府组织,民主生活十分活跃。有些人认为有这么多非政府组织一定会出现混乱。与此相反,这种情况使得我们的社会强有力地组织在一起。这意味着如果你对环境问题不满意,你可以发起一个组织,也可以参与一个相关组织,而不必使用暴力或其他手段。一些组织的历史非常悠久。有些组织是全国性的,有些是地区性的。你也可以今天在这里建立一个组织,由你自己任主席,另请某人负责账务。我们通过银行来注册组织。你还需要一个理事会。此外就没有别的程序了。大多数瑞典人,像我一样,是大概十个组织的成员,缴纳很少的会费。我对环保问题很感兴趣,所以我加入了自然之友等组织并缴纳会费。我认为这给社会带来了极大的活力。

有关瑞典的第五方面是对国际社会的贡献。我们致力于服务联合国组织。自上个世纪60年代起,瑞典所参与的联合国维和行动就多于世界任何其他国家,就像今天的中国一样。中国也参与了很多联合国维和行动,这是很好的。瑞典奉行不结盟政策,不是北约的成员国。我们1995年加入了欧盟。大家知道,今天欧盟拥有25个成员国。我们致力于发展国际贸易,希望消除更多的贸易壁垒。我们相信贸易能促进世界经济发展,消除贫困。我们反对纺织品配额。欧盟重新采用了纺织品配额,这是瑞典所彻底反对的。我们是欧盟内最反对纺织品配额的国家。丹麦也反对纺织品配额。我们曾承诺对中国的配额将在2004年年底取消。但欧盟重新启用了配额。这也只能再持续几年,到2007年年底就结束了。我们也很反对欧盟实施的农业补贴。许多国家,例如法国,对农民进行补贴。瑞典则不实行农业补贴。我们希望瑞典是一个开放的经济体。当我们加入欧盟时,我们不得不重新启用我们已经废除了的壁垒。当然,你们可能认为作为一个小国家,取得这些成就对瑞典来说很容易。不久前我会见了一位来自河北邯郸的人。邯郸市内人口为700

万至800万。而瑞典只有900万人口,比邯郸市大不了多少。当然中国的情况在很多方面都和瑞典不同。自1815年起,瑞典就没发生过任何战争。近两百年内没有任何大的战争。所以我们历史上一直很幸运。中国的历史则要复杂得多。几个星期前你们正在纪念抗日战争胜利60周年。那是一场持久而悲壮的战争。

让我们回过头来继续讨论中国的未来,这也是我讲座的最后一部分。什么是重要的呢?我会说是制度建设。建立一个有活力的金融体系,为商业活动创造有利的环境,而不区分是国有部门还是私营部门。制定对所有公司适用的统一的公司法。发展股市及其他金融部门。我认为这是根本的。我认为一个经济的关键词就是资源配置的效率。中国有着高的投资水平,非常高,但是如何确保这些投资是好的投资决策?银行是否能将资金引向好的投资项目?不是维持没有希望的公司挣扎,补贴它们,而是投资于新的工作机会。股市能否更正确地引导资金?我认为中国在改进资源配置效率方面还大有可为,从而保持高增长率。在中国,人们常常使用小康这个词,要在2000年至2020年这20年间将GDP翻两番。这是一个很高的目标。随着经济水平的提高,这项任务会变得越来越难。许多人认为至少在未来10年或15年里中国能保持7%—8%的增长率。但如果不进行改革、加强经济的竞争性,这将是不可能实现的。此外,今天的中国经济极度依赖外部需求,出口总额占GDP很大比例。从长期看来,中国必须拉动内需,改变这种依赖的现状。

第二,公平方面。我认为短期内很难减轻不公平的程度,因为中国的劳动力资源十分丰富。但我们还是可以做出一些努力的,例如最低工资、基本工作条件等。以服装厂为例,年轻女工每周可能要工作60个或70个小时。她们每年只能回家一次探视亲人。这个问题当然需要解决。但更为迫切的问题是医疗保健、教育等公共品的可获得性。你们如何使用财政收入?中国的财政收入增长很大,

9%的经济增长率开辟了新的税源。那么这些收入的用途如何呢?你们需要做出决定。我认为你们这些年轻人的想法是很关键的,你们将来想要一个什么样的中国?

第三点,环境方面,我认为在未来10年中,环境问题对中国和世界都起着决定性的作用,因为如果你们选择了一种耗费资源的长期发展模式,二氧化碳排放量将上升到很危险的高度。我相信你们是不会这么做的。我们需要新的科学技术。为了承办奥运,你们会尽量在北京使用不污染环境的汽车。希望你们能为发展环保新技术作出贡献。

至于第四点,政治改革,我认为从长期看来这将对中国十分重要。中国正经历着巨大的变化,通过因特网等技术,农村在向城镇发展,人们受教育程度在提高。中国人每个月发出200亿条短信,人们之间进行了大量通信。你们学习各种语言,发展旅游业,进行各种互动。我认为政治改革与这些变化相配套是很关键的。只有中国人自己才知道如何实现这一点。这是个极关键的问题。此外,对瑞典来说,人权是非常重要的问题。中国已经签署了人权领域最重要的一份公约——《公民权利与政治权利国际公约》,你们正在朝这份公约的方向努力。这份公约很重要,是国际体系的一个组成部分。我还认为,长期内,给非政府组织更大的舞台、树立对公众社会的信心以及对人民增进社会福利的意愿和努力的信心,都是至关紧要的。

最后,第五方面是国际秩序。同样,中国对于联合国建设以及世界贸易体系的发展等方面发挥着越来越重要的作用。15年后,2020年的世界,将与现在的世界大不相同,将会更加全球化,更加一体化。

总的说来有五点。第一点是注重制度建设——要建立一个透明可信的制度,如金融体系。第二是要建成一个包容的社会,让穷人也感觉被包容于其中。如果中国经济每年增长9%,那么穷人也应

当从中受益。第三点是要坚持保护环境。在提供更好的环境方面要把握机会站在全球的前列。第四,要建立一个真正开放的社会,建立灵活开放的政治体制,并为国际秩序的发展继续贡献力量。政治体制对中国来说十分关键。如果国际秩序相对稳定,中国可以享受对外贸易、外国投资、技术引进、教育机会等各个方面的成果。我认为这是相当关键的五点。

我已经在中国待了三年。这三年里,中国的经济增长了1/3。中国在世界中的地位也至少提升了1/3。这体现在方方面面,包括全球钢铁市场、其他农矿产品市场、原材料市场等。中国选择的前进方向对世界的未来产生着越来越大的影响。我很高兴你们在这里接受着北大优秀的教育,并将在中国未来的发展中起到举足轻重的作用。谢谢!

现场对话

听众:大使先生,我是北京大学经济学院的一名教师。你刚才提到社会福利和经济增长二者可以兼得。我猜你提到的福利系统是通过高税收而实现的。经典经济学理论一般认为高税收会降低人们工作的积极性。你如何解释经济理论和瑞典的经济现实之间的差异呢?或者你会驳斥这个理论?

雍博瑞:试图驳斥理论通常是危险的。我想如果要建立一套社会福利系统的话,必须要预见到它将如何运行。以医疗保障为例,瑞典人的平均寿命是全世界最高的。前一阵联合国发布了人类发展指数年度报告。在报告中挪威排名第一,瑞典排名第三。我们投入医疗保障的资金仅占瑞典GDP的8%,其中3/4的资金来自于政府,另外1/4来自私营部门。而美国的医疗保障费用占其GDP的13%—14%,同时他们的系统也更加私营化。然而在美国仍然有

3 000 万人没有获得医疗保障。所以我认为私营体系并非一定优于公共体系。最重要的问题是要确保这个体系是有效率的。税收并不是支持医疗体系的唯一来源，我们还有医疗保险。我知道中国并不希望实行如瑞典一般的高税率。但我很高兴纳税，因为我希望在瑞典农村的贫困人口也能够获得和我同样好的医疗保障。如果我有很好的医疗保障，但另外一个人的医疗保障却很糟糕，那么我不会认为这是个好的医疗体系。这是社会不公的表现。我希望在一个社会中公共物品的分配是公平的。对我来说，这意味着更高的生活水平。当然，为此我们必须付出代价。中国政府的财政收入占整个 GDP 的 20%。你们可以选择如何来运用这笔收入。你们可以发展医疗保险。你们必须为穷人做些事情。

听众：我是北京大学经济学院的一名教师。在最近欧盟与中国的贸易谈判中，有些评论者认为中国做出了过多的让步。而这些让步会令成千上万的中国工人失业。请问你如何看待这个问题？谢谢。

雍博瑞：我刚才谈到瑞典并不支持贸易配额制度。我认为最好能取消一切贸易限制。当然，中国的出口仍然将会继续增长。根据上周欧盟和中国达成的贸易协定，7 500 万件已经抵达欧洲港口的纺织品将被放行。在 2007 年之后，所有的贸易限制都将被取消。和美国的情况要复杂一些。中国和美国之间还没有达成类似的协议。从昨天的报纸上我得知目前中国国家主席正在墨西哥访问。访问很成功，但墨西哥人可能会感到担心。他们曾经向美国销售很多类似中国目前正在生产的产品。现在由于中国的出现，他们正不断丧失市场。中国的经济规模太大了，中国正成为世界工厂。我预计在未来中国会面临越来越多的贸易摩擦。

现在来看看瑞典的情况。在瑞典工会的力量很强。他们将开始讨论中国劳工状况的问题。他们会说，好吧，我们希望有自由竞争。

但中国的工人至少应该享受最低工资。如果中国经济每年增长9%，出口每年增长20%，那么中国必然要在世界舞台上发挥更大的作用。我想这个问题不会消失。瑞典很坚定地支持自由贸易，但同时对劳工的权利和环境问题也很重视。因此中国应该更多地发展国内需求，而不是过分地依赖出口。去年中国的出口额增长了1.5亿美元。这相当于印度一年出口额的两倍。中国一年的出口增长额比印度全部出口额还要多。

听众：谢谢，大使先生。我是北大经济学院大三的学生。我来自国际经济与贸易系。你能多谈一谈中瑞之间的贸易情况吗？另外我刚才突然有一个想法。和中国相比，瑞典是一个小而富有的国家。你认为有可能让中国的工人去瑞典工作吗？

雍博瑞：我首先要说中国和瑞典之间的贸易进展良好。两年之前中国成为瑞典在亚洲最重要的贸易伙伴，其重要性超过了日本。虽然目前从中国的进口只占瑞典进口总额的2%。

谈到劳工问题，这是一个有趣而复杂的问题。在全球化的背景下，我们允许货物和资本的自由流动，但涉及劳动力的时候，却有很多限制。欧盟国家有统一的移民政策。如果你想去瑞典，你需要申请签证。我们希望更多中国人能去瑞典观光旅游。如果中国公司去瑞典发展的话，他们可以将他们的工人带到瑞典去。假设你的建筑公司在瑞典承建了一个工程。那样你可以将你的工人派去瑞典，但你必须遵守瑞典的劳工法。曾经有个中国的富翁在瑞典建造一个叫做“瑞典门户”的工程，包括一尊巨大的佛像。他带去了一些中国工人。这些工人获得了去瑞典的签证，但他们的工资只有瑞典要求的最低工资水平的1/5。这是瑞典法律所不允许的。因此他们的雇主最后只能同意支付更高的工资。

听众：我是北大经济学院的学生。你刚才提到有些中国的亏损国有企业完全依靠银行的支持，因此他们成为银行的负担。但这些企业为很多人提供了工作。如果这些企业破产的话，那么很多人将失去工作，而这将是一个更大的社会问题。请问你怎么看待这个问题？谢谢。

雍博瑞：在过去几年中，中国国有企业雇用的工人人数正在以每年500万人左右的速度减少。从中可以看出中国企业正在经历着重组。这些工人可能转向了其他工作。中国的经济增长速度是9%，不断有新的工作机会出现。如果中国继续允许银行向那些亏损的企业贷款的话，这些企业可能会年复一年地持续亏损。这不是说只亏损一年，而是两年、三年、五年。这些是低效率的企业。在瑞典的经济体系中（将来中国经济体系也将如此），这些低效率的企业会破产。这可能听起来很残酷，但破产法是一个经济体系至关重要的一部分。如果一个企业年复一年地亏损，那么它就应该破产或者被重组。可能换一个企业主能将它经营得更好。如果银行不断贷款给那些无法偿还贷款的亏损企业，那么从长期看来这是非常浪费的。不知道你是否同意，但我认为一个企业由于各种困难而暂时的亏损是可以理解的，但如果这种亏损成了一种慢性疾病，那么它就成为整个社会和经济的负担。破产应当被看成是一个对公司进行改革，带来新主人和新资本的契机。

Steady Reform and Balanced Development

—China's Today and Future

Dr. Börje Ljunggren, Swedish Ambassador to China
September 15, 2005 in Peking University

Speech

May I first say that I am very happy and honored to be here and to have the opportunity to speak at such an institution of excellence as Peking University, an internationally very well recognized university. I think that you all should feel privileged to be students and staff at this university.

I am also proud to say that your university and Swedish universities have cooperation. We have a recent agreement between your university and the Stockholm University, one of our five key universities. We also have a program with your Law School, together with an institute at the Lund University, the second oldest university in Sweden, which concerns human rights. We are very happy with that program. It is research orientated and part of your master degree in International Law. Thirty students participated this year in the program. We just discussed a minute ago that next week on Tuesday the Crown Princess of Sweden will come to your university and meet with students in the Law School. The Crown Princess is a young lady, 28 years old. She will come to China to learn about the country and to have an official program. She is going to be the future head of state in Sweden, as queen. Coming to China and learning about the country is part of her preparations. So I am glad that I can receive her next week. The structure of my speech is that I will first comment on the socioeconomic development in China. I will do that from five different perspectives. One will be economic growth, one will be equity, or social justice you might say, the third one will be sustainable development, the fourth one will be political change and democracy, and the fifth one will be the environment. Then I will say a few words about Sweden, from the same five perspectives, trying to tell you a bit about Sweden and her modern history. Thereafter I will draw some conclusions, both regarding China of today and China of tomorrow, based on my perspective as the Swedish ambassador but also as an academic. So I will speak very freely.

Then we start with the five aspects of China. First, the economic development in China. What has happened in China in the last 25 years since 1978 is the most rapid development that we have witnessed in the world. The other week I listened to Jeffrey Sachs, the very famous American economist. He said that there is no other example in recorded history of an economy that has grown as fast as the Chinese economy for such a long period of time, 9% a year for 25 years. It is exceptional. Of course, it is from a very low base. As a consequence, China has become the fifth largest economy in the world in terms of GDP, and you will soon climb further, I am sure. You can also make an adjustment, usually called PPP, purchasing power parity. You know that concept, I am sure. If you cut your hair in Beijing, you may only pay some 20 Yuan. If you do this in Sweden, even if you have less hair like me, you pay 200. So in order to compare, you have to adjust using PPP. If you do that, then the Chinese economy has already become the second largest economy in the world, only the US is larger.

Secondly, what in a sense is even more remarkable is the way that foreign trade has developed. In 1978, China's total export amounted to 20 billion US dollars. This year it will exceed 700 billion. The old Chinese economy, before the reform started, was a very closed, inward-looking economy, with very limited foreign trade. Last year, China's exports amounted to 40% of GDP. It is a very high figure by any standard. It is higher than Sweden, which is a much smaller economy and more integrated into the world economy. It is thus a very high figure for a big economy in particular. You have become the 3rd largest trading nation in the world. You surpassed Japan, and are only after the US and Germany.

What is special about the Chinese economy is that you import a lot and then you re-export in an assembled fashion. 50% of what you import is then exported, like mobile phones. And of course, in this context, foreign direct investments play an exceptionally big role. During the last few years, China has been the largest recipient of foreign direct investments in the world. You receive 60 billion US dollars a year in foreign direct investments and that represents around 10% of the global volume of foreign direct investments. Again that is very different from the past. Before the reforms started, you did not even have a law on foreign investment and now it plays a crucial role. More than 50% of China's export is generated through foreign direct investments. Again that is a very unusual feature. Another thing that is also striking is that China has made a technological leap in a very short period of time. A lot of modern technology has been brought into China, for example, information technology. The Swedish company, Ericsson, has been in China for over a century. The first delivery of an Ericsson telephone was in Shanghai in 1892, 113 years ago. But the company did not open a representative office until 1985. At that time you had 20 million telephones in the whole of China. Now you are approaching 700 million, out of which 360 million are mobiles. That is what I mean by technology leap. A lot of technology was absorbed during a very short time span. It is part of what we have witnessed in the global economy. Of course, fundamentally it is the development of the market economy. You cannot say that China is yet a mature market economy. But the vast majority of prices are determined by the market. That is a very essential measure. The fact that you are so integrated into the world economy today, exporting 40% of your GDP, means that many prices depend on the world market. So from being a very closed economy, the Chinese economy has become a very interdependent economy, integrated into the world economy. I think this is very significant. And of course also very significant in this context is the fact that you joined the WTO three years ago. Today China plays an important role in the WTO. And we hope that you will play a role that will mean that the WTO will be strengthened further. I think it is very much in China's interest to contribute to such a development.

These are very impressive figures. If you look at the Chinese reform from an institutional perspective, like the banking system, the regulatory system and the stock market, the story is not as impressive. There are many problems here as you know. Most people would say that the biggest challenge that China is facing when it comes to economic development in the short and medium term is the financial sector and the relationship between the financial sector and the state-owned enterprises. The banks have a double role; they should perform as banks, but they also have to keep the state-owned enterprises alive, even when the enterprises are loss-making. But it is not a stagnant situation. We can see the reform of the banking system and we can see the reform of the SOEs clearly. Now if we take the four major banks, three of them have entered into cooperation with foreign banks, like the Bank of America and the Bank of Scotland. Possibly one of the big banks in China will be introduced on the stock market before the end of the year. That is very significant. Moreover you have had currency reform. You have moved from the peg that you had to the dollar to a basket of currencies, and you have adjusted the currency upwards a little bit. You can see that the administration takes a step by step approach here. This is very important.

The legal system is evolving, again from a very low level. I recently visited the Ministry of Justice here in Beijing, as our minister was here. Between 1958 and 1978 there was no Ministry of Justice in China. Only when the reform started was the ministry reestablished. And of course now legal development has a key role to play in creating good conditions that can support economic development. These are crucial things. I think in the long run, nothing is more important than a viable, transparent, trusted institution. The stock market is an interesting instance. In the past eight years you have had a 9% growth rate. But the stock market experienced its lowest level in eight years this summer. There is no other country in the world where the growth goes like this and the stock market goes like this (with gesture). This is very strange. Of course it reflects

the fact that people do not have much confidence in the stock market. They do not invest in the stock market. They invest in other things. I think it is very important to develop a stock market and a financial system that people can trust. The key word again is transparency. You must know what is happening within the company—is it making a loss or a profit? Is it reliable or not? So the whole accounting system and the annual reports of companies are important. We have a very strong law in Sweden so that every company must be very transparent. Inside trade and so forth is punishable.

So what has happened socially in the mean time? If we look at global poverty, a bit more than 1 billion people out of 6 billion people in the world are living under \$1 a day. This is \$1 a day PPP adjusted so that we can compare. A big contribution to the reduction of poverty has happened in China. You have a couple of hundred million people less under this poverty line today than you had before the reform started. This is very impressive. But you still have, depending on how you measure, roughly 100 million people living below \$1 a day. If you measure in terms of consumption, it is 150 million below \$1 a day. Using the Chinese measurement, which is 75 cents a day, you have some 35 million. So of course you still have some very poor people in China and some very poor regions. Obviously, today you have very wide disparity in China, between the rich and the poor, between the cities, especially the eastern cities and the inner part of China, as well as generally between the cities and the countryside. Normally you measure income distribution with the Gini coefficient. You know about the Gini coefficient: the lower the figure, the more equal, the higher the figure, the more unequal. According to World Bank data, China is now at 0.45; which is quite unequal. Sweden is at about 0.3, which places it among the more equal countries in the world. Brazil is at about 0.6. China is becoming more unequal, I think. Of course it is unavoidable in a sense that you have so much labor in rural China that is willing to migrate. The figure we use to quote is that you have 140 million migrant workers. It is a tremendous number. It is more than the size of most countries in the world. There are maybe 10 million migrants out of Sichuan alone. As you know many of them work under very tough conditions, below the minimum wage, without much protection when it comes to safety and little or no access to health care and education. But still, I think the fact that they can migrate is good. They earn more and they want to come to Beijing and Guangdong and they send money back home. Some of their savings are invested in small towns and villages as a consequence. So migration actually narrows the gap instead of widening it. But this is still a huge social problem for China.

Income distribution is one thing. Another dimension is access to what we call public goods, like health care and education. I think that is the government's major responsibility. If you look at China you know that if you are poor, if you are a peasant in Gansu and need a surgery in the hospital, nothing will be done unless you can pay. You need the money upfront before they will do anything. I saw a health survey recently published by the Ministry of Health. It said that 50% of the rural population cannot afford health care. And this is in a country with a socialist tradition. I think the essence of a socialist country is equity, or social justice. You cannot say that it is just if people have to get deeply indebted or have to decide against having an operation. I know the government now is very concerned about this when they talk about the harmonious society. Different ideas, like the insurance system and rural cooperatives are being formed. I think this is truly a very important issue. Education is also an important issue, but not as seriously skewed. As you know, poor kids in China cannot complete schooling because their parents do not have enough money. I know the government has added resources in the budget this year to address this. I think this is very essential. Equal opportunity is essential. You cannot demand equal outcome. Not every one can become professor, but equal opportunity, equal chance to a good start in life is crucial. So of course if you put income, health care, education and gender on top of each other you get an aggregate picture of inequality in China today, which is undeniable. Of course the vision must be what we call an inclusive society, where everybody feels part of the development process.

Then the third aspect I want to comment on is the environment. What about the environment? I think China's current growth model is unsustainable. In the long run, the ultimate goal of growth must be the well-being of society. Good cities to live in, good environment, fresh air and clean water. You cannot say that this is the situation in China today. Chinese cities are among the most polluted in the world. Water is scarce, especially in northern China. Again, the government talks about five balances. This is one of them, between man and nature. This is very important. What is encouraging is that you can address this issue. Technology is the key to many problems. China is very wasteful in energy. You use four times as much to produce 1 000 dollar worth of output as an advanced economy. And of course as a consequence, you have carbon dioxide emissions and suffix dioxide. You use a lot of coal in China. You are the second biggest importer of oil today in the world. I think this is the key when it comes to the environment. Of course, the oil price is shooting up and that puts pressure on all economies to become more efficient, including the China. But the point here is that you have can choose to address the issue before it is too late to do things.

When it comes to the political dimension, I should comment briefly on that. I think that people in China have much more freedom as individuals today than what they had 25 years ago. And I think that you are all examples of that. I think that your whole mind-set is much free than what was the case in China some decades ago. But when it comes to political institutions, in the form of a political system, as an observer like me, coming from a country with a long democratic tradition, I think this is still a very interesting area. Look at how rapidly China has been transformed as a society and compare it with the pace of political reform. This is a very important question.

Finally, the fifth perspective, the international dimension. As I said at the outset, China's current foreign policy is very different from what it used to be. I was Ambassador to Laos from 1978 to 1980. At that time, the Communist Party of China supported different movements in Thailand to undermine the government of Thailand. You had one official foreign policy but also a different policy that aimed at spreading revolution. Today China's foreign policy is very much driven by self-interest to create a stable world where China's economy can develop, grow, and get foreign investments, where trade can grow rapidly, and where technology, oil and raw materials can be made available. You see now how China is investing abroad, in mines and in oil reserves in Venezuela and so forth. So China is not only a recipient of foreign investment. Of course, I think this is very significant. What is also very important is China's commitment to the UN as a permanent member of the Security Council. As you know, there is a very important summit right now in New York. Actually I am proud to say that your president Hu Jintao is meeting with the Swedish Prime Minster in New York today. The reform of the UN system is not as profound as it should be. It has to be developed further. The results of the summit seem to contain nothing about the nuclear weapons control (and nuclear weapons can spread even to terrorists in the future). The Swedish Prime Minister was very disappointed about this.

These were my five aspects to say about China. Let me say something more briefly about Sweden from the same five perspectives. I think you all know a little bit about Sweden. Sweden is located in Northern Europe. It has a very cold climate. Winters are colder than here and longer than here, but there are wonderful summers, springs and autumns. The population is only 9 million people, even though it is a fairly big country, one of the biggest countries from the surface in Europe. The population density is high in the southern part and very low in the north. Stockholm is the capital. I think you know that Sweden is one of the more developed countries in the world. Not at the very top, but at the top when it comes to GDP per capita, roughly 30 000 US dollars per capita. The official Chinese figure is 1 250 dollars per capita, which is a big difference. But if you PPP adjust, which you should do, your income per capita today is 5 000. Comparing, 5 000 to 30 000, is not 25 times but rather 6 or 7 times. Swedish modernization started rather late, in the late nineteen century. At that time we were, together with Japan, the most rapidly growing economy in the world. Then in the 1970's we had economic difficulties and had to restructure. Now we are doing quite well, having the highest

growth rate within the EU. Not like yours, no other country can have that level for such a long period of time, 9% for 25 years it is almost impossible. The growth rate is 3% in Sweden, which is fairly good if you have reached a high economic level. But it could be better. The dilemma we have is that we the economic growth is fairly good and we have rapidly growing productivity, like 6%—7% a year, but we have too few jobs. It is sometimes called jobless growth. Because there is so much investment in technology, and when the companies invest in something more which demands a lot of labor, they do it in China, India, or East Europe where the costs are low. So we see money-outbound investment. But investments also go to Sweden. We have seen Chinese investments, like Huawei Inc. and other companies invest in Sweden. There are maybe 20 Chinese companies present in Sweden today. In China there are about 250 Swedish companies present. Ericsson has presence in 25 provinces and ABB has more than 20 factories. So you can see that Sweden is strongly committed to openness, trade, and the WTO. We are one of the four or five countries in the world that provides what the UN demands for development assistance, 0.7% or more of GDP. Many countries, like the US, are on their way down, going even below 0.1%. We have a strong tradition when it comes to international commitment.

If you look at equity, social fairness, and income distribution, I mentioned the Gini coefficient being 0.3, we have strong commitment to social justice. Sweden has had a Social Democratic government for most of the time since 1932 except for nine years. For the social democrats, high employment rates for men and women, and public education and health care have been the key. Sometimes people say that if you have a lot of welfare, growth will go down. It is not true. It is perfectly possible to have social programs committed to welfare which sustain growth. It is not at the expense of growth. That social programs would harm growth is not correct according to data. But you have to make sure that you have efficient rather than wasteful programs. Health care is not totally free in Sweden. You have to pay for part of it, medicines and so forth. We think health care should be determined by your disease, not by your purse. You should not be turned away because you do not have the money. We are continuously aware of that you have to have sound and transparent public finances. A strong economy is the foundation of a strong social system. Germany has an election coming up on Sunday. They have not done very well when it comes to these issues. They have 12% unemployment and big deficits. Their economy has not been reformed enough. Sweden carried out economic reforms because we had a crisis in the early 1990s. Notably, our pension system was reformed. Now we have a pension system that is going to last a long time. You can never say that reforms are finished. If you say that your reforms are completed, you are in big trouble.

About the environment. When I was a young student in the 1960s, the question of the environment became a big issue in Sweden. We had a lot of NGOs that got involved to show that there was pollution and so forth, like the conditions in the chemical factories where substances leaked into the ground water and so forth. They became very active. We got our first environment protection agency, like SEPA in China, and the first legislation. The Party responded to pressure from the NGOs and vice versa. The public, the grass roots, played a very important role in making people aware of all these problems. Media as well. Today we have a very strong legislation on the environment. And we have very specific targets for what is permitted. We also use a lot of incentives and disincentives to make companies and households reach those targets. We have very high petrol prices because we want to influence people's behaviors in the direction of public transport. Not use their cars all the time, but take the subway or the bus. I live in the suburbs of Stockholm. I would never go by car to my office. I would take the convenience to go by subway. That is very important, otherwise you get very congested cities like you have in Beijing today. I think it is crucial to have what we call sustainable development.

The forth dimension is the political dimension and democracy. Since 1920, Sweden is what you call a parliamentary democracy. Both men and women have the right to vote in general elections. We have an election in every four years. In our parliament we have seven parties. The Social Democrats are governing the country. But they do not have the majority in

the parliament. They have 40% of the seats. So they govern with the support of two parties, the Left Party and the Green Party. They have opposition, consisting of all the other four parties: a more conservative party, a center party, a liberal party, and a Christian democratic party. Election is very competitive. We will have an election in next September and it will be a very interesting election. If you look at the public opinion polls, the opposition is leading. So we will see what happens. But I am a civil servant. So my job does not depend on which Party is in power. I belong to a professional core of civil servants, recruited and promoted on merits. If the government changes, very few people will leave, only the ministers, vice ministers and the political advisors. That is all. The rest will remain and serve the new government, another democratically elected government, depending on the majority in parliament. Even though you have this election, it is a very stable system. We also have a very lively civil society with more than 100 000 NGOs. Some people say, how can you have so many? It must be a mess, disorderly. On the contrary, it makes the society very strong. It is very fabric. It means that if you are not happy with the environment, you form an organization or join an organization. You do not have to use violence or anything. Some organizations have been there for very long. Some are national, and some are local. You can form one here today. You are the chairman, somebody else takes care of your account. We register the organization with the bank. You have a board. No other procedures. Most people in Sweden, like myself, are members of probably ten organizations, paying small fees. I am interested in the environment, so I pay to the Friends of Nature and so forth. I think it creates great vitality.

The fifth aspect on Sweden is the international commitment. We have a very strong commitment to the UN. We have been involved in more peace keeping operations in UN operations than any other country since the 1960s. Like China today. You are also involved in a number of peace keeping operations, which is very good. We are non-allied and do not belong to NATO. We are a member of the EU since 1995. As you know, the EU today has 25 member countries. We are strongly committed to international trade. We want to remove more barriers. We believe that trade is something that can drive the world economy and reduce poverty. We are very much against the textile quotas. The EU reintroduced that. Sweden was completely against it within the EU. We were the number one country against it. Also Demark was against it. We had promised China that by the end of 2004 the quotas should be gone. But then they were reintroduced. They can only be maintained for another few years. By the end of 2007 they are finished. We are also very much against the agriculture subsidies of the EU. Many countries, like France, subsidize farmers. We do not do that. We want to have an open economy. When we entered the EU, we had to reintroduce barriers which we had already removed. Of course you may think that as Sweden is a small country it is very easy to make those achievements. The other day I met a man from Handan in the Hebei Province. Within the city limit, you have 7—8 million people. Sweden has only 9 million people. So we are not much more than Handan. So of course it is a different story in many ways in China. Sweden has not been in any war since 1815 and not in any major war in almost 200 years. So of course in our history we have been lucky. China's history is more complicated. The other week you were commemorating the 60th anniversary of the war with Japan. It was a very long and tragic war of course.

Now coming back to China, the future, the final part of my lecture. What is important? I would like to say institution building. To build a viable financial system, and to build a conducive environment for businesses, irrespective of whether it is public or private. One single company law for all companies. Develop the stock market and other parts of the financial system. I think that is fundamental. A key word in an economy for me is what you call allocative efficiency. That is because you have a very high level of investments in China, an exceptional high level. But when you invest, how can you make sure that the investments are good investments? Can the banks channel the money to good investments? And not keep hopeless companies floating, subsidizing them, but investing in the new job opportunities? Can the stock market channel the money accurately? I think there is a lot to be done in China when it comes to improving allocative efficiency, in particular to sustain growth at such a high level. One word you often use in China is Xiao Kang, to quadruple GDP in 20 years, between 2000 and 2020. It is a very ambitious task. It becomes more difficult when you climb up the ladder. Many people say that at least in the coming ten or fifteen years you can maintain 7%—8% growth. But you cannot do it without reforms and without increasing the competitiveness of the economy. And of course, today you are extremely dependent on demand from the outside. You export such a large share. In the long run, you must develop more domestic demand to not be as dependent as you are now.

As regards the second aspect in equity, I think it is difficult to reduce inequality in the short run because of the abundance in labor. But certain things can be done. For example, regarding minimum wage and basic working conditions. If you take the garment factories, the young women work maybe 60 or 70 hours a week. They can only go home once a year to visit their families. This needs to be addressed of course. But what is even more immediate is health care; access to health care, access to education, and access to public goods. How do you use your public revenue? It is growing significantly. A 9% growth generates new resources. What do you use them for? You have a choice. I think your voices are crucial. What kind of China do you want in the future?

Thirdly, when it comes to the environment, I think that in the next ten years are decisively important for China, and also for the world. If you choose a very wasteful model in the long run—I do not think you will do that—but if you would do that, the quantity of carbon dioxide would increase to a dangerous level. We need new technologies. For the Olympics, you will try to have environmentally friendly cars in Beijing. I hope that you can contribute to the development of new technology that sustains the environment.

When it comes to my fourth point, about political reforms, I think that in the long run the question will become very important. China is undergoing such a major transformation, from rural to urban, from less educated to more educated, and through technology, like the Internet. You send 20 billion SMS messages a month in China. . You learn languages, you have tourism, and other interactions in so many ways. I think it is crucial that political reform paces with this. Only you can tell how to do it. In addition, for Sweden human rights is one of the key questions. China has signed *the Covenant on Civil and Political Rights*. You are now working in the direction of that covenant. It is a very important covenant and part of the international system. I also think that in the long run it is crucial to give more scope to NGOs, to have trust in civil society, and in the intention and commitment of people to work for the goodness of society.

Finally, the fifth dimension, the international system. Again, China's role is becoming more and more important, in developing UN, and in strengthening the world trading system. The world you will enjoy in 15 years from now, 2020, will be very different from today. It will be much more globalized and much more integrated.

To conclude I have five points. One is to pay greater attention to institution building-building transparent and trusted institutions like the financial system. Second, focus on becoming an inclusive society where poor people also feel part of the development. If China grows by 9% a year, they should also enjoy it. Thirdly, do not compromise when it comes to the environment. Take the lead internationally to provide a better environment. You have the chance. Fourth, create a truly open society, with a viable open political institution, and continue to contribute to the development of the international system. The system for you is crucial. If the international system is stable, you can enjoy the fruits of foreign trade, foreign investment, the flow of technology, and education opportunities. I think these are the five key points.

I have been here for three years. In three years China's economy has grown by 1/3. Your role in the world has grown by at least that much. I can see that in so many ways. You play an important role in the world market, including that for steel, oil, commodities and raw materials. The direction China is choosing means more and more for the future of the world. I am glad that all of you are in such a great program in this univer-

sity and will become people playing an important role in the future development of China. Thank you very much.

Q & A

Audience: Mr. Ambassador, I am an assistant professor from the School of Economics of Peking University. You just mentioned that it's possible to have welfare and growth together. I assume that your welfare system is supported by high tax rates. I think in the classical economic theory, people will predict that high tax will reduce people's incentive to work. How do you reconcile the economic theory with the facts of Sweden? Or you will just refute the theory?

Börje Ljunggren: I think it would be dangerous to try to refute the theory. I think it is essential that if you develop a welfare system, you anticipate how it would work. Take health care as an example. Sweden has the highest life expectancy in the world. The other day, the UN released its annual report on the human development index. Norway is No. 1 in the report and Sweden is No. 3. We only spend 8% of GDP on health care, 3/4 public and 1/4 private money. The US spends 13%—14% and its system is much more private. And still 30 million people in the US are not covered. My point is that something private is not necessarily better than something public. The key question here is to make sure this system is efficient. To support the system, tax is not the only source. We also have health insurance. I know that in China you do not want to have high tax rates like in Sweden. I am happy to pay my tax. I want equally good health care for poor persons in rural Sweden. If I have good health care but another person has a lousy one, I do not think it a good system. It is not socially just. I like a society in which the public goods are fairly distributed. I think it gives a higher living standard for me. It costs something. In China the government revenue amounts to 20% of GDP. You can choose how to use it. You can develop an insurance system. You must do something for the poor people.

Audience: I am a teacher from the School of Economics. My question is that during a recent trade negotiation between EU and China, some commentators argued that China made too many concessions, which would cost millions of people of their jobs and will leave many in poverty. What is your comment on this? Thanks.

Börje Ljunggren: As I mentioned earlier Sweden is not in favor of these quotas. I think it would be better not to have any restrictions. Of course, China's export will continue to grow. According to the agreement reached last week, 75 million pieces of textile products in the ports of Europe will be released now. After 2007, there will be no restrictions. With the US it is more complicated. You and the US still do not have an agreement. I read in the newspaper that yesterday your president was in Mexico. It was a successful visit, but the Mexicans are very worried. They used to sell a lot to the US, the same kind of products as you have. Now they are losing market shares because of China. Your economy is so huge. China has become the factory of the world. My prediction is that you will see more trade frictions coming up in the future.

Now turning to my own country. There are very strong labor unions in Sweden. They will start to discuss conditions of workers in China. They will say, okay, we will have free competition, but the workers in China should have at least some minimum wage. If you grow by 9% a year, and if your export grows by 20% a year, you will have a major effect on the world stage. I think the issue will not disappear. Sweden's commitment to free trade is very strong, but so is our commitment to labor rights and to the environment. That is why China needs to develop more domestic demand, not to be too dependent on export. China's export last year increased by 150 million US dollars. That is twice the size of India's total exports. Your increase in one year is India's total export.

Audience: Thank you, Mr. Ambassador. I am a junior student in the School of Economics. I come from the Department of International Economics and Trade. Can you tell us something about trade between Sweden

and China? Just now an idea occurred to me. Sweden is a small but very rich country compared to China. Is it possible for some Chinese labors to migrate to Sweden? Thanks.

Börje Ljunggren: I think that, first of all, trade between Sweden and China goes very well. Two years ago, China became Sweden's most important trading partner in Asia, more important than Japan. But China's share was only 2% of Sweden's total import. Regarding labor, it is an interesting question and a complicated one. With globalization, we have free flow of goods, capital etc.. But when it comes to labor, there are a lot of restrictions. In the EU countries, we have the same immigration policy. You need a visa to go to Sweden. We want a lot of Chinese tourists. If Chinese companies establish themselves in Sweden, their workers can move to Sweden. Suppose you have a construction company and you have a contract in Sweden. If you do that, you have to respect our labor laws. Once there was a rich Chinese man who built a so-called "gateway to Sweden", with a big Buddha statue. He brought some Chinese workers to Sweden and they got visas to build this gateway. But they were only paid 20% of our minimum salary. We cannot allow this. So Chinese employers have to agree to pay much more.

Audience: I am a student from the School of Economics. As you mentioned, some loss-making Chinese SOEs are supported by the banks. They become big burdens for the bank. But those enterprises provide jobs for many people. If those enterprises die, many people will lose their jobs, which could be a bigger social problem. What do you think of this problem? Thanks.

Börje Ljunggren: I think the number of workers employed by Chinese state-owned enterprises have decreased by 5 million a year for the last several years. So there is a lot of restructuring going on. The workers possibly moved to new jobs. You have 9% growth, and a lot of new jobs will be created. The risk is that if you continue to let the banks lend money to loss-making enterprises, those enterprises will make the same losses every year. It is not just one year, but two years, three years, five years. They are very inefficient companies. In our system, also in your system in the future, such companies would go bankrupt. It may sound cruel, but bankruptcy law is a fundamental part of the economic system. If a company is doing very poorly year after year it should go bankrupt or it should be restructured. Maybe some other owner can reform it to make it more efficient. If a company is losing money year after year and the bank is forced to give loans even though the company is not going to repay the loan, then in the long run, it is even wasteful. I do not know if you agree—I think companies can make losses temporarily because of difficulty, but if the loss is chronic, then such a company becomes a burden for society and the economy. Bankruptcy should be seen as a possibility to reform companies and to bring in new owners and new capital.

加拿大驻华大使

罗岚先生 (Mr. Robert Wright)

罗岚（Mr. Wright）

罗岚先生1968年在麦吉尔大学获得工学学士。1971年作为工业贸易商业部的贸易政策官员开始了在加拿大政府的工作生涯。随后，他作为东京回合多边贸易谈判的加拿大代表团成员被派往日内瓦，先后担任过日内瓦乌拉圭回合谈判加拿大代表团副团长、加拿大驻美国大使馆经济公使兼副使(1993—1995)和外贸部副部长(1995—2001)。同时他还任出口发展公司董事、北方天然气输送管道署署长。2001年至2005年，罗岚先生任加拿大驻日本大使。2005年底被任命为加拿大驻华大使。

Mr. Wright obtained a Bachelor of Science from McGill University in 1968, and began his career with the federal government in 1971 as a trade policy officer in the Department of Industry, Trade and Commerce. Thereafter he was posted to Geneva as a member of the Canadian Delegation to the Tokyo Round of Multilateral Trade Negotiations. He was appointed Deputy Head of the Canadian Delegation to the Uruguay Round in Geneva. From 1993 to 1995, Mr. Wright served at the Canadian Embassy in Washington, D.C., as Minister (Economic) and as Deputy Head of Mission. From 1995 to 2001, he served as Deputy Minister for International Trade. In this capacity, Mr. Wright was also a Director of the Export Development Corporation and Commissioner of the Northern Pipeline Agency. Mr. Wright served as the Canadian Ambassador to Japan from 2001 to 2005, and was appointed as the Canadian Ambassador to China in 2005.

全球经济的助推器

——崛起的中国和发展中的中加关系

加拿大驻华大使　罗岚先生(Mr. Robert Wright)

2005年10月11日　北京大学

演讲全文

很高兴来到北京大学，也很荣幸能在经济学院20年院庆之际做此演讲。这周，我们加拿大驻京使馆也在庆祝周四即将到来的中加建交35周年。中加两国在过去的35年里维持了稳固的双边关系，这段合作关系前景无限。

作为刚刚到任的加拿大驻华大使，我必须说明我还不够资格以中国专家的身份来演讲。我的评论是基于我在外交外贸领域三十多年的经验，包括我在曾任WTO东京回合谈判和乌拉圭回合谈判加拿大代表团成员、加拿大驻美使馆副使、加拿大外贸部副部长，以及最近的加拿大驻日大使的过程中所取得的经验。

我最关注的问题是如何迎接九月初由胡锦涛主席和加拿大总理保罗·马丁所提出的挑战。加中关系发展得很顺利，贸易和经济数据都证实了这一点。但两国的领导人都认为这还不够。考虑到两国的经济具有互补性，两国之间悠长的文化和历史联系，以及加拿大是中国在北太平洋彼岸最近的邻居这一事实，我们需要发展更深的战略关系。我们的领导人呼吁拓展加中两国的商业、贸易、投资、科技等方面的联系。作为加拿大驻华大使，我在未来几年里所面临的主要挑战就是如何为发展双边关系作出贡献以实现这些目标。

2005 年 1 月，保罗·马丁以加拿大总理的身份首次对中国进行官方访问。上个月，胡锦涛主席也对加拿大进行了首次官方访问。这些活动建立了新的加中“战略伙伴”关系。这意味着双方政府都对拓展双边关系作出了政治承诺。在过去的五年里，我们两国的双边贸易翻了一番，两国领导人还提出了新的目标，要在 2010 年使加中贸易额再翻一番。

在进一步讨论经济事务之前，让我先强调一下作为加中两国人民之间纽带的两国关系中最重要的因素。我们两国有着长期相互合作、相互尊重的历史，这也是两国未来关系发展的基石。

事实上，中国人早在 230 年前就来到了加拿大。1788 年，英国探险家约翰·米尔斯从澳门带了 70 名中国木匠，在加拿大西海岸的温哥华岛登陆。他们在当地造船，据说还跟岛上的土著族群通婚。在过去的 150 年里，中国移民参与建设我们的国家，对我国从大西洋沿岸到太平洋沿岸的所有主要社区都作出了贡献。在加中正式建交的 35 年里，加拿大受益于来自中国内地和整个大中华区的大量华人移民作出的贡献。

据估计，加拿大人中约有一百万为华裔，他们丰富了加拿大的文化，使加拿大的经济更加有活力、更加国际化。许多华裔加拿大人致力于推进两国间的贸易和投资。他们同时了解这两个国家，并不断加强着两国之间的联系。

加拿大可能是世界上最以本国的多样性而自豪的国家。走在温哥华、多伦多或蒙特利尔的任何一条街道上，都可以发现加拿大是全球最具种族多样性的国家之一。我们认为这种多样性是加拿大外交与内政政策的基础，也指引着我们发展与中国及其他亚洲国家的紧密关系。

为了给我的评论提供一些背景支持，让我先对加拿大经济作一个简要介绍。加拿大的人口约为3 200万，经济总量略低于10 000亿美元，人均约31 000美元（而中国拥有13亿人口，16 500亿美元的经济总量，人均1 300美元）。我们拥有世界第二大的国土面积（俄罗斯国土面积最大，中国位列第三）以及大量重要自然资源储备。加拿大GDP的构成中，服务业约占70%，工业占25%，农业占2%。加拿大主要产业包括汽车、汽车零部件、采矿业、能源、伐木业和农业。加拿大的出口总额占GDP的1/3，多年来维持着对美国的巨额贸易顺差。

我对中国最深的印象就在于它的变化。作为大使，我肩负着通过开创商业机会来促进加拿大繁荣的经济任务，因此在我看来中国的变化就是机会的源泉。加拿大是一个非常依赖对外贸易的开放经济体。加拿大认识到国际商务是一条双行道：我们出口以获得外汇用于购买外国产品。我们欢迎中国的产品出现在加拿大的货架上，同样，我们也希望加拿大的产品能更多地来到中国市场。

与许多国家一样，加拿大在对华贸易中存在大额贸易逆差，2004年约为135亿美元。自1995年至今，中国对加拿大的出口增长了5倍，高达185亿美元，中国现在是加拿大的第二大进口国，仅次于美国。同一时期，加拿大对华出口翻了一番，增长至50亿美元，使中国成为加拿大第四大出口市场。尽管这些增长令人印象深刻，但事实上加中贸易关系还相对较弱，双边贸易额不到两国与其他国家贸易额的2%。

过去十年中，加拿大对华出口的结构不断改善，越来越多样化。就在1992年，小麦还占加拿大对华出口的大部分，现在这一主导地位已经被工业产品、机械设备和林业产品所替代。虽然中国仍然是一个劳动力富余国家，以出口劳动密集型产品为主，但中国出口到加拿大的产品已经变得越来越高端。2004 年上半年,中国对加拿大的出口中,机械设备产品第一次超过了消费品的比重,其中计算机和电信设备占了很大份额。

中国加入 WTO 对中国经济的开放起了巨大的作用。但希望在华进行销售的加拿大人仍然面临着市场准入的挑战。因此,我们会继续关注以确保中国实现入世承诺,尤其是在金融服务业和农产品食品领域的承诺。我们希望重新成为对华的牛肉输出国;确保保险合资企业获得国民待遇;努力降低外资银行设立分支机构的资本金要求;同时正如胡主席和马丁总理所呼吁的,我们还希望中国政府尽快核准确立加拿大的旅游目的地国地位。

两国间的外国直接投资是一项特别的挑战和机遇。2004 年,中国是世界第二大外国直接投资接受国。但是,加拿大在华直接投资总额仍然较小,2004 年仅为 5 亿美元。我们并不完全清楚为什么加拿大公司不在中国进行更多的投资。但加拿大是全球主要投资国,是净对外投资的国家。出现这种情况可能有多种原因。在采矿等行业里,加拿大居于世界领先地位。例如,加拿大在蒙古是仅次于中国的第二大投资国,主要投资于采矿业。而中国在采矿业的投资限制阻挡了加拿大公司在这一领域的投资。但现实情况是,无论是对大西洋两岸来说,还是对太平洋两岸来说,加拿大都是全球供应链的一环。加拿大与中国的联系也体现着加拿大与全球供应链的联系,需要得到发展。

问题的另一个方面是中国在加拿大的投资。中国海外直接投资总额约为 370 亿美元,但投资于加拿大的只有 1.9 亿美元,还不到总额的 1%。过去,中国在加拿大的直接投资集中于照明设备制造、交通服务、贸易和零售业。现在中国的投资开始转向自然资源。中国经济发展的重点和加拿大供应自然资源及相应产品的能力之间有明显的互补性。我们欢迎中国对加拿大自然资源领域进行投资,这将极大地促进加拿大经济在国内外的发展。

实行新的“战略合作关系”的一个关键因素在于尽早实施《外商投资促进及保护协定》(FIPA)。中国应当认识到在加拿大进行投资是通向北美自由贸易区这一世界最富有的市场的最佳桥梁。当然,我们最大的贸易伙伴和投资伙伴是美国,我们也将帮助中国企业在美国市场上获得成功。加拿大的成本比美国低9%;13年来加拿大经济持续增长,削减了30%的国债;加拿大还拥有高素质的劳动力队伍,这些使得加拿大成为八国集团中表现最好的经济体,能为中国提供所需的优良投资环境。

对中国的企业来说,北美距离中国最近的深水码头和航空港就是不列颠哥伦比亚省的温哥华。从任何一张地图都可以看到这个明显的事实:不列颠哥伦比亚使得加拿大成为来往于中国和北美之间的最佳门户。最近,加拿大政府发表了“太平洋门户倡议”,以把加拿大西海岸建设成为通往快速增长的太平洋经济体的理想门户。加拿大的国营部门和私营部门准备在不列颠哥伦比亚投资近20亿美元用于建设高速公路、铁路、港口和边境基础设施,以保证货物能在加拿大、北美和太平洋之间高效率地运输。

显然,这些统计数据表明中国在加拿大的投资是有利的。加拿大开放的态度也欢迎来自中国的投资。加拿大最近的民意调查显示,2/3的加拿大民众相信中国的经济增长是一个机遇(相反,大多数美国人认为中国是一个经济威胁)。

正如加拿大在北美自由贸易区中起着重要作用,中国也在和邻近国家进一步融合。加拿大的利益不仅在于和中国发展关系,还在于和整个东亚地区发展关系。简单的双边模式已经不够广泛,不够复杂,无法尽享全球化的益处。因此我们将致力于发展基于双边关系的更紧密的地区联系。

作为地区的领导之一,中国近期对加拿大经济的影响虽然间接,但却是很重要的。中国工业和消费的惊人增长意味着加拿大所供应的自然资源的价格会有大幅上涨。我们的自然资源,尤其是能源，占我们出口总额的60%以上。这种对农矿产品的需求复苏，给加拿大经济带来了新的增长动力。20世纪90年代，加拿大经济增长的动力在于汽车和高科技行业，现在加拿大在采矿、能源及其他自然资源领域的长期优势更加强了这一动力。

《纽约时报》的托马斯·弗里德曼曾撰文表示中国以前依靠低廉的劳动力价格来吸引工作机会。现在，中国则越来越凭借能干的、受过良好教育的、积极向上的年轻劳动力来吸引工作机会。同样，加拿大也非常注重教育，发展以创新为动力的知识经济。的确，在八国集团中，加拿大的高等教育人口比例最高。我们的高中生平均阅读水平最高，数学和自然科学的平均分数位列第二。我们的大学是世界一流的大学，尤其对外国留学生来说，在加拿大留学比美国或欧洲花费要少。

众所周知，中国面临着许多经济挑战。全球经济现在依靠中国的发展来提供增长动力。中国经济增长的风险影响到全球经济的前景。目前，中国人凭借其高明的智慧走上了经济崛起之路。25年来所维持的9.5%的增长率就是这一能力的有力证明。尽管有些人质疑中国的经济统计数据，但几周前OECD发表的研究报告表明，中国的潜在增长率确实上升到了9.5%。

然而，要保持这样的增长动力，中国必须解决一些问题，例如完全履行入世承诺——投资保护、知识产权保护、建立健全透明的监管和法律体系以及在商业争端中严格执法。我们了解为经济活动创造公平开放的环境并非一日之功，我们期望看到并鼓励为之不断努力。同时，良好的监管和商业法规对全社会也有连锁反应。

一些发达经济中的观察家强调，新兴的亚洲经济融入全球经济会给其就业以及国内生产带来威胁。当然，中国经济的崛起给我们提出了许多重要的政策问题。但加拿大对此的回应不是保护政策，而是注重于为加拿大经济长期发展做出努力。这意味着提供稳定的宏观经济环境，使我们的经济更加灵活，推进结构调整，促使资源

从夕阳产业向朝阳产业转移。

我认为21世纪早期的重要标志之一就是中国的快速崛起及其对全球产生的影响。正如马丁总理2004年所准确表述的，“中国不应再被简单地看作新兴市场；它将成为世界强国”。我想再一次强调，加拿大历来是一个开放的出口国，我们从全球格局的变化和中国经济的增长中看到了机遇。

我们认为中国的成功巩固了加拿大的成功。加拿大的自然资源领域、服务和金融领域、教育机构、旅游业、技术制造业以及其他很多传统优势行业都能从中国的发展中获益，原因非常简单——中国的经济增长就意味着对加拿大产品和服务需求的增长。

贸易和投资的增长不仅仅带来经济收益，它使各国经济相互依存，进而有助于建立稳定的、有秩序的国际关系。中国经济日益融入全球经济是中国和平崛起的重要因素。这正是我们所欢迎的。我们将致力于建立一个适应21世纪中国以及整个东亚的复杂性和日益增长的具有影响力的合作关系。这样，我们将赋予“战略合作关系”以实际的意义。

在座的很可能就是中国的下一代领导人，再一次感谢你们给我这个机会在这里演讲。我希望当你们走出这个房间时，对加拿大以及我们两国的前景会有更好的印象，这将影响你们对未来的看法，从而促进两国进一步的合作，挖掘两国巨大的潜力。

我很高兴有机会回答你们的提问。

谢谢。

现场对话

听众：我是经济学院的老师，我想提一个有关人才流失的问题。现在，发达国家，例如英国、加拿大，“窃取”着发展中国家的工程师、老师和医生。您是如何看待人才流失问题的?

罗岚:谢谢你的问题。我们并不"窃取"任何人。我们邀请想来加拿大的人到我们国家。自我们建国起就是这样了。我们欢迎世界各国想来加拿大并为我们的社会作出贡献的人。我们接受有才能、受良好教育的移民,同时也很看重移民居住并服务于世界其他地区的意愿。

因此说我们在世界各地实施活跃的"窃取"计划是错误的。我们并不"窃取"别人。我们只是邀请想来加拿大的人来我们国家进修、教学并选择任何他们所希望的职业。这是二百多年来我们一贯的政策,收到了很好的效果。我们也将继续实施这个政策。

听众:谢谢。我是今年七月从北大毕业的学生,正在准备出国学习。在讲座中,您提到加拿大是美国的石油和天然气供应大国。那在某种程度上是否可以说是美国在"剥削"加拿大?您还提到了加拿大欢迎对其自然资源投资。美国对此态度如何?例如,中国对自然资源和高科技都有很强的需求,希望在自然资源领域进行投资。美国会反对中国在加拿大的自然资源领域投资么?

罗岚:我们确实是美国的主要资源供应者。许多人没有认识到这一点,他们只想到沙特阿拉伯。但我们排名仅次于沙特阿拉伯,尽管我们的资源开发费用相对较高。但随着油价的上涨,加拿大的资源越来越富有经济价值,越来越多的公司开始投资于开发加拿大自然资源。我们在吸引自然资源领域的投资方面十分果断,因为我们认识到这将给我们带来更多的财富和就业机会。我们缺乏独自开发这些自然资源的资本和人力。

我们和美国的关系在过去的二百多年里都十分紧密。如果我没有记错的话,美国上一次入侵我们是在1807年,那是大约二百年前。当时我们把他们赶回了华盛顿,还烧毁了白宫。所以短期内他们不会再那么干了。

美国从未对加拿大吸引外国公司在自然资源领域投资表示异议,因为他们认识到我们是相互独立的国家。我们之所以向美国出口自然资源,是因为我们在经济上有利可图。我们是开放的市场、自由的市场。美国是我们最大的贸易伙伴,但我们仍是两个独立的国家。

因此我不认为加拿大吸引外资在自然资源领域投资和我们与美国之间的关系有任何矛盾和冲突。这就是北美市场的状况。

听众:谢谢。您在讲座中提到了采矿业投资的限制,您能再详细讲讲么?其他部门的投资限制如何呢?

罗岚:对这个问题我无法提供很详细的回答。在我短暂的在华期间,最明显的投资限制就是采矿业的投资限制。加拿大在智利、南非等地都有投资采矿业,是世界主要采矿业投资国。我敢肯定加拿大公司也很想在中国投资。但是这里存在投资限制。我能理解这种限制,但我也看到了两国在这个领域的巨大合作潜力。

在描述加中双边关系的所有数据中,投资数据是最低的。我不理解为什么加拿大公司不在中国进行更多的投资,也不理解为什么中国公司不去加拿大投资。部分原因可能是教育因素,或者两国商界的接触不足。胡主席和马丁总理都认识到我们必须有所作为。两国正共同努力改善投资关系。我认为很重要的一点就是实行外国投资保护协议,这份协议有望在下个月签署。此类协议能增强双边投资的信心,政府可就此做出进一步努力。

听众:我是《21世纪经济报道》报的记者。您在任驻华大使前曾任驻日本大使,请问您认为中日之间经济上最大的区别是什么?您如何看待东亚的发展及其对加拿大的影响?谢谢。

罗岚:这是一个很难的问题。有关日本和中国的区别,我的第一印象就是中国经济的活力。这是日本所不具备的。日本是一个发达经济体，它的人均 GDP 比加拿大还高。日本已经进入发达阶段很多年了，它在加拿大的投资超过了 90 亿美元。因此在投资数量上，日本要高于中国。当我来到中国，不禁对中国经济的活力印象深刻，这正是因为你们处于一个不同的发展阶段。

从个人角度来说，从我夫人和孩子的角度来说，我们在两个国家都受到了热烈的欢迎。这里的人们十分欢迎我们，加拿大在这里的声誉很好。这一点上我们并没体会到什么区别。

中国和日本的不同仅仅在于发展阶段的不同，在于中国经济所具有的活力是日本所不具有的。中国处于一个有着大量新机会的时代，并且正积极利用着这些机会。

关于东亚，我们鼓励这一地区实现一体化。过去的 15 年里这一地区取得了前所未有的成就。我们认为东亚地区的一体化对加拿大乃至全球都是有益的，因为这将带来更多的就业和机会。我们支持这一地区的一体化进程，因为我们知道一体化程度越高、进度越快，地区内国家相互了解、相互支持、相互依靠的程度就越高。我们认为东亚的崛起是一股积极的经济和政治力量。

听众：我是一名社会学的学生，因此我的问题与经济学的主题无关。您在讲座中提到加拿大是一个多样化的国家。我很赞同这一点，我的一个同学正在加拿大留学，她告诉我加拿大是一个很有吸引力的国家，在那里可以接触到各种文化。但我也看到新闻说一些加拿大官员对多样化感到担忧，他们担心文化认同感的下降和社会稳定性的恶化。请问加拿大政府如何保证多样化有一个美好的前景？谢谢。

罗岚：多样性是加拿大与生俱来的特性。目前，除了占加拿大人口很小比例的原著民之外，所有的加拿大人都是从别的地方移民过来的。法国、英国、欧洲中部……如果你去加拿大中部的省份，你就能发现许多来自俄罗斯、乌克兰、意大利的人。我们有着除意大利

本土以及希腊、土耳其之外最大的意大利社区。过去的一百年里，尤其是近三四十年，亚洲移民不断增加。中国移民是增长最快的移民群体。你会发现加拿大的许多学校内不仅仅有中国学生，还有人教中文。40 年前，我们就制定了政策，不是简单地把移民改造成加拿大人，而是在鼓励他们接受加拿大的价值观与道德观、融入加拿大社会的同时，鼓励他们维系与原住国的文化纽带。我们这样做是经过深思熟虑的，因为我们明白这对丰富加拿大文化的重要价值。因此这不是什么新政策，而是我们实行了多年的政策。这个政策完美么？不。它能解决所有的问题么？不。有些移民是不是面临着更大的困难？是的。但总体来说，加拿大的经验是十分喜人的。这就是为什么加拿大人对移民的态度非常积极。他们认识到移民对这个国家的经济、对这个社会作出了贡献，是加拿大的好公民。

事实上，在移民刚到加拿大的头几年里，他们对加拿大社会的净贡献要大于原有居民，并且增长幅度很大。移民给加拿大带来的不是需要负担的成本，而是净贡献。现实很完美么？不，我们仍然存在问题。但所有的社会都存在问题。我们以加拿大的多样性为荣，这种多样性不仅仅体现在温哥华、多伦多等大城市，还体现在全国各地的小城镇中。

很高兴你的朋友在加拿大过得开心，请替我问候她。如果她听到了那些负面评论，也不是什么令人吃惊的事情。但总的说来，多样化的政策实施得很好，并将继续给加拿大带来福利。因为这就是我们的本质——加拿大是多个社会相融合的产物。

听众：我的问题是有关教育的。您在讲座中强调了加拿大的教育、加拿大的研究生项目。请问加拿大有哪些措施鼓励外国学生留学加拿大呢？

罗岚：加拿大是一个联邦制的国家。联邦政府负责外交政策、国际贸易和加拿大政策的一致性。但教育是由各省政府负责的。我们有10个省。省政府通过省内大学制定、推出各种教学项目来鼓励外国学生到加拿大留学。

走进加拿大的任何一所大学，你就会发现我们一直致力于提升学生生活的质量，吸引尽可能多的学生来加拿大深造。相对于去美国或英国这样的国家来说，到加拿大进行本科或研究生阶段的学习，费用要低廉得多。加拿大作为留学目的地能提供更为丰富多彩的环境，因为加拿大的社会对国际留学生的开放程度要胜过其他一些国家。

来加拿大留学唯一的缺陷，就是气候太冷了。如果要来加拿大留学，就要能适应冬天的大雪，除非你去西海岸。温哥华在西海岸，那儿的气候就不那么糟糕。我来自蒙特利尔，那儿的冬天非常冷。

听众：我知道您在世界贸易谈判上有着丰富的经验。12月份将会在香港就多哈回合谈判中的发展问题举行一次会议。此轮谈判涉及取消发达国家的农业补贴。加拿大将会在12月的这次会议中有何作为呢？此外，中国是发展中国家，而加拿大是发达国家，我们应如何合作以取得更大的成功呢？谢谢。

罗岚：首先是农业补贴问题。我们是主要的农产品出口国。加拿大是多年的出口大国。我们强烈支持消除各种形式的农业补贴。这是加拿大几十年来的立场，也是目前我们所要坚持的立场。我们不认同运用补贴促进农业出口的做法。坦白说，这影响了我们的出口潜力。这也影响了其他国家发展本国生产的能力。加拿大的这一立场多年来十分明确。

至于多哈回合谈判，我们当然是强力支持的。我们认为通过国际贸易推动发展中国家发展也能给我们带来好处。这是对全球有益的。这是双赢的局面。当中国从发展中阶段迈向发达阶段时，当非洲找到解决其某些社会、经济问题的方法时，我们都能从中获益。这不仅给加拿大的经济发展创造了机会，还涉及一些影响全球的重

要政治、社会事务。因此这不是发展中国家和发达国家之间利益的交换，而是整体利益的增进，是世界净收益的增加。

这是多哈谈判早期的结论。我们在香港的会议上会继续支持早期的成功结论，这是基于我们对发展中国家获得真正经济机会的希望。这意味着，一些国家必须进行一定的结构调整，承担一定的义务，正如中国在加入世贸组织过程中所承担的义务。我们认为那是一个好的过程。我们希望看到其他一些国家也承担起类似的责任。

我大部分的职业生涯都在GAAT和WTO中度过。我仍然相信，获得经济发展的最佳方法，就是施行基于多边组织下的规则与法律所建立起来的多边贸易体系。

听众：谢谢大使先生。我今年五月刚结束在欧洲的学习回国。现在有一种说法是“高科技能改善环境”。中国现在得到了很大的发展，尤其是在技术领域。但同时也有关于大量环境污染的负面评论。我的问题是，您如何看待中国的技术水平？

罗岚：事实上，胡主席访问加拿大的时候，我听他谈过中国所面临的一些社会、经济、发展问题。他毫不隐瞒这些事实。他意识到中国面临着结构调整的问题，面临着环境污染的问题。所以中国有重要的环保问题亟待解决并不是一个秘密。而我认为发展活跃的高科技产业和解决污染问题之间没有大的冲突。事实上，我认为这两者是互补的。胡主席在温哥华走访了一家叫做Ballard的公司。这很可能是世界上最先进的生产氢燃料电池的公司。他对我国研发的这种可以消除汽车废气污染的新技术十分感兴趣。这是我们寻求和其他国家合作发展的领域，最终我们将会在全球运用这项技术来消除汽车尾气排放造成的污染。

因此我并认为不存在任何冲突。我们是《京都议定书》的签约国。我们签署了《京都议定书》，并采取了严厉的措施来降低废气排放量。即使我们的主要贸易伙伴，美国，并没有签署《京都议定书》，我们也签了。原因首先在于我们注重保护环境。加拿大是一个非常清洁的国家,我们希望能保持这一特点。此外,我们还希望促进环保领域的研发。而我们知道最好的促进方法就是将自己和《京都议定书》联系起来,努力发展相关技术解决废气排放污染问题。我们正在中国积极寻找合作伙伴,以共同努力改善中国的环境。

听众:谢谢您能来做演讲。我感到很荣幸能在这里提问。您提到加拿大是自然资源的出口大国,也很欢迎投资。这让我看到了中加两国合作的广阔前景,也想提一个关于环境的问题。我们知道在环境保护和经济增长之间存在着两难的境地。您能介绍一些加拿大在保护环境方面采取的措施么?例如教育和法律等。谢谢。

罗岚:当然。我们不认为开发自然资源和环境保护之间是相互冲突的。因为你在开发自然资源并不意味着你在污染环境。如我所说的,我们签署了《京都议定书》,因而必须在接下来的几年里大规模降低废气排放量。对加拿大来说,这不是件容易的事。幸运的是,我们有很好的大学、很好的技术,还有公司在进行大量投资以保证对自然资源的开发满足最严格的环境要求。

加拿大人为他们的环境感到自豪。如果你问加拿大人他们从哪儿来,他们总是会开始谈起清洁的国家、广阔的土地和森林。因此对加拿大人来说,环境保护是重中之重。这意味着政府必须和企业共同努力来保证金属矿产的采炼、森林的砍伐、石油和碳的提炼对环境是无害的。

我们的经济是由私有部门来推动的,政府负责制定标准。我们说,作为一个行业,你必须在下一年里实现这些目标。然后我们鼓励私有部门采取措施来实现这些目标。我们并不规定这些目标具体应该如何实现,而是在加拿大的法律体系下制定标准。

因此我们与私有部门进行合作。我们还认识到,如果我们能在加拿大做好,比如氢燃料电池这样的例子,那这将会给全球带来福

利。在这些领域我们可以输出产品和专业技能，也可以与各国合作在当地发展该技术。因此我认为，高科技产业的发展，制造业和资源产业的发展，与维护加拿大的环境是互相补充的。它们毫不矛盾。我们将会和资源产业共同努力，实现《京都议定书》的目标。

听众：我有一个关于加拿大经济的问题。我注意到加拿大在1996年结束了长达20年的经常账户赤字。1999年后贸易顺差从2%增长到约5%，而失业率则从约9%跌至6%或7%。在您看来，贸易的扩张对失业率的降低有多大程度的影响？我知道失业率对政治家来说是很重要的。

罗岚：你说得对。从1995年到2001年，我在去日本前当了六年的加拿大外贸部副部长。那段时期我们的出口每年都大量增长。我们的货物贸易盈余和我们的经常账户盈余开始增长。因此我问了我自己一模一样的问题：为什么会发生这些情况？我说这是因为政府采取了好的贸易政策。这确实是一部分原因。我认为加拿大和美国之间关于自由贸易协议的谈判起到了非常重要的作用，因为它改变了加拿大商界的心态。

传统上，加拿大商界谈起贸易，只会想到东、西之间的贸易，即从加拿大中部或东部沿海到加拿大西部沿海。当我们开始自由贸易协定谈判时，我们开始想到南、北之间的贸易，我们开始想到不仅是加拿大内部的贸易，而是和我们最大的贸易伙伴——美国之间的贸易。

我们认识到我们不仅可以竞争，而且在竞争中我们可以获胜。因此20世纪80年代后期到90年代中期，加拿大商界的心态发生了巨大的变化。当墨西哥1995年加入NAFTA的时候，我们意识到在美国市场上我们面临极佳的机会。我们拓展了自由贸易的范围，把墨西哥等有8 000万人口的市场包括了进来。这样，短期内我们就从一个3 000万人口的市场增长到了有4亿人口的市场。这给加拿大经济带来了巨大的推动力。

另一个原因是20世纪90年代初，美国走出了衰退期，并在1994年开始了持续至今的增长期。美国市场对加拿大资源和加拿大的出口有着巨大的需求。当美国经济增长时，加拿大经济迅速受到影响。如果美国经济运行放缓，加拿大经济则会遭受损失。因此我不得不说，过去几十年里我们之所以能维持对美国的贸易顺差和对全球的经常账户盈余，实现加拿大经济的增长，一方面是受到美国市场对加拿大产品需求的驱动，另一方面也是由于加拿大在北美市场上具有很强的竞争力。

另外我们还调整了经济。在1995年，我们消灭了政府赤字。之前我们像现在的美国一样每年有财政赤字。后来我们有了财政盈余，进行了减税，偿还了政府债务。我们的债务-GDP比例是八国集团中第二低的，并且这一比例还在下降。这增强了加拿大的商业信心，带动了加拿大的投资，同时这也创造了更多的就业机会和提高了生产力。这样的态势从1994年持续至今。我们非常幸运，我们也做出了正确的决策。

Booster for the Global Economy

—A Rising China and the Developing Sino-Canadian Relationship

Mr. Robert Wright, Canadian Ambassador to China

October 11, 2005 in Peking University

Speech

I am very happy to be here at Peking University and it is an honor for me to speak at the College of Economics as you celebrate your 20th anniversary. At the Canadian Embassy here in Beijing, we are celebrating our own anniversary this week. This coming Thursday marks the 35th year since China and Canada established diplomatic relations. Our bilateral relationship has remained strong over the last 35 years, but the potential for the future for this North-Pacific partnership is enormous.

I should mention that having only just arrived here in China as the Canadian Ambassador, it would be pretentious of me to speak to you as a China expert. My remarks are, however, informed by thirty-plus years of experience spent in foreign affairs and international trade, including terms as a member of the Canadian Delegation to both the Tokyo Round and Uruguay Round under the WTO; Deputy Head of Mission at Canada's Embassy in Washington, DC; Canadian Vice Minister of International Trade; and most recently, Canada's Ambassador to Japan.

The issue I am most focused on is how to respond to the recent challenge set out in early September by President Hu Jintao and Canadian Prime Minister Paul Martin. The Canadian-Chinese relationship is working just fine, and the trade and economic numbers bear this out. But both countries' leaders have said that this is not enough. Given our complementary economies, given our long cultural and historical ties, and given that Canada is China's closest neighbor across the north Pacific, we need to attain a deeper, strategic relationship. Our leaders have called for an expansion of Canadian and Chinese commercial ties, trade, investment and science and technology linkages. As Canada's Ambassador to China, my main challenge over the next several years will be to contribute to a bilateral strategy to achieve these objectives.

In January, 2005, the Right Honorable Paul Martin made his first official visit to China as Canada's Prime Minister and just last month, President Hu Jintao made his first official visit to Canada. These missions have resulted in the establishment of a new Canada-China "Strategic Partnership." This means that both governments have made a political commitment to expand the bilateral relationship. While bilateral trade between our countries has doubled over the last 5 years, our leaders have challenged us to double Canada-China trade again by 2010.

Before addressing economic issues in more depth, let me first stress that the most important factor in the Canadian-China relationship are the ties between our two peoples. Our countries have a long history of mutual cooperation and respect, which serves as an important guidepost for future relations.

The Chinese presence in Canada actually stretches back 230 years. In 1788, British explorer John Meares landed on Vancouver Island on Canada's west coast, with 70 Chinese carpenters from Macao. They built a boat there, and then it is believed they married into the native communities on the island. Over the last 150 years, Chinese immigrants have helped build our country and have contributed to all our major communities, from the Atlantic to the Pacific. More recently, over the past 35 years of official Canada-China diplomatic relations, Canada has benefited from many immigrants who have come to Canada from China's mainland and from the wider Chinese Diaspora.

There are an estimated one-million Canadians of Chinese ancestry who have enriched our culture and helped make the Canadian economy more dynamic in nature and international in scope. Many Chinese-Canadians are engaged in the promotion of trade and investment between Canada and China. They know and understand both countries and they reinforce the strong and growing bonds between our two lands.

Perhaps more than any other nations in the world, we in Canada celebrate our diversity. A walk down almost any street in Vancouver, Toronto or Montreal will tell you that Canada is one of the most ethnically diverse nations on the planet. We see our foreign and domestic policies as being rooted in this diversity and this helps to guide our close ties with China and the rest of Asia.

An economic snapshot of Canada provides useful context to frame my remarks. Canada is a country of roughly 32 million people with an economy of slightly under US $1 trillion, or US $31 000 per capita. (This compares with China's 1.3 billion people, US $1.65 trillion economy, or US $1 300 per capita.) We have the second largest land mass in the world (Russia is the largest, China is the third) and we have an enormous reserve of critical natural resources. In Canada, the services sector accounts for roughly 70% of GDP, industry 25% and agriculture 2%. Major Canadian industries include automobiles, and auto parts, energy, minerals, lumber and agriculture. Exports account for roughly a third of our GDP and we have enjoyed for many years a substantial trade surplus with the US.

My dominant impression of this country is one of change. To an Ambassador charged with an economic mission of promoting increased Canadian prosperity through the development of commercial opportunities, I see this change as a source of opportunity. Canada is an open economy, heavily dependent on foreign trade. Canadians recognize that international commerce is a two-way street: we export to earn the foreign exchange that allows us to buy foreign goods. We welcome Chinese products on our store shelves and equally we would like to see more Canadian products here in China.

Like many countries, Canada is running a sizable trade deficit with China—roughly US $13.5 billion in 2004. Since 1995, Chinese exports to Canada have grown by over five fold to US $18.5 billion and China is now Canada's second-largest source of imports, after the US Over the same time period, Canadian exports to China have doubled to US $5.0 billion, making China our fourth largest export market. Despite this impressive growth, the Canadian-Chinese trade relationship is in fact relatively small, less than 2% of both our countries' total trade with other countries.

The composition of Canadian exports to China has evolved during the past decade and become more diversified. Whereas wheat accounted for the bulk of Canada's exports to China as recently as 1992, it has been replaced by exports of industrial goods, machinery and equipment, and forestry products. While China remains a labor-abundant country exporting predominantly labor-intensive goods, the range of goods that it exports to Canada has become considerably more sophisticated over time. In early 2004, China's machinery and equipment exports to Canada surpassed consumer goods for the first time, with computers and telecommunications equipment accounting for a significant share.

China's accession to the WTO contributed importantly to the opening up of this economy. But market access challenges remain for Canadians looking to sell here. Consequently, we will continue to focus on ensuring the effective implementation of China's WTO commitments, especially in the financial services and agri-food sectors. We are seeking to re-establish our position as an exporter of beef to China; ensure national treatment for foreign-invested insurance joint ventures; reduce capital requirements on foreign bank branches; and we would like to see the Chinese government quickly finalize approved destination status for tourism to Canada, as called for by President Hu and Prime Minister Martin.

Bilateral foreign direct investment (FDI) presents a particular challenge and opportunity. In 2004, China was the world's second-largest recipient of FDI. However, the overall level of Canadian direct investment in the Chinese economy is relatively small, totalling about US $500 million in 2004. We are not entirely sure why Canadian firms do not invest more aggressively in China. We are, after all, a major force for investment in the world, and a net outward investor. There are probably a number of reasons. In certain sectors such as mining, Canadians are world leaders. For example, Canada is the second largest investor, after China, in Mongolia—mainly in the mining sector. However Chinese investment restrictions in this sector effectively prevent investment by Canadian firms. But the reality is that Canada is part of global supply chains, whether we look across the Atlantic or across the Pacific. Canada's linkages to global supply chains are also linkages into China and need to be developed.

The other side of this coin is Chinese investment in Canada. China's total overseas FDI is estimated at about US $37 billion; however, Canada's share is US $190 million, less than 1% of the total. Chinese FDI in Canada has focused in the past on light manufacturing, transportation services, trading and retail. Now it is moving into resources. There is an obvious fit between China's economic development priorities and Canada's capabilities in supplying natural resources and resource-based products. We welcome investments in our resource sectors that are of significant benefit to Canada both domestically and in terms of our international economic reach.

A key element to the implementation of the new "Strategic Partnership" will be the early completion of a Foreign Investment Protection and promotion Agreement (FIPA). China should take note that investment in Canada is the best bridge into the world's richest market, the North American

Free Trade Agreement (NAFTA). Our largest trade and investment partner is, of course, the United States, and we can help Chinese businesses succeed in that market. With an overall Canadian cost advantage of 9% over the US; our 13th year of uninterrupted growth, a remarkable 30% reduction in our national debt, and with our highly-educated and productive workforce, Canada is the best-performing economy in the entire G8—offering just the kind of investment climate that China needs.

For businesses in China, the closest major deep-water port and the closest major international airport in North America are located in Vancouver, British Columbia. The facts are evident on any map: from British Columbia, Canada is the ideal gateway from China to North America and from North America to China. The government of Canada has recently announced a major "Pacific Gateway Initiative" to make the west coast of Canada the gateway of choice to the rapidly growing Pacific economies. The public and private sectors in Canada are already investing close to $2-billion in highway, rail, port, and border infrastructure in British Columbia to ensure that goods move efficiently across Canada, North America and the Pacific Ocean.

Clearly the numbers support Chinese investment in Canada, but so to does the Canadian attitude of openness. In Canada, recent polls found that by a 2:1 margin Canadians believe that China's economic growth is an opportunity (In contrast, a majority of Americans believe China to be an economic threat).

Just as Canada is now a key member of NAFTA, China, too, is becoming more integrated with its neighbors. Canada's interests lie not only with China but with all of East Asia. A simple bilateral approach to doing business is no longer broad enough nor sophisticated enough to capture all the economic benefit of a globalized world. We will therefore continue to work on developing closer regional ties that build on bilateral relationships.

As one of the region's leaders, China's recent impact on Canada's economy has been indirect but nevertheless important. China's remarkable in-

dustrial and consumer growth has meant that Canada is seeing a significant increase in the prices of the natural resources it supplies. Our natural resources, notably energy, now account for more than 60% of our exports. This resurgence in commodities is driving growth in Canada's economy. Canadian engines of growth in the 1990s—the auto and high-tech sectors industries—are being complemented by longstanding Canadian strengths in mining, energy and other resource sectors.

The New York Times' Thomas Friedman has written that China used to attract jobs because of its inexpensive labor. Increasingly now, China attracts jobs because of its talented, educated and highly motivated young labor force. Canada, too, places great emphasis on education and has expanded and diversified into a knowledge-based economy, powered by ingenuity. Indeed, among G8 countries, Canada has the highest proportion of people with a post-secondary education. Our high school students have, on average, the best scores in reading and the second highest scores in math and science. Our universities are recognized as being among the best in the world-and for foreign students, they are considerable less costly than in the United States or Europe.

As you well know, China faces many economic challenges ahead. The global economy has come to depend on China's development as an independent engine of growth. Risks to China's growth have thus become risks to world growth prospects. To date, China has managed its economic renaissance with skill. Its ability to sustain 9.5% growth for a quarter of a century is strong testimony to that. While some doubt China's economic statistics, a survey of China conducted by the Organization for Economic Cooperation and Development released just a few weeks ago confirmed that China's potential growth rate has in fact risen to the 9.5% level.

However, to maintain this momentum, China will have to tackle such issues as full implementation of WTO commitments—investment protection, intellectual property protection, the development of more transparent regulatory and legal systems, and the full application of the rule of law in commercial disputes. We know that the creation of a level and open playing field for economic activity does not happen overnight, but we expect and encourage ongoing progress. Good governance and the rule of law in commerce also have a ripple effect across society and we will encourage this as well.

Some observers in developed economies have emphasized the perceived threat to jobs and domestic production from the growing integration of the emerging Asian economies into the global economy. To be sure, China's economic rise poses a number of important policy issues for my country. But Canada's policy has been to respond not with protectionism, but instead by focusing on doing what is right for our economy in the long run. This means providing a stable macroeconomic environment, making our economy more flexible, promoting structural adjustment and facilitating the transfer of resources from shrinking to expanding sectors.

I believe one of the defining features of the early 21st century will be the rapid emergence and global impact of China. As Prime Minister Martin accurately noted last year, "No longer can China be considered simply an emerging market; it has established itself as a world power." I want to stress once again that given Canada's history as an open, exporting nation, when we look out at the shifting global landscape and China's economic ascent, we see opportunity.

We see your success as reinforcing our success. Canada's natural resource sectors, our services and financial sectors, our educational institutions, our tourism industry, our technology-driven manufacturing sectors and our many other areas of traditional Canadian expertise all stand to benefit from China's emergence for one very simple reason—economic growth in China means increased demand for our products and services.

But growth in trade and investment goes beyond mere economic gain: it creates economic interdependence that in turn is the cement that helps build stable, orderly international relations. China's increasing integra-

tion into the global economy has been a major factor in its "peaceful rise." This is something that we welcome. We will work to build a partnership that embraces the complexity and the growing influence of 21st century China, and East Asia as a whole. In doing so, we will give meaning to the new "Strategic Partnership" announced last month by President Hu and Prime Minister Martin.

I suspect that this room contains many of China's next generation of leaders, and I thank you again for giving me the opportunity to speak to you. I hope you leave this room with a slightly better appreciation of Canada and our prospects and that this will shape your perspectives in the future and foster further cooperation to tap our huge potential.

With that, I would be happy to answer your questions.

Thank you.

Q & A

Audience: I'm an academic member of the School of Economics. I want to put forward a debatable issue about brain drain. You know, developed countries like Britain, Canada, etc. "poach" engineers, teachers and doctors from developing countries. What do you think of the brain drain? Thank you.

Robert Wright: Thank you for the question. We don't "poach" anyone. We invite people to come to Canada if they want to come to Canada. This has been the case since our foundation, and this has been the case for many years. We welcome people from many countries who want to come and contribute to our society. We accept immigrants recognized by talents, recognized by education, but also recognized by the interests of living in and serving other parts of the world.

So it is wrong to charge that we have an active program going around the world to "poach" people. We don't do it. We just invite people who want to come, to come to our country, to study in our country, to teach in our country, and to practice whatever profession they want. This has been our policy for more than 200 years and has worked well for us. And this is the policy we will continue in the future.

Audience: Thank you. I'm a student graduated from PKU this July, and now preparing to go aboard for further study. In the lecture, you mentioned that you are a big oil and gas supplier to US. So is Canada exploited by US in a sense? Also, you said Canada welcomes investment in natural resource sector. What's the US's attitude towards your decision? For example, China has strong demand for natural resource and high tech, and wants to invest in natural resource. What's the US's attitude towards this? Will it be opposed?

Robert Wright: It's true that we are a major natural resource supplier of the US. A lot of people don't see it. They think about Saudi Arabia. But we are second only to Saudi Arabia, though the resources in Canada is relatively expensive to develop. Given the rising price of oil, it has become economic and more and more companies around the world are putting money in developing these natural resource bases. We have no hesitation in inviting countries to invest in our natural resource sector, because we realize that will bring us more wealth and more jobs. We don't have the capital base and people to develop the resources by ourselves.

As for the relationship with the US, we have been extremely closed for more than 200 years. The last time when the US invade us was 1807, if I got my days right, which is more about 200 years ago. And we drove them back to Washington and burnt the White house down. So they're not going to do that again in a short period.

The US has never raised any concerns about the need of Canada in inviting investments to natural resource sector, because they recognize that we are independent countries. We're exporting natural resource to America,

because we see economic advantages in doing it. We are open markets, we are free markets. The US is our biggest trading partner, but we're still two countries.

So I don't see any contradiction between our inviting companies all over the world to invest in our natural resources and our relationship with the US. That's a natural part of the North America market.

Audience: thank you. In the lecture, you mentioned the restriction on investment in mining here. Would you elaborate that, please? Are there restrictions on investment in other sectors?

Robert Wright: I don't have a detailed answer to your question. As for the short period I'm here, the most obvious restriction to me is on mining. We are in Chile. We are in South Africa. Canada is a global leader in investing in mining. You can see us all round the world investing in mining. I'm sure Canadian companies would like to invest in China. But there are restrictions. I understand this, but I see great potentials in this area to do more than what we've done before. I see terrific potentials in this area for us.

Among all the figures that show bilateral relationship between Canada and China, investment is the weakest. I don't understand why Canadian companies don't put more money here and why Chinese companies don't invest in Canada. Part of that is education, or contacts between business communities. Both President Hu and Premier Martin recognize this as something to be addressed. We've been working together to find a way to improve the investment relationships. And I think it's important to put in place a foreign investment protection agreement, which is probably coming out in a month. This kind of agreement can increase confidence in bilateral investments. And these are the steps that can be taken at the government level.

Audience: I'm a journalist from the 21st Century Economic Report newspaper in China. I know that before you came to China, you were Ambassador to Japan. So what do you think the economic difference between China and Japan is? How do you predict the development of East Asia and what's the impact of development of East Asia on Canada? Thank you.

Robert Wright: That's a very difficult question. My first impression of the difference between Japan and China is no question the excitement and dynamism you see here. You don't see these in Japan. Japan is a well developed economy. It's GDP per person is even higher than the number of Canada. It has been a well developed economy for many decades. Japan has invested more than 9 billion dollars in Canadian market. So in the magnitude of investment, Japan is of a higher level than China. But when you come to China, you can't help being impressed by the excitement and dynamism here. It's simply because you're at a different stage of development.

At a personal level, from my wife and my children's view, we feel warmly welcomed in both countries. The welcome we receive from people here is very warm. Canada has a very good reputation. So we don't see a big difference.

You are just different in the stage of development, in excitement and dynamism. You don't see this excitement in Japan because it's at a different stage of development. You are in an age of great new opportunities and you are moving very fast to take advantage of them.

As for East Asia, we encourage integrations in this region. What happened in this region in the past 15 years was unparalleled. We see that the integration of this region will bring benefits to Canada and to the world, because it will bring more jobs and thus more opportunities for us and the world. We support integration in this region because we know the more integrated you are, the faster you get integrated, the more you will understand each other, the more you will support each other, the more you will depend on each other. We see the emergence of East Asia as on-

ly a positive economic and political force.

Audience: I'm a student of sociology. So my question is not related to the topic of economy. You mentioned in the lecture that Canada is a diverse country in the world. I agree with that, because one of my friends is now studying in Canada, and she told me Canada is a very attractive country where you can touch different cultures. But I read about a piece of news yesterday that some Canadian officials are worried about the diversity, the culture identity, and the stableness of the society. How will Canadian government ensure the diversity towards a good future? Thank you.

Robert Wright: We are a country born with diversity. Every people other than our original people, who are now making a relatively small portion of the population, come from somewhere else. France, UK, Central Europe. If you go to central provinces in Canada, you will find lots of people coming from Russia, Ukraine, and Italy. We have the biggest Italian community outside Italy, Greece and Turkey。 And over the last 100 years, mainly last 30—40 years increasingly from Asia. The fastest growing community is Chinese community. And you will find in many schools around the country, there are not just Chinese students, there are people teaching Chinese. As long as 40 years ago, we put in places in government policies not to try to change immigrants, not to just change them into Canadian. But to encourage them to become Canadians, to achieve our values and ethics, and work with our system, but at the same time maintain their ethnic ties and culture ties with the country they're from. We did this deliberately, because we see the value in maintaining this context for the enrichment of the Canadian community. So this is not a new policy. It's a policy we've had for many years. Is it perfect? No. Does it work every time? No. Are there some communities that have more difficulty than others? Yes. But in general, the experience has been very positive for Canada. That's why, when you ask Canadians about immigration, they respond very positively. Because they recognize that the immigrants contribute to the economy, contribute to the society, the immigrants are good citizens.

In fact if you look at the net contribution of immigrants to the Canadian society, it is always very high relatively and increases dramatically over the first few years when they come. It's not net cost, but net benefit to the Canadian community. Is it perfect? No, there are problems. There are always problems in every society. We are very proud of the way it's working in Canada. And we're very proud of the diversity we have coast to coast. And you will find it not only in Vancouver, not only in Toronto, but in small cities and towns right across the country.

I'm pleased that your friend is enjoying her stay and please give her my best wishes. If she's hearing some of these comments, it's not surprising. But in balance it's working extremely well in Canada and it'll continue to work because it's by nature who we are. We are a product of many many societies.

Audience: My question is about education. In the lecture you emphasized on education, post graduate programs in Canada. What kind of advantage do you offer for students to study in Canada?

Robert Wright: Canada is a federal state. The central govern has certain responsibilities in foreign policies and international trade and harmonies of Canadian policies. But it is provincial governments—we have 10 provinces, that are responsible for education. Education is control at a provincial level. So it is the provincial institutions, through their universities, that develop all kinds of programs to encourage foreign students.

But if you go to any university, you'll find that we are working hard to add valuable contribution to student life to attract as many students as we can. It's much cheaper to go for graduate studies or undergraduate studies in Canada than it is in US, and in UK, for example. It's also, we think, a more enriched environment to do it, because the society is more open to international students than societies in some other countries.

The only drawback is that it's cold. You have to get used to snow in the

winter if you came to study in Canada, unless you go to west coast. Vancouver is not quite as bad. I'm from Montreal. Montreal is a cold city in the winter.

Audience: I know you have much experience in world trade negotiation. And you know, in December there will be a meeting in HK about the Doha Round in development. This round of negotiation tries to address agriculture subsidies in developed countries. What will Canada do in that meeting? China is a developing country and Canada is a developed country, what can we do to have more achievement?

Robert Wright: Well, first on agriculture subsidies. We are a major agriculture exporter. We've been an exporter for many years. We have been a strong proponent of the elimination of all forms of agriculture export subsidies. That has been Canada's position for many decades. It is the position we continue at this point of time. We do not believe in the use of subsidies for exports of agriculture products. Frankly, that disturbs our export potential. It also disrupts the ability of other countries to be able to develop domestic production capacity. That's clear position which has been very clear with Canada for many many years.

In terms of the use of Doha Round to promote development, this is something of course we strongly support. We think promotion of development in developing countries through international trade benefits not just developing countries, but it benefits us as well. It benefits the globe. To use the English expression, we see this very much as the win-win situation. It benefits us when China moves from a developing stage to a developed stage. It benefits us when Africa finds solution to some of its enormous domestic social and economic problems. It provides not just economic opportunities for Canada, but it comes to term with some major political and social issues that are affecting the globe. So this is not a question of trade-off between developing and developed. This is a question of total benefit, of net benefit to the world.

That is the early conclusion of the Doha Round. In HK, we'll promote early conclusions, successful conclusions of the Round on the basis that prove we hope for real economic opportunities for developing countries. That means, some countries has to undertake certain structure adjustment and undertake certain obligations that make sense. Just as China undertook certain obligations in its accession to WTO. We think it's a good process of accession. We'd like to see some of these undertakings applied to some other countries around the world.

I spent most of my professional career in the GAAT, in the WTO. I remain very confident that multilateral trade established by rules and laws through multilateral institutions is the best way to achieve economic development.

Audience: Thank you Mr. Ambassador. I've just finished my education in Europe and came back in May. Today there is a saying that "Technology will bring the environment condition to a higher level". China has changed a lot, especially in technology sector. Meanwhile, there is negative comment that China has a lot of pollution. My question is how do you see China's technology level?

Robert Wright: I think, in fact I heard President Hu, when he visited Canada, talked about some of the social, economic and developmental problems you face here. He realized these facts, quite openly. He realized that there are some structure adjustment problems here, there's pollution problem here that have to be addressed. So it's not a secret that China has some major problems in environmental protection to be dealt with. But I see no contradiction between the development of an active high tech sector and the work to resolve pollution. In fact, I think they're very complementary. In Vancouver, he visited a company called Ballard in west coast, just outside Vancouver. It's probably the most advanced company in the world in the production of hydrogen fuel cells. He was very interested in the use of this new technology, which has been developed in my country, as a way to eliminate all pollution from motor vehi-

cles at some point in the future. Here is a field we search for development in Canada, in association with other countries, to develop a product that eventually could be used not only in this country but around the world to eliminate one of the major sources of pollutions through motor vehicle emissions.

So I see no contradictions. And we're a member of Kyoto Accord. We have signed Kyoto Accord and have undertaken very strict obligations to control emission level. Even though our major partner, our trading partner, the US did not sigh it, we did. And the reason why we did it is: First, we believe in the environment. Canada is a very clean country and we want to keep it that way. But also because we want to encourage research and development in the area of environmental protection. And we knew a good way to do that was by associating ourselves with Kyoto Accord and working towards the development of these technologies as one way to resolve the emission and pollution problems.

We are actively looking for partnerships here in China that allows us to work with you to contribute to environmental improvement here in China.

Audience: Thank you, sir. Thank you first for the great honor to be here and the benefit from your lecture. And it's greater honor for me to raise my question here. You've mentioned that Canada is a great exporter of natural resources, and you welcome investment very much. So I can see the brilliant prospect of partnership between China and Canada. So that raises my question about the environment. We all know that there's a dilemma between environment and economic growth. Would you introduce some of the measures you've taken to protect the environment, like education, laws, etc.? Thanks.

Robert Wright: Sure. Again we don't see a contradiction between natural resource development and pollution. Just because you are developing your natural resources does not mean you are polluting the environment. As I said, we have signed the Kyoto Accord, so we have to reduce our emissions of pollution products by a fairly significant level over the course of coming years. This will not be easy for Canada to achieve. We're fortunate, because we have good universities, good technologies and companies who are investing heavily in means to ensure that the extraction of these resources is done in a way that confirms to the highest environmental standards.

Canadians are very proud of their environment. If you ask Canadians where they're from, they always start by talking about clean country, open spaces and forests.

So for Canadians, if you ask them, among all of their priorities, they always put environment on the top, which means the government must work with the private sector to establish a very specific way to ensure the extraction of metals and minerals, the harvesting of our forests, the extraction of oil and carbon is done in a way that is environmentally friendly.

In our economy, which is driven by the private sector, the governments set standards. We say, as an industry you must achieve these over the course of next year. Then we encourage the private sector to take action to achieve these targets. We don't dictate precisely how these should be achieved, but we do set standards under Canadian law legislation.

So we do it in cooperation with the private sector. We also do it in the recognition that if we do it right in Canada, like the hydrogen fuel cell, it could be a benefit to the world. In these sectors we can export products and export that expertise or we can work with our partners around the world to develop the expertise in other countries as well. So I see the development of high-tech sector and manufacture sector and resource-based sectors and the good stewardship of Canadian environment are perfectly complementary. They're not in contradiction at all. We will achieve our goal in Kyoto Accord, and we'll do it with corporation with our resource-based sector.

Audience: I've got a question about Canadian economy. I noticed from the data that Canada has ended about 20 years of current account deficit in 1996. The trade balance has gone up since 1999 from around 2% to around 5%. In the meantime, the unemployment rate has gone down from around 9% to 6% or 7%. To your experience, to what degree has the trade expansion contributed to unemployment decline? Because I know unemployment is a primary issue to politicians.

Robert Wright: You are certainly right about that.

I spent 6 years as Vice Minister of Trade of Canada, from 1995 until 2001, before I went to Japan. Every year over that period, our export increased dramatically. Our merchandise trade surplus and our current account surplus started to increase. So I asked myself precisely that question. Why has this happened? I'd like to say it was because of good trade policies of the government. And that was part of it. I think the negotiation of free trade agreement with the US played a very important role, because it changed the psychology of the Canadian business community.

Historically, the Canadian business community thought in terms of trade east and west, from central Canada to west coast Canada, from east coast Canada to west coast Canada. When we negotiated the free trade agreement with US, we started to think north south. We start to think about not just trade within Canada but the trade with our largest partner, the US.

And we realized that we could compete, not just compete, but we could win. So the psychology of the Canadian business community changed very dramatically through late 1980s to mid 1990s. And we realized the US market had great opportunity for us when Mexico joint NAFTA in 1995. We expanded that scope to include Mexico and other markets of 80 million people. So we grew from a market of 30 million people to market with 400 million people through over, after a short period of time. That gave us an enormous burst and enormous energy to Canadian economy. That's one reason for it.

But the second reason is that US came out of a period of recession in early 1990s and then came into a period of growth that lasts from 1994 through till now. The US has been an enormous draw on Canadian resource and Canadian exports. It is true that when the US economy grows, the impact on Canadian economy is very fast. It has an immediate impact. If the US economy slows down, that hurts us. So I have to say a lot of growth in the Canadian economy over the past decades including the fact that we now run a consistent balance of trade surplus with US and the fact we run a current account surplus with the world has been driven by the growth in US market and by the draw on Canadian products and the fact that Canada has been extremely competitive, very competitive in the North America market.

We also adjusted our economy to it. We also eliminated our national deficit, the government deficit in 1995, I believe. We were running annual deficit like US is now and we eliminated it in 1995. Since then we run government surplus, we reduce taxes, we pay down government debts. Our debt/GDP ratio in Canada is the second lowest in the G8, and it is going the right direction, it is going down. And this has increased business confidence in Canada, has increased investment in Canada. As a result there is more employment, there is more productivity coming out of Canadian economy. So all of the right things happened to us over a period of 10 years, from 1994 through to date. And it's continuing to have a positive effect on Canadian economy. So we've been lucky, but we've also made right decisions.

英国驻华大使

韩魁发爵士 (Sir Christopher Hum)

韩魁发（Sir Christopher Hum）

前英国驻华大使韩魁发爵士于 2003 年被授予爵士爵位。韩魁发爵士在剑桥潘布洛克学院主修现代和中世纪语言，之后进入英国外交部工作。他曾任纽约英国驻联合国常驻代表团政务参赞 (1989—1992)、外交部亚太司司长（1992—1995）、英国驻波兰大使（1996—1998）、外交部副主任（1998—2001）等要职。他现任英国剑桥冈维尔与凯斯学院——组成剑桥大学的最古老的学院之一的第 41 任院长。韩魁发爵士于2002年3月至2006年1月担任英国驻华大使。

Sir Christopher Hum was made KCMG (Knight Commander of St. Michael &.St. George) in 2003. He studied Modern and Medieval Languages at Pembroke College, Cambridge University, before joining the Foreign and Commonwealth Office (FCO). Other positions he has held include Deputy Under-Secretary of State and Chief Clerk, FCO (1998—2001), British Ambassador to Poland (1996—1998), Assistant Under-Secretary of State (North Asia/Pacific), FCO(1992—1995), Political Counsellor and Head of Chancery of United Kingdom Permanent Mission to the United Nations in New York(1989—1992) and so on. He is now the 41st Master of Gonville and Caius College, one of the oldest colleges which make up Cambridge University in Cambridge, England. Sir Christopher Hum was the British Ambassador to China during 2002 the March to 2006 the January.

开放的世界　开放的中国

英国驻华大使　韩魁发爵士(Sir Christopher Hum)

2005年11月24日　北京大学

演讲全文

副校长,院长,女士们,先生们:

下午好!首先非常感谢你们邀请我来演讲。能和美国大使、其他国家的大使——这些杰出的同事、朋友一起参与这个系列讲座是我的荣幸。我和他们非常熟悉,也非常看重他们的意见。他们的讲座无疑有着很大的价值。我也很荣幸能有机会和北京大学的师生进行交流。北大是一所世界一流的大学,拥有一个实力日益强大的经济学院。我知道贵校和英国的大学有很多联系,尤其是你们和英国声望最高的学府之一——伦敦经济学院的密切合作。北大—伦敦经济学院暑期学校已经是一个成熟的项目,相信在未来的几年中它的成果将更加丰硕。我还了解到两校正在就合作办学进行讨论。

伦敦经济学院对与中国建立合作关系的兴趣反映了英国乃至世界的趋势。基本上所有的部门,包括政府、公司和学术机构都认识到他们必须有一个中国策略。他们或者把中国看成是一个前所未有的机会,或者把中国看成是一个威胁。对一些公司来说,中国策略涉及利用中国价格低廉的货物和服务;对一些公司来说,这意味着调整自身生产方法和生产成本以应对中国比较优势的挑战;对另一些公司来说,这意味着向一个有着13亿消费者的市场进行销售。而对于学经济的学生来说,中国是一个更简单易懂的词。他们讨论全球化时,很大程度上就与中国有关。因为中国是当今世界经济中最重大、最激动人心的传奇。

我很有幸能够近距离观察到中国的崛起。1970年,我第一次来到北京时就感觉中国经济具有巨大的潜力,但这潜力被今天看来是错误的经济社会政策所制约了。80年代初期,我再次来到中国时,中国正在邓小平的领导下开始改革开放。农业改革的试点让农村经济走上了增长的道路。而当我以大使的身份在2002年第三次来到中国的时候,中国正逐步发挥它的经济潜力,恢复其世界主要经济体的地位。中国对世界经济的影响无疑是巨大的,并且多年来不断增强。

而今,我们认为中国影响着世界经济活动的方方面面。中国已经是全球谷物、煤和钢铁的最大消费者。它还是世界上最大的手机市场,这也许说明了中国人数之众。中国奢侈品市场已经达到了整个欧盟的规模,并将在几年内超过美国市场的范围和规模。无怪乎绝大多数流入中国的外国投资都服务于中国国内市场。同时,众所周知,中国在出口方面令人震惊的表现远远超出了它对进口资本货物和消费品的高涨的需求,这使得中国成为包括英国在内的大多数工业国家的主要贸易伙伴。

2010年,中国将成为全球最大的出口国。去年,中英双边贸易额超过了200亿美元。今年,这一数字将达到250亿美元,向两年前温家宝总理和布莱尔首相所设定的2010年400亿美元的目标又近了一步。这个数字还不包括中英之间日益紧密的投资关系。目前中国已有超过4 400个英国投资的企业。我很自豪在所有欧盟国家

中，英国是中国的最大投资者，也很高兴看到越来越多的中国公司到英国投资，比如华为，因为我们希望当中国企业越来越多地响应“走出去”的号召时，我们可以扮演一个合作者的角色。

我们看到，英国消费者正受益于中国制造的价廉物美的产品。许多英国公司也从中国的比较优势中获利，他们集中精力在本国进行研发，而将生产的其他环节转移到了中国。在我们看来，这是十分自然的事情，也是我们所欢迎的。随着中国政府对科技投资的注重，一些英国公司也在中国寻求合作研发的机会。这些都说明，我们认为中国的崛起是增进我们自身福利的一个机会，而不是一种威胁。这是全球化的自然结果，而全球化是需要管理和探索的。这也正是我们的经济、我们的公司所正在努力的。

中国的成功对所有人都产生了深刻的影响。只需关注全球资源市场即可认识到这一点。中国的自然资源相对短缺，并在不断减少，这限制了中国经济的发展。如果中国要保持之前的增长速度，则势必转向国际市场以满足其原料需求。这就对已经持续下滑了100年的全球商品价格产生了重要影响。中国强劲的需求已经引起了若干种商品价格的上涨，如原油和铜。中国目前的能源消费占全球能源消费的10%，仅次于美国。在未来十年，这个数字有可能上升到14%。2020年，中国将消费全球煤产量的40%以上。许多分析家认为，15年后中国的原油消耗将相当于目前整个沙特阿拉伯的石油产量。即使中国政府实现了在2010年将每美元GDP能耗降低20%的目标，中国对国际资源市场的影响仍然不可忽视。

中国对全球影响的第三个方面体现在外界对中国成功的兴趣。过去几年里，我们就全球经济事务与中国政府进行了非常紧密的合作。我们的独特优势在于英国主办了8国集团会议，而中国主办了20国集团会议。因此我们共同就贸易、债务、发展等问题进行了努力。我们为中英两国在这些问题上立场的一致性而感到非常振奋。

我们也很了解中国在反贫困方面取得的前所未有的成就。我们非常了解中国在近几十年将成千上万人从贫困中解脱出来的惊人成果,这是我们国际发展部所特别关注的。我们希望能与中国合作并探索是否能将中国经验能运用于世界其他地区,如非洲。

随着中国经济的进一步开放,世界各国都将与中国经济休戚相关。毕竟这些年来,中国贡献了全球经济增长的1/3。难怪政策制定者、资本家、金融分析师及其他评论者都会有“中国经济能否继续强劲增长”的疑问。撇开一些外部因素,这个疑问的答案很大程度上取决于中国能否处理好它在经济结构方面的一些重大问题。

去年,不可持续的固定资产投资增长水平使中国经济面临过热的严重危险。中国经济面临硬着陆的风险。中国政府对此采取了多种宏观调控措施,成功地抑制了投资。但中国政府的评估也认为,中国经济还没有实现均衡的增长。要实现这一点,就要保证自改革开放以来出现的收入不平等问题得到解决。我们认为中国领导人将减少不平等作为下一个五年计划的重点是十分正确的。

在大多数人日益致富的情况下出现的收入不平等现象恶化,是有多种原因的。在某种程度上这是发展初期的必经阶段。中国成功的沿海发展策略、城市化进程以及正在进行的城镇工人工资改革都构成了收入不平等的原因。出于政治和社会稳定的考虑,这种不平等现象不能再继续恶化。收入不平等的扩大也有其经济上的后果,对于一个2/3的人口仍居住在农村的国家来说,保证农民获得包括医疗、教育在内的社会服务和金融服务是十分重要的。否则,国民经济的整体效率将降低。在城镇,中国政府也正确地认识到居民并没有更自由地消费,而是将钱储蓄起来。当然,消费确实有所增长,包括急剧增长的汽车消费和住房开销。但对于中国这样一个成功地实现了脱贫和收入增长的国家来说,消费者需求并没有像人们所想的那样腾飞。对工作前景和社会保障的担忧,使得人们不得不积累预防性储蓄。那么政府能做些什么呢?毕竟这是近年来许多国家,比如日本,所共同面临的问题。我的建议是,政府应该为提高

经济活动参与率做出更多努力，通过发展教育和医疗帮助农村失业人员在城镇中获得工作，这需要加强农村和私有经济领域的社保安全网，需要鼓励私有经济的发展以推动国民经济，加快国有企业重组改造。

银行应当在国民经济调整中起到主要作用，这要求银行以更加商业化的姿态面对风险和投资。我们了解到，对许多中国私企来说，尤其是中小型的私企，获得银行融资十分困难。中国积极的财政政策不应依赖于通过银行来向低效率的行业提供补贴。中国所急需的是有效的金融中介。否则，中国超过20 000亿元的储蓄将不能得到最好的运用。按照WTO的要求，在2006年年底中国将开放银行业，这应当会给中国金融业带来发展的契机。

中国银行业改革已经取得了可喜的成果。中国政府成功地吸引了包括三家英国银行在内的外国股东投资四大银行。这一事实说明了中国金融业改革已经初见成效。但是我们还不能说中国已经拥有了一个坚实的、没有系统风险并对外国参与者完全开放的银行系统，还不能说中国银行系统为将储蓄转化为生产投资提供了有效率的中介。在广义的资本市场发展方面，中国还应努力推动股票市场，发展公司债券市场，解决保险等领域的市场失效问题。市场失效并不是金融部门特有的问题。我们相信中国还应进一步努力，制定以市场为基础的经济政策，完善公司及破产方面的立法，以及实现社会体制的现代化。现有财政补贴制度造成的扭曲也是刚刚开始的财政改革所应解决的问题。中国还应通过运用实行自由的汇率制度来实现更有效的货币政策。

其他一些领域也值得一提。如前所述，软性贷款政策已经支撑了那些亏损的国有企业太长时间。刚刚开始的以有效配置能源为目的的能源价格改革，是我们所认为的下一个五年计划的重点。对宏观调控政策的依赖使企业未能对它们的生产和投资决定负责，导致了资源配置缺乏效率。英国政府相信中英双方可以在很多领域进行交流，中国可以借鉴英国的经验。我们乐于提供技术上的帮助，并提供建议和支持。我们曾将30年的大好时光用于痛苦地改革英国本国经济。经历了这一改革阶段，我们成为自由市场改革的支持者。因此我们非常乐于与中国分享我们在国有—私营部门关系、市场监管、劳动力改革等方面的经验和教训。这样做对我们将有教育的意义，同时也希望这些经验能帮助中国更好地利用全球市场的机会。

总而言之，鉴于过去25年里中国在经济体制改革中体现出的创新能力和毅力，我对中国成为世界经济强国很有信心。如我所说，中国还需进行一些艰难的改革。但中国已经证明了它应对经济挑战的能力。毫无疑问，积极的改革措施将继续实施。经历了25年的成功，改革的进程将不可逆转。新的五年计划指出的道路将能够进一步地深化这些改革，同时实行一系列更加均衡、更加人性化的政策。总的来说，这些改革对中国有益无害。而对中国有益的，就是对国际社会有益的。谢谢。

现场对话

听众：非常感谢大使先生。我叫吴志攀，是法学院的教授和北京大学的副校长。感谢您为我们演讲。我的问题是，您在讲座中提到英国是在中国的最大的欧洲投资者。但我记得德国是欧洲在华投资第一大国，是这样么？

韩魁发：我和德国大使讨论过这个问题。你可以问他同样的问题，但我相信他的答案和我一样。我们都是依据中国商务部的数据得出的结论。商务部的数据显示，英国在华投资总量大于德国在华投资总量，而近年来德国在华投资的流量大于英国在华投资流量。因此我们都可以说自己是欧洲最大的在华投资者，也毫无疑问都能

得到可靠数据的支持。

关于英国在华投资，我还想补充一点。当我在演讲中提到英国是如此大的在华投资者时，听众们常常会感到吃惊，而事实正是如此。我认为造成这种现象的原因之一是与我们大量投资的领域有关。可以说，其他欧洲国家的投资要更"可见"一些，因为他们投资的是日常消费品。英国主要投资在两大领域。一个是能源领域。我们在这个领域最大的两项投资是BP石油和壳牌石油，他们在大型石化设施领域投资了大量资金。但这些设施建在郊外，普通的消费者看不到它们。我们还大量投资于服务业。我们的银行在这里投资，我们的保险公司、会计师、律师都在这里。随着中国经济越来越依赖服务业，我们看到了无尽的机会，因为服务业正是英国企业的优势所在。

听众：谢谢您精彩的讲座。我来自国际贸易系。我的问题是，在您的任期内，您和您的同事能为进一步发展中英经济关系做出什么贡献呢？因为英国是中国的一个非常重要的贸易伙伴。谢谢。

韩魁发：我的任期马上就要结束了，我将在一个月内离开北京。那让我来谈一谈在过去四年里我们努力做过些什么吧。我们和商务部一起就双方互有所长的领域进行了大量研究。

英国首相两年前访问中国回国后，专门成立了一个小组来研究如何加强和中国的关系问题。组员来自政府内外、商界、学界以及自然科学领域。他们从各个方面考虑如何加强与中国的联系。

关键的合作领域当然包括贸易。此外，在和中国商务部协商之后，我们确定了5个重点领域。让我看看是不是还想得起来，这些领域包括：信息产业、能源、医疗服务、水资源等。我们将精力集中在这几个领域是因为我们非常有信心在这些领域中确实能有所作为。中国的企业和公共服务部门都对接受投资很感兴趣。这就是政府部门所能做的。我们深深感到不能替我们的公司做生意，我们只能为他们提供建议。我们所能做的,就是找出存在机会的领域,然后让我们的公司自己进入该领域。这就是我们的政府和我们的公司正在做的。

从大使和使馆的角度来说,在中国经济中,商业行为仍然可能被许多政治因素所影响。因此,有时候我们需要和中国政府进行交流以保证自由贸易的有效进行。

最后一方面是我们积极促进投资。我们组织论坛、会议或者研讨会,使得那些潜在的英国投资者可以了解中国的投资机会。另外我们也在开始做相反方向的工作,虽然一切还在起步阶段。我去过一些中国的城市,召集当地的企业家开一些研讨会,向他们解释当他们的企业发展壮大后要走出去的话,为什么英国是一个特别好的投资目的地。我们相信英国有很多可以提供给中国企业的东西。我们有着非常灵活的经济。在英国,管理费用和税收都比较低,劳动力成本也相对低廉,同时科学技术非常发达。我们试图吸引那些我们认为能够通过在英国投资而获利的中国企业去英国。这些就是政府、大使馆和大使应该继续做下去的工作。

听众:我来自北京大学经济学院。我的问题是现在英国的新工党政府强调知识经济,有一个口号是"教育、教育、教育",在你看来,英国在社会福利方面花费的巨大开支的成本与收益是什么?在你看来,中国应该如何改进其教育系统和医疗福利系统?

韩魁发:你讲得很对。工党政府确实实施了一系列政策来满足人们的社会需要。我们感觉有时,特别是在欧洲,人们并没有很好地理解这样的政策。有些其他的欧洲政府持一种更加保护主义的态度。某些时候他们会称英国政府的做法为"过度开明"。我们试图让经济更加自由化,以促使货物、劳动力和资本更加有效地流动,同时还要保证经济的参与者获得足够的社会保障。我认为我们在这方面取得了一定的成功。在过去的几年中,英国的经济增长率当

然比不上中国，因为英国的经济已经是一个成熟的经济，但我们的经济增长速度已经大大高于欧盟国家的平均水平，比一些主要欧盟成员国都要高。我们在教育和医疗方面投入了大量的资金。如果说英国人民目前还没有完全认同这样大的投入已经带来了同样多的效率方面的回报，这种说法是对的。我想这对政府来说是件令人沮丧的事情，他们也还没有找到问题的答案。医疗开支增长了许多，教育开支增长了许多，但人们普遍认为虽然这两方面有了一些提高，但提高得还不够。首相非常明确地表示，在他的第三个任期里将致力于将这些额外的投入更好地转化为消费者的有效收益。

我觉得我无法对贵国应该如何在教育及医疗领域进行额外投资提出什么建议，如果那样做的话就显得我太自以为是了。不过我们通过我们的国际发展部参与了中国的教育和医疗体系的工作，比如，我在包括甘肃省在内的一些地方度过了一段非常有意义的时间，了解农村的教育和医疗状况。我们试图做出一些贡献。当然，资金还是要来自于中国的中央政府和地方政府。这些资金正在增加，我们也看到了一些变化。这些都是令人振奋的。

听众：谢谢你，Hum 先生。我是一名来自清华大学的学生。自1978 年以来，中国的经济建设取得了巨大的成就，我认为那是一个奇迹，作为中国人，我们都感到自豪。但同时也出现了一个问题，那就是贫富差距以及东部和西部的差距增大了。你能为如何缩小这个差距提出一些建议吗？

韩魁发：我一直有些担心会遇到听众要求我给中国政府提出一些建议，因为这只有一名非常称职的发展经济学家才能胜任。不过中国有一个问题有些引起我们的担忧，那就是有关税收和政府支出。中国的地方政府收入十分有限，但它们同时担负着非常重要的提供社会保障的责任。这一点令我们感到震动。地方政府在很大程度上要负责提供医疗服务和教育。这令基层政府在提高这些福利方面产生了问题。当然,中国也有一些机制使得富裕的省份可以帮助贫困的省份,但似乎这种转移支付的幅度还不足以满足西部贫困省份的要求。我们认为如何增大这种转移支付的力度从而使东部富裕省份和西部贫困省份缩小差距是一个值得考虑的问题。

从英国政府的角度,我们试图通过两个途径来为解决这个问题做出一些小小的贡献。正如我刚才提到的,我们有一个援助计划,针对西部和西南的贫困地区,主要是甘肃和湖南。同时,我们也鼓励英国公司考虑在中国西部投资的优势。目前对外国公司来说,在中国西部而不是东部投资将获得很可观的优惠。除了日常费用比较低以外,还有政策上的优惠。我们试图让我们的公司注意到这一点。作为单个公司在中国西南部投资最多的就是一家英国公司,BP石油。他们在重庆有非常大的投资,也做得十分成功。我们把它作为一个其他英国公司可以考虑仿效的例子。

Open World, Open China

Sir Christopher Hum, British Ambassador to China

November 24, 2005 in Peking University

Speech

Vice president, dean, ladies and gentlemen,

good afternoon. I'd like to begin by thanking you very much for inviting me to speak here today. I feel honored to follow in a series of so many distinguished colleagues and friends of mine, the ambassadors from the United States and other countries. They are all people I know well and whose views I value very much. And I know they've given you very good value indeed. I'm honored for I had another opportunity to meet students and staff here in at Peking University, a world class university with an economics department which has gone from strength to strength in recent years. I know you have many contacts with British universities, and I welcome in particular your strong collaboration with the London School of Economics, one of Britain's most prestigious academic institutions. The LSE Summer School at Beida, is a well established program, and I'm sure it will flourish in the years ahead. And I understand that now there's discussion under way about a joint-program between Beida and LSE.

The LSE's interest in developing partnerships with China is a reflection of what is happening not just in Britain, but worldwide. Virtually all sectors, governments, companies and academic institutions feel they must have a China strategy. Your country is seen either as an unprecedented opportunity, or sometimes as a threat. For some companies, a China strategy may involve taking advantage of the opportunity to source cheap goods and services here. For others, the challenge is adjusting their own production methods and costs to beat the competitive advantages which China enjoys. For others, it's about selling to a market of 1.3 billion customers. For students of economics, China is perhaps a more straightforward word. When they talk about globalization, they're talking in a large part about China, for what China really represents is the most significant and exciting story in the global economy today.

I have been privileged to watch much of China's rise at close quarters. I first came to Beijing in 1970. When I lived in Beijing in that period, it was obvious to me that China's economic potential was immense, but it was stifled by economic and social policies which are now regarded as mistaken. I then returned in early 1980s, the opening and reform were beginning under the leadership of Deng Xiaoping. The agriculture policies set the rural economy on the path of growth. By the time I came here for the third time as Ambassador in 2002, China was well on its way to realizing its potential and to reclaiming its position, a position which historically it held as one of the world's leading economies. China's impact on the world economy has, of course, been significant and has been growing for a number of years.

Now, it seems to us that it influences every aspect of global economic activity. China's already the largest global consumer of commodities such as grain, coal and steel. It is the biggest market for mobile phones in the world, probably a reflection of the fact that there are so many people in China. China's market for luxury goods is already almost as large as that in the entire European Union, and within decades could out stride the US market in scope and size. So no wonder the majorities of foreign investments coming here now is being directed towards servicing the domestic markets. At the same time as you all know, China's heightened demand for imports of capital and consumer goods is more than matched by its as-

tonishing export performance, making it a leading trade partner for most industrialized countries, Britain included.

China is well on the way to becoming the world's largest exporter by 2010. Last year, 2-way bilateral trade between the UK and China was 20 billion dollars. This year, it looks like to top 25 billion dollars, putting us on track to meat the 40 billion dollars target for 2010, which Premier Wen Jiabao and British Prime Minister Tony Blair set 2 years ago. And that does not include our burgeoning foreign investment relationships, which has so far produced over 4 400 UK invested enterprises. I'm proud to say UK is the largest European investor in China. I'm delighted also to see the investment is increasingly going the other way, with Chinese companies like Huawei investing in Britain. Because we want to play a role of partner as Chinese companies follow the call to go out in increasing numbers.

As we see it, the UK consumer is benefiting from low-cost, high-quality manufactured goods produced here. Many UK companies have taken advantage of the competitiveness gains offered by production in China, concentrating their research development at home and outsourcing other aspects of the production cycle to China. That is something we truly regard as natural and we truly welcome. Other companies see scope in R&D collaboration with Chinese partners, as Chinese government steps up in investment in science and technology. All these demonstrate how we in Britain see China's rise. We see it as an opportunity to enhance our own economic welfare. We don't see it as a threat. We see it as a consequence of globalization, and we see globalization as something that has to be managed and exploited. That's what our economy and our companies are doing.

China's success has profound implications for everyone. We need only to look at the global markets for natural resources to see this. China is relatively low and downward to natural resources. This is becoming a constraint on economic growth. As long as it aims to keep up the pace of economic growth as it lasts, it will go increasingly to world markets to meet its material needs. And this fact is inserting a powerful influence on world commodity prices, after 100 years of commodity prices historically trending downwards. Strong growth in Chinese demand has contributed to record prices of a number of commodities, such as oil and copper. China currently accounts for 10% of world's energy consumption, second only to the US. And this is likely to rise to 14% over the next decades. By 2020, it will consume over 40% of the world's total coal production. In 15 years, many analysts expect China to be consuming the equivalent of Saudi Arabia's entire current oil production. And even if the Chinese government could reach its objectives of reducing energy consumption by 20% for every dollar of GDP by 2010, China's significance on international resource markets will be undiminished.

A third reflection of China's global impact is the interest being taken externally in the Chinese economic success story. Over the past few years, we have worked particularly closely with Chinese governments on global economic issues. We have been uniquely well placed to do so because Britain is known to hold G8 presidency and China has held the presidency of the G20. So we have worked side by side on a number of different current issues relating to trade, to debt, and development. And we have been very impressed by the degree of agreement which Britain and China have on all these issues.

We're also well aware of the unprecedented success which China has had on poverty alleviation. We know very well the stunning achievements of China over the past several decades in lifting hundreds of millions of people out of poverty. That is something of great interest to our Department of International Development. We want to work with China to see how some of the lessons of China can be applied to regions such as Africa.

The rest of the world feels that it has a stake on China's economic success, reflecting an increasing openness of your country's economy. In recent years after all, China has contributed something like 1/3 of all the

world's economic growth. No wonder the policymakers and capitalists, as well as financial analysts and other commentators asked "Can China continue to grow so strongly?" Leaving aside external factors, much depends on the extent China is able to tackle major structure challenges.

Last year, the economy was in seriously danger of overheating, given unsustainable levels of fixed asset investment growth. And there was a risk of hard landing the economy. In response, your authority implemented broad macroeconomic controls that seem to have succeeded in dampening investment. But I think it is the assessment of the Chinese government that we have not got to the stage that there is balanced growth in the economy. And to achieve that, China needs to ensure that first and foremost the income inequalities that opened up since the reform began are addressed. And we feel it is absolutely right that your leaders have identified the reduction of the inequality as the priority for the next five-year plan.

There are many reasons why the inequality has worsened when the majority of the population has got progressively wealthier. In some ways, it's an inevitable function of the initial stages of development. China's successful coastal development strategy, the process of urbanization and ongoing reforms to the way urban workers are rewarded have also contributed. There are political and social reasons for not allowing the situation to get worse. But there are also economic consequences of growing inequality. In a country where 2/3 of the population still lives in the countryside, it is important that rural inhabitants' access to social service, such as health care and education and to finance, is improved. Otherwise, the risk is deterioration of economy efficiency of the country as a whole. In urban areas too, the government is quite right to be concerned that people are not spending more freely, but rather locking up their earnings in savings. Sure, there has been consumption growth, with sharp increases in automobile consumption and spending on household improvement. But consumer demand has not taken off in the way you might have imagined in a country with such successful track records of poverty reduction and income growth. It seems that many people worried about job prospects and poor social security provisions and have built up precautious savings. So what can the government do to address this? It is, after all, a problem that has affected many other countries, such as Japan, in recent years. I suggest the government could do still more to raise participation rates in the economy, and to help the rural unemployed to find jobs in urban areas, and by improving education and health care. It needs to strengthen the social security safety net, particularly in the countryside, with an active role for private sector provision. It also needs to encourage the private sector to act as the engine of the economy, and continue urgently with the restructuring of state-owned enterprises.

Banks needs to be playing a major role in reorienting the economy towards greater dynamism. But to do so, the banks, too, need to develop a more commercial orientation towards risks and investments. We hear from many Chinese private sector companies, particularly small and medium sized ones, that it remains difficult for them to secure bank finance. There is no case-now that China has an active fiscal policy-to rely on banks to provide fiscal subsidies in order to prosper inefficient industries. What China needs broadly is significantly better financial intermediation. Otherwise, you can't be sure that your over 2 trillion dollar savings are being put to the best use. The liberalization of the banking sector, which will come about under the WTO provisions at the end of 2006, should provide a much needed boost to finance in China.

And already there is encouraging progress in banking reforms. The fact that Chinese government has been successful in attracting foreign stake holders to four large banks, including 3 British banks among the investors shows that reforms in finance are starting to take hold. But there is still some way to go before we can say China has a consolidated banking sector posing no systemic risk that is fully open to foreign participants, providing efficient intermediation of savings into productive investments. Where the wider capital market development is concerned, China still needs to work hard to get the stock market moving, to develop a corporate bond market, and to address market inefficiency in areas such as insurance. The issue of market failure is not just apparent in the financial sector. We believe

there's also more can be done to put in place a market approach to economic policy, sound corporate and bankruptcy legislation, and modernization of social provision. The distortions caused by the current quasi-fiscal system of subsidies also need to be addressed as part of the fiscal reform, which is now only getting on the way. China also needs to take advantage of greater liberalization of exchange rate to deploy a more efficient monetary policy.

There are other areas to be addressed, too. As I indicated, the soft-loan approach has sustained loss-making SOEs for too long. The government's approach to energy sector price reform, which is now just beginning, needs to lead to energy efficiency, which we also see as a priority for the five-year plan. Dependence on macroeconomic controls discourages enterprises from taking responsibility for production or investment decisions and all these contribute to a less efficient allocation of resources. The British government believes that there are ways in which we might be able to engage, where our own experience can be brought to play. We are ready to offer technical assistance; we are ready to offer advice and support. We have spent the best part of 30 years in Britain, painfully transforming our own economy. And having come out of that process, we are firm advocates of liberal market reforms. So we are very ready to share our experience of success and failure in areas such as public-private partnerships, market regulations, and labor reform. We hope all of these would be educational to us and might also help China to take better advantage of wider global market opportunities.

To sum up, I have confidence that China is well on its way to become a global economic powerhouse thanks to its innovation and perseverance on economic and structural reforms over the past 25 years. There are certainly tough reforms still to be addressed and I have mentioned some of those. But China has shown that it can rise to economic challenges and I have no doubt that the positive approach to reform will continue. After 25 years of economic success, the reform process is entrenched. The indications of the path to be followed under the new 5-year plan should take these reforms further, while looking at the same time at a more balanced and humane series of economic policies. In sum, we believe these reforms can only be good for China. And what is good for China, can only be beneficial to international community. Thank you very much.

Q & A

Audience: Thank you, Mr. Ambassador. My name is Wu Zhipan and I'm a professor of Law School and Vice President of Peking University. Thank you for giving the lecture. My question is, in the lecture, you mentioned that UK is the largest investor in China. But I recalled that Germany is the number one European investor in China, am I right?

Christopher Hum: I had this discussion with German Ambassador. You can ask him the same question, but I think he has the same answer that I have. We both worked with the Chinese figures, figures from Ministry of Commerce. It shows that the accumulative stock of the investments from Britain is higher than the accumulative stock of the investment from Germany. The figures also show that in recent years, the flow of investment from Germany is higher than the flow of investment from Britain. This puts us both in a position that we can claim to be the European leading investors in China, and that is what we do. There's no doubt that we can both base ourselves on the reliable statistics.

If I can say another thing about British investment in China. It often comes to a surprise to the audiences when I say Britain is such a big investor in China, which it is. I think one of the reasons is to do with the sectors in which we heavily invest. It is right to say that investments in some other European countries are perhaps more visible on the street. They're more visible in terms of everyday commodities that people use. The British investment is very strong in particular two sectors. One is power and energy. The two biggest investments we have are BP and Shell. So they have invested huge sums of money in large petrochemical facilities, for example. They're out of town, no one noticed the system. So they're not visible to average consumer. Another sector in which our

investment is very strong is called services. So our banks are investing here. Our insurers, our accountants, our lawyers are here. As China becomes a more service-based economy, we see enormous potential because that will be going to play to the strength of British companies.

Audience: Thanks for your very interesting lecture. I'm from the Department of International Economics and Trade. My question is, in your time of office, what kind of contribution can be made to further improve Sino-British economic and trade relationship, because Britain is a very important trade partner of China? Thank you.

Christopher Hum: My term of office is coming to the end. In fact, I'll leave China in one-month time as I finish my job as ambassador. So let me say what we have tried to do over the last 4 years. We have done a lot of work with Ministry of Commerce to investigate in the areas we have complementary needs and skills.

My Prime Minister came to China 2 years ago. And when he returned to Britain, he set up what he calls a task force. A small group of people, in Chinese we call it "Xiao Zu", coming from the government and outside the government, from business, from academic world, and from world of science and technology. They look across the broad at ways in which we could strengthen our relationships with China.

The important areas include trade, of course. And we established, in consultation with Chinese Ministry of Commerce, 5 priority areas. I have to see if I can remember them. They are IT, energy, healthcare, and water among them all. We have tried to focus efforts because we are confident now we have established areas where we have something to offer now. Chinese companies, Chinese utilities are interested in investments. So that is the sort of things governments can do. And we feel very strongly that we cannot do business for our companies, we can only advise them. What we can do is to map up for our companies, areas we think there are our opportunities, and leave our companies to move in. That is what our companies are doing at the moment.

As for what we can do as ambassador and embassy, this remains an economy that a number of political factors continue to affect the conduct of trade. There are moments at which, in order to enable liberal trades to take place effectively, you need to talk to the Chinese government.

The final thing we try to do is to facilitate investments. We have tried to create forums, conferences, seminars and so on, where potential investors from Britain can come out and learn about the opportunities of investment in China. What we also started to do, at quite early stage, was to do the opposite. I have been out to cities in China where we held seminars for local businessmen and have tried to explain to them as their business grow and develop and go out, why Britain is a particularly good place for them to invest. We believe Britain does have a lot to offer to Chinese companies. We have a rather flexible economy. We have low overheads, low taxes, and relatively low labor costs. And we have very high science and technology. We are trying to bring in to Britain Chinese companies which we think will benefit from investing in Britain. These are the sort of things that the government, the embassy and ambassadors can continue to do.

Audience: I am from the School of Economics, Peking University. My question is that the new Labor government emphasizes the knowledge economy, emphasizes education, education, and education. In your view, what is the cost and benefit of this large spending on the welfare system? In your view, what Chinese government can do to improve its education system and also the medical welfare system?

Christopher Hum: You are quite right. The Labor government has tries to put into place a series of policies that enable social needs of the people to be met. We feel sometimes, especially in Europe, this is not very well understood. You have other European governments, who have a rather more protectionist approach to life, who have referred in cases to British ultra-liberalism. What we have tried to do was to free up the economy to make the economy is more efficient, to enable goods, labor and capital to move freely, while at the same time ensuring there is sufficient social pro-

tection for the people who are involved in the economy. We feel we have had reasonable success in doing that. Over the last few years, the growth rates in Britain are nothing compared to the growth rates in China as we have a mature economy. But our growth rates have been considerably higher than the average in European Union, higher than other major European countries. We have put a lot of money into education and a lot of money in health. I think it is right to say that British people are not yet convinced that this very high level of spending on education and health have resulted in a proportional amount of extra efficiency. I think this is a real frustration for the government. They haven't really got an answer for that. The spending on health has got up a great deal, the spending on education has got up a great deal, but the perception of the people is that while there has been some improvement, but the improvement is not so great. What the Prime Minister has made it clear he wants to do, in his third term in office, is to make sure the new spending is better translated into effective gains for the consumer.

I don't think I would have any suggestions for how your own additional investment in education and health would be undertaken. I think that would be rather presumptuous for me. We are trying, through our Department of International Development, to involve ourselves into both the health sector and education sector. So I have spend some fascinating days in places like Gansu Province, for example, looking at rural education and rural health. We are trying to make a contribution, but clearly funding has to come from the central government and the local government. This funding is going up and there are changes which we see on the ground and those are very encouraging.

Audience: Thank you, Mr. Hum. I am a student from Tsinghua University. My point is that China has made great achievement in economy since 1978. I think that is a miracle. As Chinese, we are proud of it. But there is a problem arising, that is, the gap between rich and poor and between east and west is getting bigger and bigger. Could you please give any suggestion how to reduce this big gap?

Christopher Hum: I am always a little bit worried that I'd see questions asking me to give advice to the Chinese government because that requires an extremely competent development economist. One thing which has concerned us a little is the problem with taxation and expenditure. It struck us in the rural areas the local government, in particular, have rather limited sources of income, and they are at the same time responsible for the very important areas of social provision. So it is at the local government level that health care is met very largely and education. And this creates problem at the local level in raising the level of provision. There are, of course, mechanisms whereby richer provinces can contribute to the poorer provinces. But it seems to us that the volume of funds that are transferred in that way does not match up to the requirement of the west, the poorer areas. We feel it would be worth looking at ways ensuring there is a larger volume of flows, and then the sort of equalization goes on between the poorer provinces primarily in the west and the richer provinces in the east. So that is one area that might be worth looking at. As far as the British government is concerned, we try to make a small contribution in two ways. One is, as I said, our assistance program, which is now devoted entirely to the provinces of the west or southwest, primarily Gansu and Hunan. Also, we are trying to encourage our companies to look at the advantages that come from investment further west. There are now quite considerable concessions available for foreign companies that invest in the western part of China as opposed to the east. Of course, overheads are low and there are certain concessions. We try to bring that to the attention of our companies. As it happens, there is a British company, which has the largest single investment in the west and southwest of China. That's BP. They have very large investment in Chongqing. That has been very successful. We point to that as an example that other British companies could think about to follow.

澳大利亚驻华大使

唐茂思博士 (Dr. Alan Thomas)

唐茂思 (Dr. Alan Thomas)

唐茂思博士受教于西澳大学和澳大利亚国立大学，获优等文学学士和历史学博士学位。他曾任澳大利亚外交部副秘书长、管理司司长、外交部人事司司长与澳大利亚总理内阁部国防分部部长。唐茂思博士曾任驻巴西大使 (1992—1995)，并曾在东京(1986—1989)和新加坡 (1979—1983) 任职。唐茂思博士于2003年3月至2006年11月担任澳大利亚驻华大使。

Educated at the University of Western Australia and the Australian National University, Dr. Thomas holds a Bachelor of Arts degree with First Class Honors, and a PhD in History. Positions he has held include Deputy Secretary, Head of Coorporate Management Division, Head of Staffing Branch, and Head of the Americas and Defense Branch in the Department of the Prime Minister and Cabinet. Overseas, Dr. Thomas served as Ambassador to Brazil (1992—1995) and had postings in Tokyo (1986—1989) and Singapore (1979—1983). Dr. Thomas was the Australian Ambassador to China during March 2003 to November 2006.

合作与双赢

澳大利亚驻华大使　唐茂思博士(Dr. Alan Thomas)

2006年3月16日　北京大学

演讲全文

我很高兴今天来到北大,我喜欢被这么多明清建筑所包围。春日的温暖驱逐了冬日的寒冷,这是一个美好的日子。我很高兴能够参与你们三月的系列讲座。四月份我将陪伴温家宝总理正式访问澳大利亚,然后再来中国迎接一位澳大利亚部长过来参加博鳌亚洲论坛。

温总理的澳大利亚之行会使两国亲密的合作关系更上一层楼。2005年中国是澳大利亚的第二大贸易伙伴,而澳大利亚是中国的第九大贸易伙伴。中国也是澳大利亚最大的外国留学生来源国。2005年底,中国留澳的学生超过了81 000名。

你们希望我谈谈澳大利亚人眼中的中国经济。我这里先谈谈澳大利亚人对中国经济的感觉,然后再谈一下中国经济在区域经济中发挥的作用。接下来,我将侧重阐述中国举世瞩目的经济增长所带来的机遇与挑战,以及中澳两国正在谈判的自由贸易协定如何帮助中国迎接挑战。这会带来一个双赢的结果。

澳大利亚人眼中的中国是一个有着13亿消费者、庞大的并且还在不断增长的市场,其新兴的中产阶级比整个澳大利亚的所有人口——2 000万——还要多得多;澳大利亚人眼中的中国是一个对能源和资源有强劲需求的国家,她推动了世界商品价格,如石油和铁矿石的价格。这种世界价格的增长给澳大利亚一部分地区带来了繁荣,比如我的家乡澳大利亚西部就从中受益。澳大利亚提供很多中国经济持续增长所需要的资源。今年中国将首次从澳大利亚进口液化天然气,以帮助广东省解决能源短缺问题。澳大利亚欢迎中国的经济增长,在我们看来,它既有益于中国本身,也有益于世界。

经过几十年的经济改革,澳大利亚已经建成了一个几乎没有什么贸易壁垒的开放型经济。这是一个艰苦的过程,因为它强迫企业重组,导致劳动力失业。举个例子来说,澳大利亚商场里70%的服装来自中国;澳大利亚曾经有生产大蒜的企业,但他们的产品现在被从中国进口的大蒜所代替。澳大利亚认识到,不管是对消费者来说,还是对提高经济效益而言,一个开放透明的市场和货物自由流动的机制都是更好的。政府一直帮助企业重组,培训工人以实现再就业。我们可以理解由于改革带来的政治上和经济上的社会压力,但我们仍然认为前进的最好办法是坚持改革,融入更开放、更一体化的世界经济体系。所以,虽然很多澳大利亚人依然深情地回忆起工业保护的年代,但总体而言,这些年来,经济是繁荣了。澳大利亚通过努力,已经成为经济发展水平最高的发达国家之一,并已将失业率降到了30年来的最低水平。

中国在现代化和改革进程中面临着与澳大利亚相似的问题。挑战是非常多的:扩大的贫富差距、失业、城乡分配不均加剧、环境退化与污染(这对农业和中国人的健康都存在潜在的威胁)、老龄化、由固定资产过度投资带来的经济增长、银行业高水平的坏账呆账,拖拉经济后腿的庞大的官僚机构和不挣钱的国有企业,等等。但中

国政府正采取一系列措施来应对这些挑战。澳大利亚也可以帮助中国。

正如我刚才所说的，澳大利亚能够可靠地、稳定地为中国提供其经济增长所必需的能源和资源。澳大利亚也能够为中国提供高质量、低数量的工业产品，以及食物和纤维产品，以填补中国生产和消费的缺口。而且，澳大利亚的服务业也十分乐观，他们希望通过两国正在谈判的自由贸易协定，使之在中国有更多扩展业务的机会。

2005 年 4 月，中国总理温家宝和澳大利亚总理霍华德决定两国需要通过谈判，达成一项囊括商品、服务和投资的自由贸易协定。澳中两国已经有一个很密切的贸易关系。在过去的 5 年里，双边贸易年平均增长率高达 20%。澳大利亚的公司期待着一个更广泛的自由贸易协定，能使他们在优惠的基础上更好地进入中国市场。

有些人说，农业问题是中国的敏感问题，不应该纳入自由贸易协定体系。但实际上，澳大利亚农产品数量只有中国的 1/10。澳大利亚只会帮助中国填补国产农产品生产与消费的缺口，而不会替代中国的产品。也有人说，服务业也是中国的敏感问题。但事实上，澳大利亚的服务业对中国是十分合适的。澳大利亚能够给中国市场带来世界一流水平的技术和管理经验，这有助于发展服务行业，而不会给中国的公司带来威胁。比如说，澳大利亚银行在处理呆坏账方面被评为世界最佳。澳大利亚的银行有各种不同的应对中国情况的操作方案，他们已经表示愿意与中国银行一起工作，以提高风险管理能力和完善贷款程序。但两国的双边投资关系比令人印象深刻的双边经贸关系要落后得多。这方面比较令人遗憾。下个月温总理访问澳大利亚时，将会签署很多协议，这将促进双边投资关系。我们希望这会带来双方投资合作的新纪元。

自由贸易协定可以在优惠基础上提高市场准入，从而提高两个国家的经济一体化的水平。允许澳大利亚公司以优惠条件进入中国市场,可以帮助中国全面扩大市场,提供新的就业机会和创造更多的财富。我坚信双方的谈判代表一定能达成一个真正自由、全面和双赢的自由贸易协定。

Win-Win Cooperation

Dr. Alan Thomas, Australian Ambassador to China

March 16, 2006 in Peking University

Speech

It is a great pleasure to be at Peking University today. I enjoy being surrounded by so many Ming and Qing Dynasty buildings. It is a good time to be here as the spring warmth drives away the winter chills. I am glad to be part of your seminar program in March. In April I will accompany Premier Wen Jiabao during his official visit to Australia before returning to China to welcome an Australian minister to the Boao Forum for Asia.

Premier Wen's visit highlights the close, cooperative relationship our two countries enjoy. In 2005 China became Australia's second largest trading partner. And Australia became China's ninth largest trading partner. China is also the number one source of overseas students in Australia with over 81 000 students enrolled in Australian institutions at the end of 2005.

You have asked me to talk about the Chinese economy through Australian eyes. I will first talk about Australian's perceptions of China's economy and its role in the region. I will focus on some of the opportunities and challenges from China's impressive economic growth. Then I will explain how the free trade agreement, which our two countries are negotiating, can help China meet some of its challenges and provide a win-win outcome.

Australians see China as a large and growing market of 1.3 billion consumers, including a new middle class far greater than Australia's own population of 20 million. Australians see China as a country where growing demand for energy and resources is pushing up world commodity prices such as oil and iron ore. The increase in world prices is creating a boom in some parts of Australia, including Western Australia which is my home state. Australia supplies many of the resources that China needs for its continued economic development. And in the middle of the year, China will take its first shipment of LNG from Australia to help ease the energy shortage in Guangdong. Australia welcomes China's economic progress, which we see as good for China and good for the world.

After decades of economic reforms, Australia has an open economy with few trade barriers. This has been a difficult process, as it has led to forced industry restructuring and job losses. For example, some 70 per cent of the clothing in Australian stores now comes from China. And Australia used to have a garlic industry but that has been replaced by garlic imported from China. Australia recognizes that it is better for consumers and overall economic efficiency to have open and transparent markets and a free flow of goods. The Government has provided assistance to allow industries to restructure and workers to retrain. We can understand the pressures generated by reform-political as well as economic and social pressures—yet we consider that the best way forward is to continue reforms, in the context of an open and more integrated global economy. As a result, although numbers of Australians still recall fondly the past era of industry protection, on the whole, the economy has flourished. Australia has managed to achieve one of the highest levels of economic growth of any developed country and driven unemployment to its lowest levels in 30 years.

China faces some similar issues as it proceeds with its modernization and reform program. The challenges are enormous: A rising rich-poor gap, unemployment, rising income disparity between city and country residents, environmental degradation and pollution (which has serious implications for agricultural production as well as the health of Chinese peo-

ple), an ageing population, growth generated by over investment in fixed assets, high levels of non-performing loans in the banking sector, a huge cumbersome bureaucracy and unprofitable state owned industries that drag on the overall economy. But the Chinese government is putting in place measures to deal with these challenges. Australia can assist China in meeting these challenges.

As I mentioned earlier, Australia is a reliable and stable trading partner providing the energy and resources that China needs for its continued economic growth. Australian firms also supply China with high-value, low-volume industrial products and food and fiber commodities to meet the gap between production and consumption. Further, Australia's service firms are optimistic about emerging opportunities in China for them to grow their business, including through a bilateral Free Trade Agreement which our two countries are negotiating.

In April last year, Premier Wen Jiabao and Prime Minister Howard decided out two countries would negotiate a Free Trade Agreement that included goods, services and investment. Australia and China already have strong trade relations. Bilateral trade has grown at an annual average of nearly 20 per cent over the last five years. Australian firms are looking for a comprehensive Free Trade Agreement that will offer improved access to China's market on a preferential basis.

Some people have said that agriculture is sensitive for China and should not be included in an FTA. But Australia's agriculture production is only one tenth the size of China's. So while Australia can help China meet the gap between domestic agriculture production and consumption, Australia can not displace Chinese production. Some have also said that services are sensitive for China. But Australian service firms are a good fit for China. Australian firms can bring world class technology and managerial experience to the China market to help grow the sector without being a threat to China's own firms. For example, Australian banks are rated best in the world in terms of non-performing loans. While Australian banks have differing plans for their China operations, they have already shown their willingness to work with Chinese banks to improve risk management and lending processes. To date our bilateral investment relationship has lagged behind the impressive trade relationship. This is disappointing. During Premier Wen's visit, a number of agreements will be signed that will provide a boost to bilateral investment. We hope that this will usher in a new era of close cooperation on investment.

By allowing improved access on a preferential basis, a free trade agreement can increase the level of economic integration between our two economies. Allowing preferential access for Australian firms will help to grow the overall market, providing new jobs and wealth-creation opportunities. I am confident that our negotiators will be able to reach agreement on a free trade agreement that is truly liberalizing and comprehensive, with win-win outcomes for both sides.

瑞士驻华大使

马提内利先生 (Mr. Dante Martinelli)

马提内利（Mr. Dante Martinelli）

丹特·马提内利大使在巴黎政治研究学院获荣誉学位，有丰富的外交经验。他的外交生涯包括瑞士驻美国大使馆经济商务参赞（1985—1989），瑞士驻法国大使馆参赞（主管经济金融服务）（1989—1993），瑞士外交部外交顾问(1993—1996)，瑞士驻意大利大使馆、瑞士驻马耳他大使馆、瑞士驻圣马力诺大使馆大使(1996—1999)，他还曾担任世界银行集团多边投资保证代理处轮换行政总监(1988—1989)和瑞士驻欧盟使团大使(1999—2004)。丹特·马得内利先生现任瑞士驻中国大使馆、瑞士驻蒙古大使馆、瑞士驻北朝鲜大使馆大使，官邸在北京。

Mr. Dante Martinelli graduated from Institut d'Etudes Politiques de Paris with honors. He has abundant experience with diplomacy. Overseas, Mr. Dante Martinelli served as Ambassador of Switzerland to Italy, Malta and San Marino with Residence in Rome (1996—1999), Diplomatic Advisor to the Minister of Foreign Affairs of Switzerland (1993—1996), Counsellor, Head of the Economic & Financial Service of Embassy of Switzerland in Paris (1989—1993), Counsellor, Deputy Head of the Economic & Commercial Office of the Swiss Embassy in the United States (1985—1989). Other positions he has held include Alternate Executive Director of the Multilateral Investment Guarantee Agency (World Bank Group) (1988—1989), and Ambassador, Head of the Mission of Switzerland to the EU, Brussels (1999—2004). Mr. Dante Martinelli is now Ambassador Swiss to the People's Republic of China, Mongolia and the Democratic People's Republic of Korea with Residence in Beijing.

多样化与国际化

——走近瑞士

瑞士驻华大使　马提内利先生(Mr. Dante Martinelli)

2006年4月6日　北京大学

演讲全文

下午好！很高兴能和大家相聚在这里。感谢北大的邀请，也感谢孙教授精心组织这个系列讲座。在我看来，这个名为"外国驻华大使眼中的中国经济"的系列讲座在选题方面给了演讲者极大的自由，所以，我决定多谈谈瑞士这个你们也许不是很熟悉的国家，而不是你们非常熟悉的中国。

瑞士是一个非常有特色的国家，这些特点影响着瑞士在国际关系和世界经济关系中的地位。我希望向你们展示瑞士的地理概况和面积是如何影响其在世界舞台上的地位的。

作为介绍，我想先唤起一些有关瑞士的经典形象。瑞士最著名山峰之一马特洪峰的景色、巧克力和奶酪、手表和瑞士军刀，这些都是瑞士闻名于世界的东西。但瑞士不仅是你们想到的这些传统形象，她还拥有高科技产业、高质量的教育与研发等。

除了在工业和服务业表现出色，瑞士在很多方面都力争上游。世界排名第一的网球选手罗杰·费德勒来自瑞士。瑞士的阿灵基帆船队是2003年美洲杯（世界最享盛誉的航行赛事）的得主，现在他们是2007年美洲杯组委会的主席。阿灵基帆船队的胜利是由高质量的船只保障的，而这些船只是由瑞士名列前茅的工程学院——洛桑的联邦技术学院设计。对卓越的不断追求使瑞士成为一个产生高质量的平台。

再多了解一点瑞士，让我们来看看她的多样性。瑞士位于欧洲中部，邻国包括法国、德国、奥地利和意大利。瑞士国土面积只有4 100平方公里，仅占世界土地面积的0.15%，和中国的情况大相径庭。瑞士是个高山国家，有阿尔卑斯和汝拉两大山脉，但也有重要的平原。由于地处欧洲中部，瑞士被称为欧陆的水塔。大多数流向欧洲西部海洋的河流都发源于瑞士。

瑞士有限的面积更突出了她引人入胜的多样化的特点。瑞士与邻国分享文化，使用四种语言：德语、法语、意大利语和拉丁罗曼语。拉丁罗曼语是少数瑞士公民使用的一种语言，直接来源于拉丁语。这种文化上的多样性对于只有750万人（大致相当于北京人口一半）的瑞士来说尤为难能可贵。而且，瑞士人口中的20%由外国人组成。由于国土面积有限，瑞士的人口密度在欧洲国家中属于最高的几个之一。

瑞士联邦诞生于13世纪，今天瑞士建立在联邦制度基础上的联邦政体形式是于1848年正式创立的。瑞士联邦由26个州组成，各州有自己的政府结构，在教育、公共安全等很多事务中有主要决定权。各州间的团结机制确保资源从较富有的州转移到较贫穷的州，从而保证联邦内部地区之间的差异得到平衡。

18岁以上的瑞士公民都拥有选举权和被选举权。此外，瑞士的政权通过“半直选民主”由人民决定，这意味着集齐100 000个签名后，有选举权的公民可以要求就改变联邦宪法进行投票，集齐50 000

个签名，就可以要求重新审议甚至反对议会已通过的法律。半直选民主制度存在于联邦和州两个层面。在两个州，全体公民直接就制定法律进行投票。他们在城市公共广场集会，就法律或地方政府的政策直接投票。

联邦议会由两个议院组成：国民议院和联邦议院。议会议员都不是职业政治家，除了议会职责外还保留各自的职业。他们在联邦首都伯尔尼每年聚会四次，每次大约三周。两个议院拥有同等的权利和地位。国民议院的200名成员直接代表瑞士人民，根据各州的居民数量分配席位，其议员任期为四年。国民议院并不是职业议院，成员仅获一些费用开销的补贴而不是工资。联邦议院代表各州，各州无论大小各拥有两名代表。

瑞士联邦政府又称联邦政务会，有七名成员，由两个议院共同选举产生，任期四年。瑞士总统由两个议院在七名政府成员中选出。他既担任总统，同时也是七个政府主要部门之一的首脑。2006年，瑞士总统在履行联邦总统职务的同时继续管理联邦环境、交通、能源及通信部。

审判体系由洛桑的联邦最高法院、卢塞恩的联邦保险法院、贝林佐纳的联邦刑事法院组成。正如你们注意到的，这三个法院对应于瑞士三个不同地区：洛桑对应法语区，卢塞恩对应德语区，贝林佐纳对应意大利语区。

中国的GDP增长率远高于瑞士，2005年两国分别增长9.9%和2.8%，但人均GDP就反之，2005年购买力平价调整后两国分别是6800美元和32000美元。瑞士人均GDP的高数字来自国家经济实力。瑞士有着悠久的高质量工业制造的传统，还拥有重要的服务业如旅游、银行、保险等，出口导向的制造业和服务业是瑞士经济的主要力量。瑞士是机械、化学制品、医药、手表、珠宝等的重要出口国，这些产品都在各自的领域中处于领先地位。

瑞士经济首先是以服务业为基础的经济，GDP总值的70%来源于服务业。制造业也依然十分重要，主要由高科技产业构成。受限于国土面积狭小多山，农业规模十分有限，是资本密集型产业。瑞士发展成为高附加值和高科技经济的部分原因是由于国土面积狭小，此外，瑞士除水力资源外，其他自然资源匮乏。有限的国土和较少的人口规模造就了瑞士经济的竞争力。容量很小的国内市场使得瑞士无法像中国同业一样进行大批量生产。瑞士企业必须极富竞争力，在国际市场上出售高质量产品及服务，以弥补国内市场不能满足产业利益的缺憾。这就必须对教育和研究进行大量的投资，这一点我稍后会再详细展开。

由于瑞士企业需要具有强大的竞争力，瑞士经济发展成为高附加值的、高度专业化的经济。除了银行业、金融服务业和保险业，瑞士在制药、环境技术、高级化工产品、医学科技、信息及通讯技术和奢侈品等方面也居世界领先地位。然而有趣的是，瑞士经济的98%由中小企业组成，这证实了创新不仅存在于先进的跨国公司，而且渗透到经济的各个层面。中小企业多数产品用于出口，成为特定市场和大型跨国公司的供应商。

因此，国际贸易对瑞士至关重要。欧盟目前是瑞士最重要的贸易伙伴，占有近62%的瑞士出口额和约80%的瑞士进口额。2005年，瑞士与中国（含香港地区）的双边贸易额是120亿美元。中国是我们迅速成长的贸易伙伴，虽然它在我们的全球贸易中所占份额还很有限。但这一份额会随着中国经济的增长而增长。中国（含香港地区）已经是我们在亚洲最大的贸易伙伴。

瑞士通过在国外进行直接投资广泛地参与海外经济。有270多家瑞士公司在中国设立了超过600家分支机构，主要集中在北京、上海和广州地区。瑞士是中国第15大外国直接投资者。有些规模巨大的著名瑞士企业已经在中国经营了几十年。例如雀巢公司已经进入中国市场20多年，拥有超过10 000名在华员工。

瑞士的经济实力也源自作为高质量旅游胜地的发展潜力。原生

态的环境、优美的风景、顶尖的观光设施、冬夏季节的丰富变化和体育活动,都是瑞士旅游业主要财富。

瑞士经济的潜力依赖于创新。因此,教育和研究是最重要的。教育方面,瑞士拥有12所大学,60所高等教育学院和一些大型研究设施,许多都处于国际领先地位。瑞士大学的教席也很多样化,4 800多名教授中的1/3是外国教授。公共和私人在教育方面的投资也是成功的重要原因。瑞士是世界上教育投资占GDP比例第三高的国家。

教育和研究是息息相关的,因此瑞士对研究也进行了大量投资。瑞士对研发的投入占GDP的2.6%,是世界研发投入最高的国家之一。这说明瑞士在专利保护和科技投入所带来的研究结果与实际应用方面处于世界领先地位。瑞士每百万人口的科技出版物数量居世界第一,这说明了研究的质量。瑞士有23位诺贝尔奖获得者,这也进一步证明了这一点。爱因斯坦曾是瑞士公民,他得知自己获得诺贝尔奖的消息的时候正在上海。他可能是我们的诺奖得主中最著名的一位。

瑞士的研究中心在生命科学、纳米技术、信息和通讯技术和环境科学等方面硕果累累。这些研究中心与国际研究网络相融合。以日内瓦的欧洲粒子物理研究所为例,那里有着世界最大的粒子加速器,协调着许多国家在粒子物理领域的研究合作。此外,瑞士是欧盟第六个科技研发框架计划的成员。

透明性和知识产权保护对我们来说十分重要。我们出口的高质量产品需要大量研究的支持,所以我们投资的研究必须受到保护。我相信随着中国研发质量的提高,中国将会越来越重视知识产权的保护。

现在我想讲一下瑞士的外交政策。国际社会正面临着和平安全的威胁以及经济不平等、环境污染、移民、公众健康等问题的挑战,这些问题需要一个相互依赖的国际社会共同应对。作为国际社会的一员，瑞士也极其重视这些问题，积极参与建设一个更安全、稳定、繁荣的世界。

因此，瑞士十分重视其外交政策，我们追求五项目标。第一，作为具有长期中立传统的国家，瑞士提倡国家之间的和平共处。第二，是尊重人权和民主，瑞士的人道主义传统可以上溯到1863年国际红十字会组织在日内瓦成立。我想指出，瑞士和中国从1991年开始就进行着非常有建设性的人权方面的对话。第三，是保护自然资源，瑞士认为合理利用地球的自然资源是至关重要的，我们抓住一切机会宣传可持续发展的开发。瑞士的科技创新对发展更环保的技术和工业加工程序贡献良多，这也是我们这一目标的体现。我们的第四个目标是在世界经济中建立更好的框架条件，以保护瑞士的海外经济利益。第五，是我们通过积极的发展援助政策来对抗贫困。

最后，说到瑞士的外交政策就不得不提"国际化瑞士"的传统。这与瑞士在许多政府性和国际性组织中的主持人地位密不可分。我们的主办国传统可以追溯到19世纪。比如1863年国际红十字会组织在日内瓦成立。之后的一个世纪里，许多国际组织在瑞士成立，其中包括：1919年，国际联盟；1920年，国际劳工组织；1979年，多边裁军谈判会议；1995年，世界贸易组织。当然，国际化瑞士的核心因素是1945年联合国欧洲总部在日内瓦成立，七个专门机构随之而来。今天，有近2/3的联合国活动在日内瓦举行。

中瑞两国关系根深蒂固。我们早在1950年1月就承认了中华人民共和国，并于1950年9月建立了外交关系。中国是瑞士在亚洲最大的贸易伙伴。我们也一直在努力加深中瑞在政治、经济、科学、教育、文化和环境等方面的合作关系。在环境问题、联合国在多边合作中所起的作用及和平解决冲突等方面，中瑞双方具有广泛共识。我们正就朝鲜半岛的核危机以及其他国际事务与中国进行讨论。

你们可以在瑞士的门户网站上了解更多关于瑞士的信息，但我也十分乐意回答你们现在提出的问题。谢谢。

现场对话

听众：马提内利先生，您好，我是经济学院大三的学生。我知道您主要在欧洲接受教育，来中国任职之前在欧洲生活了很长时间。我想请问您认为欧洲和中国最大的差异在哪里？这些差异会影响您的决策么？您对增进欧洲和中国的经济合作有何见解？谢谢。

马提内利：谢谢你的问题。对第一次来中国的人来说，可以在中国看到现在欧洲所没有的无限生机与动力。欧洲是一个成熟的经济，过去几年增长率很低，在1%到3%的水平。在中国，所有的事物都在变化发展，而且不局限于东部沿海地区。我曾去过中国内陆，中国的西部地区，那里也在不断进步。来到中国不仅可以看到一个强大的经济体的活力，也可以看到一个日新月异的社会。

当然，在这强大的经济和不断变化的社会中也存在着不平衡，有着许多差异，这些差异组合在一起并被中国的高增长率所放大。但同时，中国的高增长率也应该能解决这些不平衡问题。因此中国继续增长不仅对中国十分重要，对这个地区和世界的其他国家也很重要，因为他们在和中国进行贸易往来，他们需要中国继续增长来为自身的经济增添动力。

听众：谢谢大使先生。我是经济学院的教师，来自风险管理与保险学系。很高兴您在演讲中多次提到保险业。我的问题是，您如何看待保险业在瑞士国民经济中的地位？您还提到了联邦保险法院，这是专门处理保险纠纷的法院么？谢谢。

马提内利：第二个问题很容易回答。是的，这是一个专门处理保险纠纷的法院。

保险在瑞士具有双重地位。对瑞士人来说，保险是一个庞大的社会保障系统，保障范围包括所有人，是全体人口的安全网。当然，我们和其他一些欧洲国家一样在为这个系统融资方面遇到了一些困难。这是保险作为社会保障网络的一面。

另一方面是保险产业。由于银行业给国际性公司的资本需求以强有力的支持，瑞士的保险业特别发达。自工业革命开始，保险业就是瑞士产业历史上的重要部分。瑞士是继英国之后第二个完成工业革命的国家，瑞士保险业伴随着瑞士工业的发展而发展。如前所述，由于国内市场规模有限，瑞士工业在发展初期就必须走向海外谋求盈利，保险业者则跟随瑞士公司走向海外进行投资，并在近到邻国、远到拉美国家的范围内进行销售，这使得瑞士保险公司在全球业界中举足轻重。瑞士保险公司也是第一批在中国开设办事处的公司之一，中国政府颁给外资保险公司的第一批执照里就有瑞士的保险公司。

听众：我是北大法学院的学生，专业是国际法。我想问一个有关欧盟宪法的问题。我们知道，受一些国家否决票的影响，欧盟宪法的起草最近遇到了一些阻碍。您是如何看待欧盟宪法的前景的呢？谢谢。

马提内利：瑞士并不是欧盟成员。尽管我们和欧盟之间有着千丝万缕的联系，我们和欧盟之间的贸易十分可观，并与欧盟国家在各个领域中有超过一百项的协议。

欧盟一体化的趋势是渐进式的。有时这一进程推进了，有时又陷入僵局，有时需要一段时间巩固已有的成果，这种反复持续了好些年。一体化程度深化到许多新领域，一体化的范围也得到了扩大，欧盟从最初6个国家组成的经济体扩充到了现在的25个成员国。当然，在过去的三四年里，欧盟的活力不那么明显，这与其在一

次重要的扩张中吸纳了10个发展程度迥异的新成员有关。因此，这是欧盟将面临的一大挑战。

然后是欧盟的政治问题。随着欧盟的扩大，各成员国对一体化的看法不同，这需要时间来磨合。因此，欧盟的改革近期看起来进展缓慢。欧盟因新宪法在去年未获通过而遭到批评，但是宪法的挫折很大程度上与某些投否决票国家的内部事务有关。我认为大家可以想象出欧盟的缓慢地走向一体化的前景，同时在这个过程中会逐步解决面临的挑战。根据历史所呈现的态势，在未来几年里欧盟会有新的进步，展现新的活力。

听众：谢谢您，大使先生。我是经济学院的教师。您在讲座中提到瑞士经济是高价值驱动的，而我们知道，中国经济主要依靠低廉的劳动力价格。您如何看待两国经济合作的前景？

马提内利：瑞士和中国之间的经济合作是很良好的，还存在着进一步发展的潜力。我们经济的特点决定了我们不会遭遇大量中国产品抢占我们的市场、威胁我们产业的问题。比如我们没有很大的纺织业。我们没有碰到别的欧洲或北美国家在该产业里碰到的难题。瑞士有一个小规模的纺织业，但该行业专门供应巴黎、罗马时装界的高级服装所用的布料。因此我们不会为纺织业的贸易所伤。

这也解释了我们能够不对中国进口的纺织品使用配额。即使在WTO或GAAT允许配额的情况下，瑞士也从来没有使用过配额。我们的市场一直对中国的出口商品自由开放。

同时我们还向中国输出高品质的产品，投资高质量基础设施，因为我们认为中国经济需要这些产品和服务。这就是我们在中国的贸易和投资如此成功的原因。由于瑞士公司集中生产高科技产品、提供高质量服务，我们是少见的能维持对中国贸易顺差的国家之一。

现在中国产业在不断升级,中国开始出口越来越多的高科技产品。因此瑞士企业开始在中国设立研究实验室,目标是在中国生产高科技产品来供应中国国内及海外市场。

Diversity and Internationalization

—Approaching Switzerland

Mr. Dante Martinelli, Swiss Ambassador to China

April 6, 2006 in Peking University

Speech

Good afternoon. I'm very pleased to be here with you this afternoon. I would like to thank the University for its Invitation and Professor Sun for organizing the "Chinese Economy in the Eyes of Foreign Ambassadors" lectures. I understand that total liberty is given to the speaker to choose his subject. Hence, I have decided to speak not about China, which I am sure you know well enough, but rather about a country you might know less about, namely Switzerland, my country.

Switzerland has very specific characteristics and those have an impact on Swiss positions in international relations and global economic realities. I hope to show you in what way the geography and size of Switzerland influence its place in the world and its policies.

By way of introduction, I would like to evoke some well-known images of Switzerland. The mountain scenery of Matterhorn, one of Switzerland's most famous peaks, is one of them. Chocolate and cheese also come to mind, as well as watches and Swiss army knives. But there is more to Switzerland than those traditional images would lead you to think. Switzerland also stands for high performance, high technology and top quality education and R&D, among other things.

Switzerland embodies an idea of high performance, and does so not only in industry and services. The world's number one tennis player, Roger Federer, is Swiss. Team Alinghi from Switzerland was the winner of the 2003 America's Cup, the world's most prestigious sailing event, and is now chairing the organizing committee of the 2007 America's Cup. Alinghi's victory was obtained thanks to its high grade boats which were developed in cooperation with the Federal Institute of Technology in Lausanne, one of Switzerland's leading engineering schools. This constant quest for excellence defines Switzerland as a high quality environment.

To learn a little more about Switzerland, let us examine its diversity. Switzerland lies in the middle of Europe and shares borders with France, Germany, Austria and Italy. Its size is only 41 000 square kilometers, only 0.15% of the world's total surface, quite unlike China. It is an alpine country with two chains of mountains, the Alps and the Jura, but also possesses important plains. Due to its geographical position in the middle of Europe, Switzerland is known as the "water tower" of the continent. Most of the rivers flowing to the seas of Western Europe take their source in Switzerland.

Switzerland's limited size only serves to highlight the fascinating diversity of the country. It shares the culture of its neighbors. Thus, there are four national languages in the country, namely German, French, Italian and Rumantsch, the latter being a language coming directly from Latin and spoken by a small number of citizens. This cultural variety is exceptional for a total population of 7.5 million people only, about half of the population of Beijing. Besides, 20% of the population is composed of foreigners. Due to the limited size of its territory, Switzerland has one of Europe's highest population densities.

The Swiss Confederation was born in the 13th century. The structures of the present Federal state, based on federalism, were created in 1848.

The Confederation consists of 26 cantons that have their own governmental structures and retain major decision-making powers in certain fields of competence like education or public security. A solidarity mechanism ensures resources are spread evenly among richer and poorer cantons in order to keep the balance between different regions of the Confederation.

Swiss citizens 18 years and older can vote in elections and be elected to office. Additionally, Switzerland's political rights rely heavily on the people through what is known as "semi-direct democracy". This means citizens can ask for a vote to change the federal constitution by collecting 100 000 signatures, while with 50 000 signatures a group of citizens can ask for a vote to change or oppose a law which has been voted by Parliament. Semi-direct democracy exists both at the federal and the canton levels. In two cantons, the population participates directly in the vote of laws. They meet in the city's public square and vote directly on laws and local Government decisions.

The Federal Assembly, the Swiss parliament, is composed of two Chambers: the national Council and the Council of States. Parliamentary deputies are not professional parliamentarians, but instead retain their own occupation alongside their parliamentary mandate. They meet in Bern, the federal capital, for four sessions per year, each one lasting about three weeks. Both chambers have equal rights and equal status. The National Council is the direct representative of the people and consists of 200 members. The seats are distributed according to the number of inhabitants in each canton. The legislative mandate is four years. The National Council is not a professional chamber; its members only receive a compensation for their expenses as opposed to a wage. The Council of States represents the cantons. Each canton, large and small, is entitled to two representatives.

The Swiss Government is the Federal Council, which consists of seven members elected by the two Chambers of the Federal Assembly for a four-year term. The President of the Swiss Confederation is elected by the Chambers among the seven members of the Federal Council. He holds this office and at the same time continues to head one of the seven major Government departments. In 2006, the President of the Swiss Confederation is also the Head of the Federal Department of Environment, Transport, Energy and Communications.

The judiciary is composed of the Federal Supreme Court in Lausanne, the Federal Insurance Court in Lucerne, and the Federal Criminal Court in Bellinzona. As you may notice, the three head courts are spread over three different regions of Switzerland: French-speaking in Lausanne, German-speaking in Lucerne and Italian-speaking in Bellinzona.

GDP growth is much faster in China than it is in Switzerland, at 9.9% and 2.8% respectively in 2005, but GDP per capita is the other way around, standing at US $6 800 and US $32 000 respectively (2005 purchasing power parity). This towering GDP per capita figure for Switzerland is due to the strength of the national economy. Switzerland's economic might rests on a liberal economic system. A long tradition of high-quality industrial manufacturing and an important services sector (tourism, banks, insurance to name but a few), both of which are export-oriented, are the main strengths of the Swiss economy. Switzerland is an important producer of machinery, chemicals, pharmaceuticals, watches and jewelry. Those products are often leaders in their respective fields.

The Swiss economy is first and foremost a service-based economy. The services sector accounts for close to 70% of total GDP. The manufacturing sector is still very important and is composed of high-tech industries, while the agricultural sector, due to small and mountainous surfaces, is both very limited and capital intensive. Switzerland has developed into a high-value, hi-tech economy partly as a consequence of its size. Additionally, the country lacks natural resources, with the only exception of hydro-power. Limited territory and a small population are important explanatory elements for Switzerland's competitiveness. A small domestic market means Swiss industries cannot mass produce, unlike their Chinese counterparts. Because the domestic market is too small to meet the interests of the local industry, Swiss firms need to be extremely competitive

and go abroad to sell high-quality goods and services. This in turn entails substantial investments in education and research, a point I will come back to in more detail later.

As a result of Swiss firms' need to be tremendously competitive, the Swiss economy has developed into a high-value, specialized economy. Switzerland is among the global leaders in pharmaceuticals, environmental technologies, high grade chemicals, medical technologies, information and communication technologies and luxury products, as well as in banking, financial services and insurance. Interestingly, however, small-and medium-size enterprises represent 98% of the Swiss economy. This testifies to the fact that innovation has permeated the economy at all levels, not only leading multinationals. SMEs export most of their products and services, acting as providers for niche markets and large multinationals.

As a consequence, foreign trade is of major importance to Switzerland. The EU is by far the most important partner of Switzerland, accounting for almost 62% of exports and close to 80% of imports. Bilateral trade between Switzerland and China, including Hong Kong, stood ad US $12 billion in 2005. China is growing rapidly as one of our major trade partners, although for the time being it still represents a small share of our global trade. But this share will expand along China's own growth. China, including Hong Kong, is already Switzerland's first trading partner in Asia.

Switzerland has a strong presence abroad through its foreign direct investment (FDI). In China, over 270 Swiss companies are present with more than 600 branches spread out on the Chinese territory. The Beijing, Shanghai and Guangzhou regions take the lion's share of this presence. Switzerland is the 15th most important foreign direct investor in China. Some of the largest and best-known Swiss companies have been operating in China for decades. Nestlé, for example, has been in China for more than twenty years and employs over 10 000 people.

Switzerland's economic strength is also due to its potential as a magnet for high-quality tourism. A pristine environment, scenic landscapes, top notch infrastructure and a large variety of winter, summer and sports activities are Swiss tourism's main assets.

The underlying quality Switzerland relies on is innovation. Consequently, education and research are of paramount importance. As far as education is concerned, there are twelve universities, sixty institutes of higher education and several major research facilities in Switzerland, many of which are leading global institutions. University staff is very diverse: 1/3 of 4 800 professors are foreigners. Public and private investments in education are a key part of this success. Switzerland is the third country of the world in terms of education expenditure as a percentage of GDP.

Education comes hand in hand with research, and Switzerland also invests heavily in the latter. With R&D expenditure representing 2.6% of its GDP, Switzerland has one of the highest R&D spending in the world. This translates in Switzerland being the world leader in terms of patents granted and shows the practical implications of research and the results achieved by investment in scientific innovation. Switzerland's status as global leader in terms of scientific publications per million population highlights the quality of research. Switzerland's 23 Nobel Prize winners are an additional proof. Albert Einstein, who was a Swiss citizen and learned he had won the Prize when in Shanghai, is probably our most famous Nobel laureate.

Swiss research centers have created clusters of excellence in life sciences, nanotechnologies, information and communication technologies and environmental technologies, among others. Those centers are integrated to international research networks. The CERN research center in Geneva, for example, which has the world's largest particle accelerator, coordinates the participation of several countries in the field of particle physics. Furthermore, Switzerland is an associate country of the European Union's 6th Framework Program for technological R&D.

Transparency and intellectual property rights are very important to us, of course, since our exports of high-quality goods are research-intensive. Therefore, the research we are investing in needs to be protected. I am convinced intellectual property protection will grow as a major priority in China alongside the growth of quality R&D.

I now wish to address the topic of Swiss foreign policy. Transnational challenges ranging from threats to international peace and security to the fight against economic inequalities via pollution, migration and public health concerns call for a concerted response from an interdependent international community. In this context, it is in Switzerland's vital interest, as a responsible member of this community, to actively engage in promoting a more secure, stable and prosperous world.

Hence, Switzerland grants a central importance to its foreign policy and pursues five defined objectives. The first, owing to Switzerland's longstanding tradition of neutrality, is to promote peaceful coexistence among nations. The second is the promotion of respect for human rights and democracy, stemming from a humanitarian tradition going back to the founding of the International Committee of the Red Cross (ICRC) in Geneva in 1863. I would like to point out that Switzerland and China have been engaged in very productive exchanges through a human rights dialogue since 1991. The third objective is the preservation of natural resources. Switzerland considers that the rational use of our planet's natural resources is of paramount importance and we promote a sustainable development based approach whenever we can. The contribution of Swiss technology and innovation in developing ever-more environmentally friendly techniques and industrial processes also serves this aim. Our forth objective is to safeguard Swiss economic interests abroad by working for better framework conditions in the global economy and the fifth is our policy of need alleviation and fight against poverty through an active development aid policy.

Finally, one cannot speak about Swiss foreign policy without making mention of what is traditionally called "International Switzerland." This relates to Switzerland's role as host nation for a great number of governmental and international organizations. Our host-nation tradition dates back to the 19th century. The ICRC, for instance, was founded in Geneva in 1863. Over the course of the next century, many international organizations established their seat in Switzerland: the Society of Nations in 1919, the International Labour Organization in 1920, the Multilateral Disarmament Conference in 1979 and the WTO in 1995 are some of them. Of course, the central element of International Switzerland is the establishment of the United Nations' European seat in Geneva in 1945. Seven specialized institutions followed in its wake. Today, about two-thirds of UN activities are carried out in Geneva.

The Sino-Swiss relationship is deep-rooted. We recognized the People' Republic of China very early on, in January 1950, and established diplomatic ties in September 1950. China is our first trading partner in Asia but we are constantly deepening this relationship at the political, economic, scientific, educational, cultural and environmental levels. We share common aspirations for the environment, the role of multilateral cooperation in the United Nations and the peaceful solution to conflicts. For example, we are discussing the Korean nuclear crisis with China, as well as other events unfolding around the globe.

You will find more information about Switzerland on the Swiss web portal, but I would be very pleased to take your questions right now. Thank you very much for your attention.

Q & A

Audience: Bonjour, Mr. Martinelli. I'm a junior student from the School of Economics. I know you receive the majority of your education in Europe, and you spend a lot of time in Europe before you come to China. So what do you think is the most significant difference between Europe and China? Do these differences affect your decision-making? And what ideas do you have in mind to further improve the economic cooperation between

Europe and China. Thank you.

Dante Martinelli: Thank you very much. When you come to China for the first time, it's to see and to witness the enormous dynamism which is going on in China, which you don't see in Europe now. The European economy is a mature economy, where the growth rate is very low, especially low in the last few years, 1% to 3% in maximum. Then you come to China and you see that everything is moving, and everything is growing. Not only, of course, mostly, in the east coast. I've been inside of China. I've been in the western part of China. Things are moving there too. By coming to China you witness not just the dynamism of the economy, but dynamism of the society. You're a witness of this dynamic society which is changing quite a lot.

Of course, dynamic economy and dynamic society have unbalances. You have quite a lot of differences which are structured in a way that is amplified by the high growth rate of China. But at the same time the Chinese high growth rate should also be able to fight against these unbalances. Therefore it is important that China continue to grow for China and for countries outside China, because they're trading with China and they need this Chinese growth to go on.

Audience: Thank you Mr. Ambassador. I'm a faculty member of the School of Economics. I'm from the Department of Risk Management and Insurance. I'm very happy that in the presentation, you mentioned insurance industry many times. So my question is what kind of role do you think the insurance industry play in the Swiss national economy? And you also mentioned the federal insurance court. Is that a court specifically deals with insurance deputes or something else? Thank you.

Dante Martinelli: The second question is easy to answer. Yes, it is a specialized court focused on insurance conflicts.

The role of insurance is double. Insurance means, for Swiss people, a very extended social security system, covering all the population, which gives a safety net to the population. We have, by the way, some problems financing the system, of course, like some other European countries nowadays. This is one aspect of the coverage as a safety net.

The other aspect is the insurance business. The insurance industry is particularly developed in Switzerland, because of the existence of a strong industry, and with the banking system providing the capital. Insurance has been covering the Swiss industry since the beginning of our industry. Switzerland was the second country in Europe to have Industrial Revolution after UK. Therefore, the development of the Swiss industry has been followed by the development of the insurance industry. As I said, Swiss industry has to go broad to have some profits. And the insurers followed the Swiss industry to cover the companies going abroad to Latin America or to neighbor countries. So we are very important in the insurance sector. Swiss insurers are everywhere in the world. They were one of the first to establish themselves in China, too. One of the first licenses given by the Chinese government to foreign insurers was to a Swiss company.

Audience: I'm a student from the Law School of Peking University, majoring in international law. I want put forward a question about the EU constitution. As we know, the draft of the EU constitution encountered setbacks recently because of the veto in some countries. Would you predict the future of the EU constitution? Thank you.

Dante Martinelli: Thank you very much. That's a very difficult question. The Switzerland, of course, is not a member of the European Union. Although we've seen very strong ties between Switzerland and the EU, not only in trade, but that we have over 100 agreements with EU in every field of activity. And all these since the establishment of the EU. EU follows a trend of integration which is done step by step. Sometimes it goes forward and sometimes it stays a little bit, a little bit less dynamic and consolidates the state taken previously. It has been going on that way for several years. Integration has been deepened. It

has been widened by the enlargement from the original economic community of 6 European countries to today's 25 member states. Of course, in this lasts 3 or 4 years, the dynamic of the EU has been less evident, due to the fact that there was very important enlargement with 10 new countries of very different level of development. For example, with large agriculture sector, poor agriculture sector in the case of Poland. This has to be integrated and adjusted to the higher level of the rest of the EU. So this is a major challenge for the EU to solve.

And then you have the political problems of the EU. While being larger, being composed by large number of the states, the idea and objective of EU itself is not exactly the same for everybody. Germany, France, UK, Italy, Poland, Spain, are not exactly on the same level of intention of the integration. And this requires some time to be adjusted and to be assimilated. Therefore, the evolution of the EU seems to be a little bit slow these days. It takes blames in part in failure to adopt the new constitution last year. This failure is due to some European issues, but it also dues a large part to the domestic issues that are within these two countries which has refused to adopt the constitution. So we can imagine the prospect that the EU will slowly integrate and confront these challenges that have to be dealt with. In a few years, according to the pattern in the history, we will go again forward and have some new dynamics.

Audience: Thank you, Mr. Ambassador. I'm a faculty member of the School of Economics. In the lecture, you mentioned that Switzerland is a high-value driven economy And as we know, the Chinese economy is mostly based on low labor costs. So how would you envision the future economic cooperation between these two nations?

Dante Martinelli: The economic cooperation is very good, but it does need improving. Due to our economic characteristics, we are not confronted with the problem of Chinese mass products covering our markets and endangering our industries because we don't have a huge textile industry for example. We're not confronted with problems that other European or North American countries may have in these sectors. We still have a small sector of textile, but highly specialized in providing materials to Paris and Rome, to the very high-value dresses in fashion made there. Therefore we're not touched by this kind of trade.

Therefore we could afford not to have quotas in textile trade, for example, even if the agreement within WTO or GAAT at that time permitted the use of quotas, Switzerland never introduced quotas. And we keep the market free for the Chinese exports.

And we've been exporting and investing high-quality products in China, because we feel that the Chinese economy needs and wants these goods. That's been the case. That's why our trade and our investment have been so successful. And we are one of the rare countries that have a positive trade balance with China, due to this specific sitution of Swiss economy producing high-tech products.

And we see now the Chinese industry is becoming more and more sophisticated and the Chinese economy is exporting more and more high-tech products. Therefore Swiss enterprises are creating research labs in China, to produce in joint-venture the high-tech products to serve the Chinese domestic market and for exports.

以色列驻华大使

海逸达博士 (Dr. Yehoyada Haim)

海逸达 (Dr. Yehoyada Haim)

海逸达博士在耶路撒冷的希伯来大学获得一级荣誉学士学位，在美国乔治敦大学获得中东及亚洲研究专业博士学位。他曾任以色列外交部研究与政策分析中心主任、副总司长、外交部中东司司长、以色列外交部联合国政治事务处主任。海逸达博士的外交生涯包括以色列驻印度大使(1995—2000)、以色列驻英国使馆政务参赞(1982—1986)和以色列驻纽约总领事馆政务参赞(1981—1982)。海逸达博士于2002年9月被任命为以色列驻华大使。

Educated at the Hebrew University of Jerusalem and the Georgetown University, Washington, Dr. Yehoyada Haim holds a Bachelor of Arts degree with First Class Honors, and a PhD in Middle East & Asian Studies. He was Head of the Center for Research & Policy Analysis, Deputy Director General. Other positions he has held include Foreign Ministry Director of Middle East Department of Israel, Foreign Ministry Director of Division for Political Affairs at the United Nations. Overseas, Dr. Yehoyada Haim served as Ambassador to India (1995—2000) and Political Counsellor of Embassy of Israel in Britain (1982—1986) and Consulate-General in New York (1981—1982). Dr. Yehoyada Haim was appointed as the Israeli Ambassador to China in September 2002.

高科技是核心，劳动力是关键

——以色列经济发展概况

以色列驻华大使　海逸达博士(Dr. Yehoyada Haim)

2006年5月12日　北京大学

演讲全文

自建国以来，以色列的经济由依赖农业转变为立足于高科技。在过去的50年中，以色列的经济获得快速发展，使其站到高科技创新的前沿，现在以色列被公认为世界上重要的科技中心之一。

以色列1992年高科技方面的出口额是20亿美元，而在2004年迅猛增长到115亿美元。在过去的几十年里，得益于高科技出口，以色列的工业出口也有了长足的发展，2005年达260亿美元。目前，高科技产品约占国民生产总值的15%，比10年前增长了5%。

现在，很多产业，比如信息技术、软件、医疗设备、生物技术和安全保障等，正在经历突破型的创新和发展，前景非常乐观。现在投资者审视他们的投资策略时，我所看到的情况是，很多以色列公司都是依托可靠和创新的技术发展建立的。

这些成功的重要因素是政府在产业研发和企业创新方面出台了

明确的领导、支持和鼓励政策。在鼓励投资方面的立法将继续对吸引外国企业进入以色列发挥重要作用。我们决心保持我们的发展势头,进一步增强在全球经济中的地位。我们在促进私有化、产业自由化以及与更多的国家和地区签订自由贸易协定方面的政策将进一步推动我们的成功。

外国投资在以色列经济发展中占据十分重要的地位。以色列现在有60支活跃的风险资本基金,为科技部门注入稳定的必要的资源。同时,除美国外,以色列企业在纳斯达克(NASDAQ)上市的数量也最多。很多在以色列投资的国际大公司都纷纷从善于经营、充满活力、不断创造高附加值的科技的从业人员那里获益。

我相信以色列的经济能够继续保持其生机活力、发展势头和领先地位,继续成为外国投资的首选之地。

中以经贸关系

中国与以色列间的经贸往来早在1992年建立正式外交关系之前很久就开始了。虽然最初的统计数字并不起眼,然而2005年双边贸易额已经达到26.3亿美元。

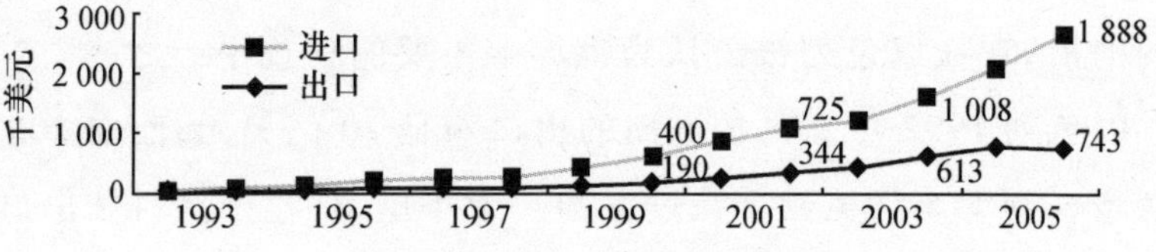

中以贸易发展(1992—2005)

以色列对中国的出口反映出他们领先行业的竞争优势:电信及信息技术、农业科技及医疗设备。以色列以滴灌及育种为代表的农业科技,在全世界范围内都居领先地位,同时也是中以合作的首要领域。在其他诸如电信、软件及医疗设备等领域,以色列企业也通过努力占据了一席之地,甚至在某些细分部门取得了主导地位。以色列企业提供的创新科技及产品能够满足中国市场快速增长的

需求。

中国对以色列的出口在过去几年中有了相当可观的增长，出口产品的组成也从低科技含量产品（纺织品、机械等）转向了更高端的产品。

中国是以色列在东亚地区最重要的贸易伙伴。由于中国市场的迅猛发展及其在国际贸易中发挥的重要作用，以色列工业贸易和劳动部已经启动了一个专门项目，以增进两国之间的贸易关系。2004年6月，当时的以色列副总理兼工业贸易和劳动部部长埃胡德·奥尔默特（Ehud Olmert）先生率领由二百多家企业代表组成的商贸团访问了中国，着眼于在中国寻求贸易及商务合作机会。

中以之间签署的主要双边经贸协议有：

- 经贸合作协议（1992）
- 投资保护协议（1995）
- 财政合作协议（1995，2004）
- 避免双重征税协议（1995）
- 研发合作协议（2000）

全球研发中心

顶级公司为什么选择以色列

受过高等教育、充满智慧、多元化的劳动力，令人惊叹的赢利性的科技发展轨迹，高水平的科研，现代化的基础设施和提供支持的政府都为创新提供了良好的环境。微软（Microsoft）、惠普（HP）、思科（Cisco）、摩托罗拉（Motorola），英特尔（Intel），西门子（Siemens）、通用电气（GE）、飞利浦医疗（Philips）、IBM 公司和 eBay 是众多投资于以色列科技的知名的国际化大公司中的几个。

企业精神

以色列的企业精神有助于产生下一个全球成功范例，就像Checkpoint（领先的防火墙互联网安全系统）公司和泰沃（Teva）制药

（世界上最大的通用药商）一样。

不断创新

以色列是世界上在研发方面投资占人均国民生产总值比例最大的国家。为了进一步培育企业精神和创新精神，在过去的十年里，以色列23个高科技孵化器为那些刚成立不久的公司提供支持。这些公司负责200个有效项目和735个成熟项目。

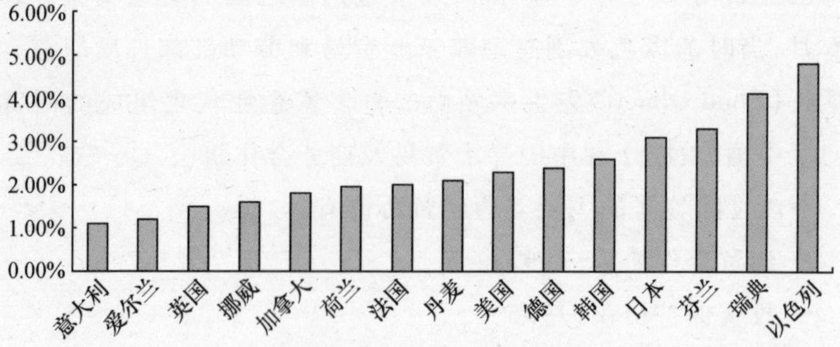

提高竞争优势的研发投入

以色列在研发方面的投资占其国民生产总值的4.8%，这个比率是全世界最高的。

来源：OECD和国家统计局。

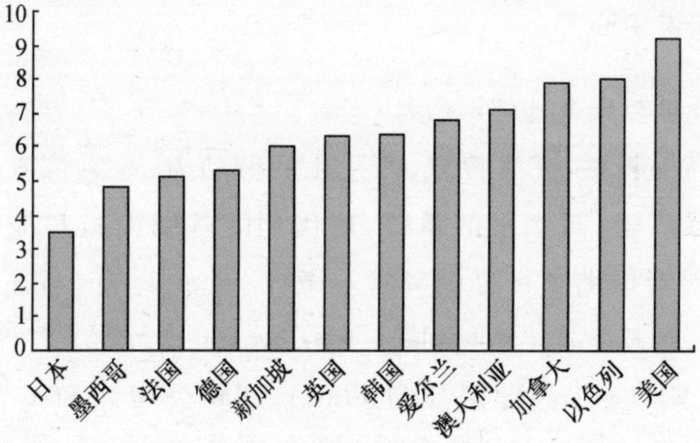

以色列在企业精神方面排第三位

来源：IMD世界竞争力年鉴。

受过高等教育的劳动力

顶级教育

作为世界上劳动力受教育程度最高的国家之一，以色列能够拥有如此众多的赢利性创新毫不奇怪。以色列是世界上拥有工程师比率最高的国家，在世界上人均教育程度和学术论文发表的比率也都是最高的。

产业和学术间的合作

以色列魏兹曼（Weitzman）科学院在技术转让创收方面位居世界第三。

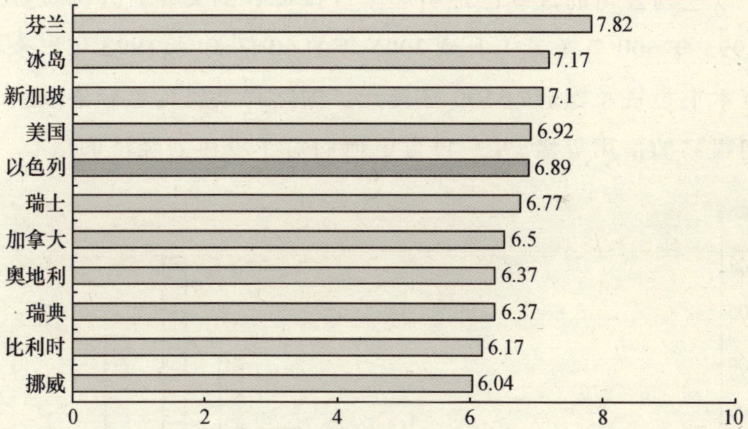

知识转让（大学—产业）

产业与学术间的合作

资料来源：IMD 世界竞争年鉴（2004）。

解决问题—创造机会

以色列国防军将高超的解决问题的能力与超凡的创造力充分结合，以色列许多最精良的创新都源于这里。在以色列国防军里受过严格培训的毕业生将所学的尖端的国防科技应用到符合市场需要的民用技术上。

以色列人能说您的语言

以色列人可以说英语和世界上多种语言,因此也可以掌握您的语言和商业文化。每年成千上万受过良好教育、野心勃勃的移民更使跨国间交流变得更容易。

骄人的成绩

以色列在以创造市场、赢利为主的创新上有长期良好的记录。现在世界闻名的以色列公司有 Checkpoint、Teva 制药、Comverse、ECI 电信、Keter 塑料、Iscar、Netafim、Amdocs、Orbotech 和许多其他的公司。

以色列公司的成绩已经引起全球投资界的关注。外国投资总额从 1993 年 600 万美元上升到 2005 年的 60 亿美元,1993 年以来在风险资本上投资总额超过 100 亿美元。国际评级机构已经连续给予以色列很高的信用等级,并一再肯定他们对于以色列经济的信心。

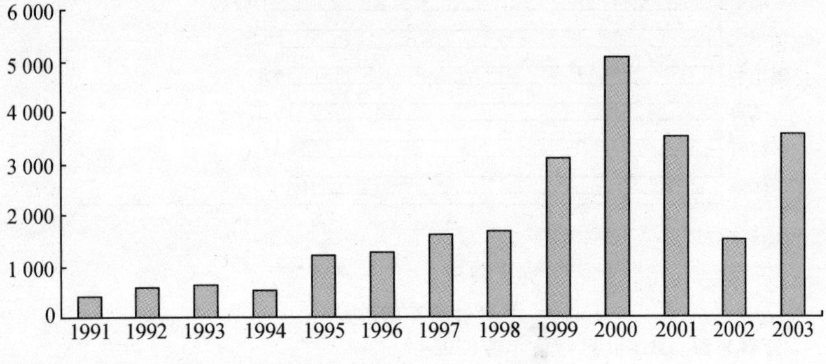

在以色列的外国直接投资

来源:以色列银行。

在产生赢利性创新方面的世界领袖

以色列的 M 系统是首个提供移动硬盘和闪存芯片磁盘产品的,改变了人们存储和处理信息的方式。

以色列通用电气（GE）医疗集团中心负责将世界上第一个微缩便携式心脏超声波系统推向市场。

产于以色列的飞利浦 Brilliance CT 扫描摄影仪为病人拍摄一张综合图片只需要几秒钟，不像以前那样需要几分钟，该仪器运用于急救室，那里是分秒必争之地。

IP 技术由两名以色列人发明，他们后来成立了 VocalTec 科技公司。

ZIP 压缩技术由以色列的 Technion 技术研究所的两名教授发明。

以色列的格文图像公司（Given Imaging）生产了第一个摄取成像相机，医生使用它能够从内部看到小肠，有助于医生诊断癌症和消化系统紊乱。

美国在线（AOL）的即时通讯工具 ICQ 技术由四名以色列的年轻人于 1996 年发明。

以色列的卡姆沃斯公司（Comverse）发明了语音通讯。

英特尔以色列公司发明了迅驰和奔腾 4 微处理器。

以色列的 Insightech 图像处理发明了一种通过超声波直接针对目标，而不是用进入体内的方法消除肿瘤的方法。

Aaron Ciechanover 和 Avram Tehnion 公司的两名教授获得了 2004 诺贝尔化学奖，他们的成绩是确认泛激素系统，对研究癌症、大脑退化疾病以及其他疾病是一个突破。

耶路撒冷希伯来大学的 Robert Aumann 教授荣获 2005 年诺贝尔经济学奖，Aumann 先生在对策论领域是世界著名的研究者。

以色列胜出的领域：

- 农业技术
- 生物技术
- 数据安全
- 计算机辅助教学

- 互联网技术
- 医疗设备
- 纳米技术
- 光学
- 安全与保卫
- 半导体
- 软件
- 电信
- 水处理技术

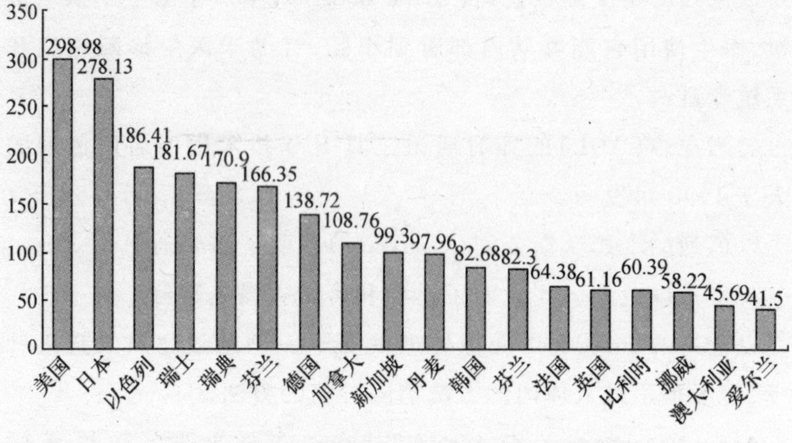

平均每年每百万人口设备专利权拥有比率图

来源：2005 年 WEF 全球竞争力报告。

支持商业发展的环境和基础建设

国际贸易和经济合作

以色列与北美、欧洲和亚洲国家签订了广泛的协议，包括：

- 《自由贸易协定》，涵盖了以色列外贸的 80%
- 联合研发项目，促进工业化合作，为这些项目提供 50% 的费用支持

• 避免双重课税的条约

现代化的基础设施

以色列为保证商业活动顺利高效地开展,提供现代化的基础设施和服务。

• 高效完善的通讯系统

• 可靠的能源设施

• 现代化的、发达的、国际化的交通系统

• 商标、专利以及其他知识产权保护

• 高度发达和透明的财务系统以及建立在普通法系和公司法基础上的司法体系

• 活跃和完善的资本市场:公司可以在 Tel Aviv 股票交易所和国外交易所双重上市。

以色列支持《OECD 国际投资暨跨国企业宣言与决议》。该宣言为国际投资的顺利进行构筑了框架。

政府支持

以色列一直致力于鼓励外资直接投资的成功开展,它通过一系列政策变化,使经济自由化发展。

• 实施自由外汇管理,使以色列国内和国外的资本存量平稳增加

• 减少关税壁垒和非关税壁垒

• 改革税法,减征劳工税、资本收入税和全球税收,出台鼓励投资于高科技产业的措施

• 将国有企业私有化,促进私营部门的发展,提高竞争力

以色列通过鼓励资本投资的立法,向外国投资者提供大量的投资补贴、纳税优惠和豁免。

鼓励产业研发的法律,对得到批准的项目提供最多可达 50% 的有条件的研发补助。

发展

以色列的国际化贸易和经济协定

- 自由贸易协定
- 双边关税互免
- 研发协定

以色列工业,贸易和劳工部下属的投资促进中心为那些有意直接投资或者建立合资企业的外国投资公司或者投资者提供全面的"一站式"服务,为潜在的投资者提供广泛的人性化服务、辅助和信息服务,它也是以色列投资信息的来源。

在此,我只是对以色列经济做一个简单的介绍。事实上,真正的蓝图更为宽广。毫无疑问,中国可以结合以色列经济方面的优势,使两国在多个领域中共同受益。愿所有的同学学有所成,毕业后可以为中以经济的发展有所贡献。

现场对话

听众:以色列的主要产业是什么?

海逸达:建国以来的很多年里,以色列最重要的产业都是农业、轻工业和劳动密集型产业。作为一个自然资源有限的小国家,以色列所依靠的是其受过良好教育、技能高超并且富于创新意识的劳动力资源。结果建设成一个在电信、IT、电子、生命科学等产业方面技术一流、以知识为基础、科技高度发达的市场经济。

听众:以色列主要的自然资源是什么?

海逸达:以色列最大的自然资源是其独立、聪慧、工作热情高的熟练劳动力大军,他们使以色列得以在竞争中领先。以色列劳动者

拥有大学文凭的比例和学术出版物的数量是世界最高的，我们因拥有人均世界最多的工程师、科学家和医生而感到自豪。

以色列的劳动力极富竞争力，这是由于我们有高效而务实的文化、超凡的独创性和企业家精神。文化、技术和主动性的结合创造了一个灵活有效的具有适应性的系统，使我们能够获得技术突破并对市场作出快速反应。

听众：以色列政府是如何支持和鼓励外国投资的呢？

海逸达：以色列集中了才华横溢和勇于创新的人，这使其成为投资的理想地点。因为开创性的企业家精神，以色列产生了领先的科技、有利商机和高投资回报。

以色列政府通过在《鼓励资产投资法》中向投资者24%的有形固定资产提供税收减免和其他税收优惠来鼓励国内外投资。《鼓励产业研发法》对50%的批准项目提供有条件的优惠。

以色列提供高效管理企业所需要的现代化基础设施和服务，包括成熟高效的通信系统，可靠的能源设施，有着现代化国际化高速公路的发达交通系统，商标、专利、知识产权保护，高度发达透明的金融系统和建立在民商法基础上的法律系统。

听众：旅行者会在以色列发现怎样的地形特征呢？植物和动物又有何特点？

海逸达：尽管面积狭小，以色列拥有大陆的多样化的地形和气候。北部森林覆盖的加利利高地与丰饶的绿色山谷相接，地中海沿岸平原是沙丘和农田，撒马利亚和犹太山岩峰横亘国土中部，在亚热带约旦峡谷和世界最低点死海方向骤降，多山的沙漠向内盖夫和阿拉瓦方向延展，结束在红海的最北端埃拉特湾。

有关您问题的第二部分，以色列动植物的丰富多样性是地理位置、多种地形和气候的反映。以色列境内有超过500种鸟类、200余种哺乳动物和爬行动物、2 600种植物，全国有超过150个自然保护区和65个国家公园，占地约1 000平方公里。

听众：海逸达大使，您能就以色列的人口问题展开介绍一下吗？

海逸达：以色列的人口在种族、宗教信仰、文化和社会背景方面十分多元化。以色列是一个有着悠久历史根源的新社会，并且还在不断地融合和演进。在近700万人口中，77%是犹太人，19%是阿拉伯人，多数是穆斯林，其余的4%由德鲁兹教派穆斯林、切尔克斯人，以及一些没有按宗教划分的人口组成。这个相对年轻的社会的特征是其对社会及宗教的承诺、政治意识形态、丰富的经济和富有创造力的文化。这些因素给社会继续发展提供了动力。

听众：以色列的文化又如何呢？

海逸达：以色列是一个有着古老历史的新国家，虽然领土很小，但文化十分活跃且多样化。4 000年的犹太文化遗产，超过一个世纪的犹太复国主义和半个多世纪的现代国家发展都对以色列的文化有贡献。七十多个不同的社区各自保留了它们的独特性的同时，整个国家发展出了自身的个性特点。

作为一个有着大量移民的国家，以色列的创造力吸收了很多来自不同文化和社会的影响，她将传统和创新相融合，并努力在保持以色列的独特性和世界的普遍性之间寻求平衡。

对文化认同的不断探寻表现在各种艺术形式的创造上。欣赏和享受这些创造的成果成为了很多人日常生活的一部分。

High-tech Is the Core, Work Force Is the Key

—Israel's Economic Situation

Dr. Yehoyada Haim, Israeli Ambassador to China
May 12, 2006 in Peking University

Speech

Since the establishment of Israel, we have turned our rural economy into a high-tech economy. In the past fifty years, the Israeli economy has experienced fast growth, which made it a leader in high-tech innovation. Now Israel is recognized as one of the important technology centers around the world.

In 1992, Israel exported US $2 billion of high-tech products. In 2004, this number increased to US $11.5 billion. Thanks to high-tech export, Israel's industrial export also gained great growth in the past decades. In 2005, the industrial export was US $26 billion. High-tech products now made up to 15% of GDP, 5% more than ten years ago.

Now, many industries are experiencing breaking-through innovations and development, expecting a bright future. While investors are reviewing their investment strategy, I see that a lot of Israeli companies are built on reliable and innovative technology.

Important factors of these successes are the policies that Israeli government put in force to lead, support and encourage industry R&D and enterprise innovation. Legislation to encourage investment will continue to play an important role in attracting foreign companies. We are determined to keep our development, strengthen our role in global economy. We made policies to promote privatization and industry liberalization, and to reach free-trade agreements with more countries and regions, which will further promote our economy.

Foreign investments are of key importance in Israeli economic development. There are 60 active venture capital funds in Israel that provide necessary resource for the technology sector. At the same time, the number of Israeli companies listed in NASDAQ is only second to the number of US companies. Many international companies gain from energetic and high-valued scientists and technologists with good managerial skills.

I believe the Israeli economy will keep on its activity, its growth and its leadership to be a first choice of foreign investments.

Economic relationship between Israel and China

The economic relationship between Israel and China started long before the establishment of formal diplomatic relationship in 1992. Although the initial figure was not that significant, the bilateral trade in 2005 was worth US $2.63 billion.

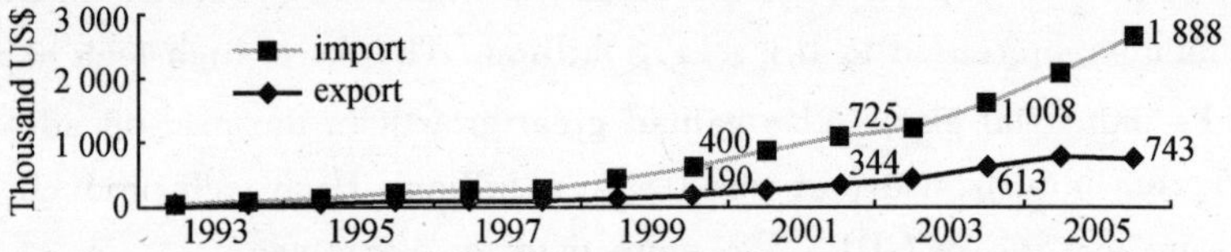

Trade Development, Israel-China 2005 (1992—2005)

Israel's export to China reflects its competitive advantages in industries like telecom and communication technology, agro technology and medical instruments. Israel is the leader in agro technology, represented by the drop irrigation and breeding techniques. This is also the prime area for cooperation between Israel and China. In other areas like telecom, software and medical instruments, Israel companies also gain a position, in

some subsections even leading positions. The innovative technology and products offered by Israel companies can meet the fast growing demand in the Chinese market.

China's export to Israel has increased significantly in the past few years, with the products going from textile and machineries to more sophisticated products.

China is the most important trading partner of Israel in East Asia. Considering the rapid growth of the Chinese market and the important role it plays in international trade, the Ministry of Industry, Trade and Labor of Israel have started a special program to enhance the trade relationship between the two countries. In June 2004, the Vice President of Israel and the Minister of Industry, Trade and Labor at that time, Mr. Ehud Olmert visited China with more than 200 representatives from the industry, to seek trade and business cooperation opportunities in China.

Major bilateral economic and trade agreements between Israel and China include:

- Agreement on Economic and Trade Cooperation(1992)
- Agreement on Investment Protection(1995)
- Agreement on Public Finance Cooperation(1995,2004)
- Agreement on Avoiding Double Taxation(1995)
- Agreement on R&D Cooperation(2000)

Global R&D center

Why top companies choose Israel?

Highly educated, intelligent and diverse workforce, amazing development of profit-making technology, high-standard research, modern infrastructure and supporting government all provide favorable environment for innovation. Microsoft, HP, Cisco, Motorola, Intel, Siemens, GE, Philips, IBM and eBay are some of the famous international companies that have invested in technology in Israel.

Business Culture

Business cultures in Israel help to create the new example of global success, like Checkpoint (leading Internet security system developer) and Teva (the biggest universal pharmaceutical company) did.

Unceasing Innovation

Israel invests a bigger part of its GDP per capita in R&D than any other countries around the world. To further cultivate business culture and innovative spirit, 23 high-tech cultivator in Israel provided support to newly found companies in the past decade. These companies are responsible for 200 effective programs and 735 mature program.

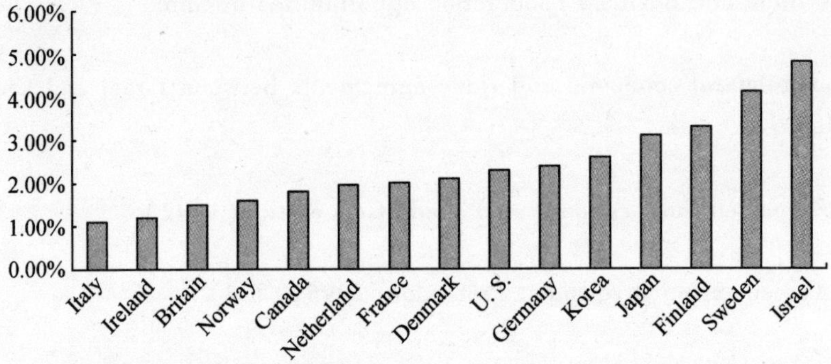

R&D investments to enhance competitive advantages

Israel invests 4.8% of its GNP in R&D, which is the highest ratio in the world.
Source: OECD & National Statistic Bureau.

High-educated workforce

Top education

As one of the countries that have the most educated workforce, it's no wonder that Israel has so many profitable innovations. Israel has the most engineers per capita in the world. The average rate of high education and academic publications per capita of Israel also top the world.

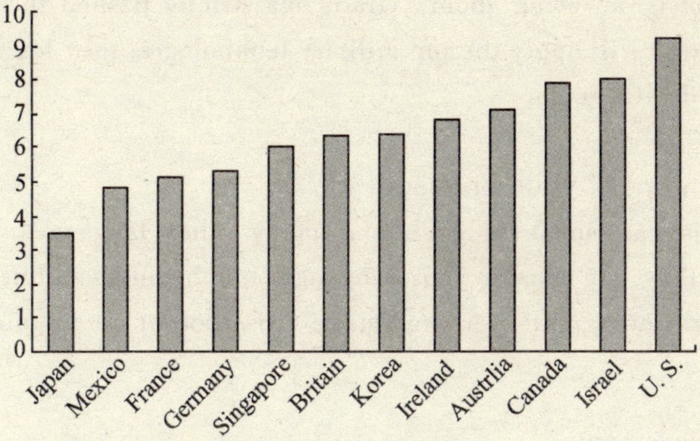

Israel ranks third in business culture

Source: IMD World Competitiveness Yearbook.

Cooperation between industry and academia

The Weizmann Institute of Science in Israel makes the third highest income in the world from technology transfer.

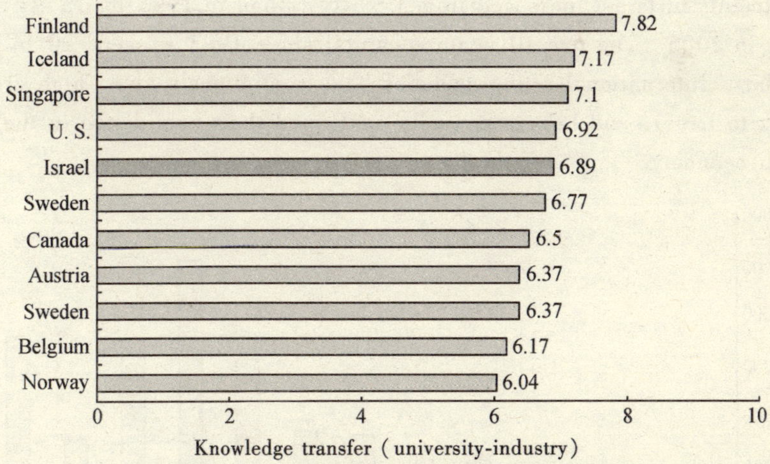

Cooperation between industry and academia

Source: IMD World Competitiveness Yearbook (2004).

Problem solving-Create opportunities

The national defence forces of Israel fully combine excellent problem solving ability with transcendental creativity, from which many excellent innovations of Israel come about. Graduates strictly trained in the national defence forces will apply the top military technologies they learned to market-oriented civil sectors.

Israelis can speak your language

The Israelis can speak English and many other languages around the world, so they can master your language and business culture. Tens of thousands of immigrants per year make cross-border communication even easier.

Proud achievements

Israel has a long-term good record in market-oriented and profit-making innovations. Now we have world famous Israeli companies like Checkpoint、Teva Pharmacy, Comverse, ECI Telecom, Keter Plastic, Iscar, Netafim, Amdocs, Orbotech and many other companies.

The success of Israeli companies has drawn world attention. Foreign investments in Israel increased from US $6 million in 1993 to US $6 billion in 2005. The overall venture capital since 1993 exceeds 10 billion dollars. International rating agencies have continuously given high credit rank to Israel, and have repeatedly confirmed their confidence in the Israeli economy.

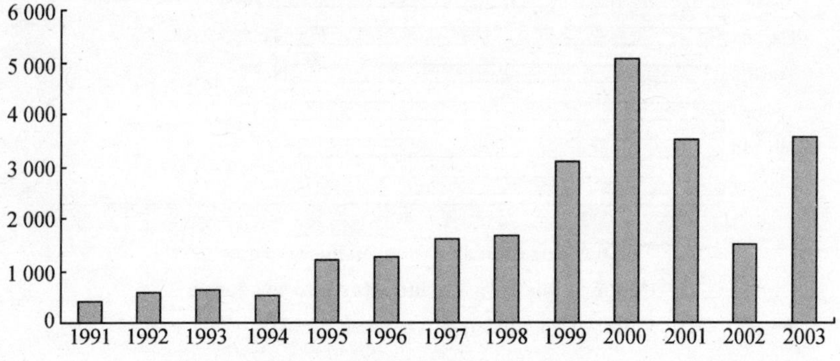

foreign direct investment in Istael

Source: Bank of Israel.

World leader in profitable innovation

M System of Israel was the first to supply the mobile hard drive and flash memory disk product, which have changed the way we store and process information.

GE Healthcare in Israel was responsible for promoting the first micro portable ultrasonic cardioscope in the world.

The Philips' Brilliance CT Photographic scanner produced in Israel costs only a few seconds to screen a synthetical picture of the patient, while it costs several minutes before. The instrument can be used in the emergency room where there is not a second to be lost.

The IP technology was invented by two Israelis, who set up VocalTec.

The ZIP compress technology was invented by two professors of Technion Institute of Israel.

Given Imaging of Israel produced the first imaging camera through which doctors can see the small intestine from inside, helping diagnosing cancer and malfunction of digestive system.

AOL's instant communication tool ICQ technology was invented by four young Israelis in 1996.

Comverse of Israel invented phonetic communication.

Intel-Israel invented Centrino and Pentium4 micro processor.

Insightech of Israel invented a method to eliminate tumors by directly aiming at the target with ultrasonic instead of operating inside of the body.

Two professors from Aaron Ciechanover and Avram Tehnion gained the

Nobel Prize in chemistry in 2004 for affirming ubiquitin-mediated protein degradation, which is a breakthrough in research of cancer, cerebral retrogression and other diseases.

Professor Robert Aumann from Hebrew University in Jerusalem, who is a famous researcher in the field of game theory, wan the Nobel Prize in Economics in 2005.

The fields in which Israel has advantages:

- Agro technology
- biotechnology
- data security
- computer-assisted education
- Internet technology
- medical equipment
- nanotechnology
- optics
- security and safeguard
- semiconductor
- software
- telecommunication
- water treatment technology

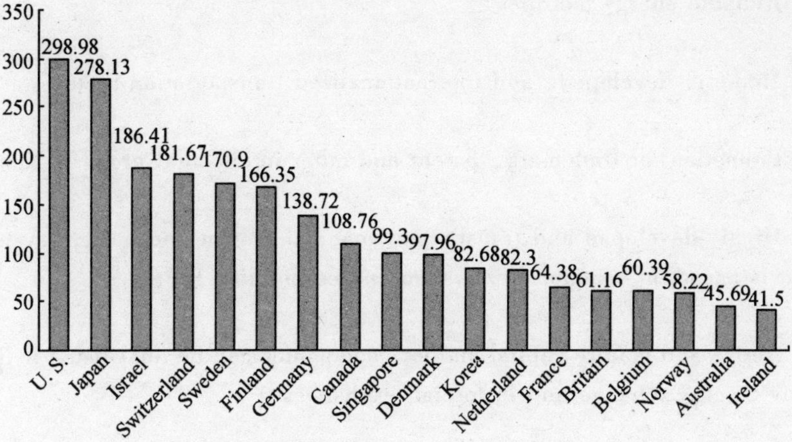

Equipment patents per million per year

Source: WEF Global Competence Report 2005.

Business-supporting environment and infrastructure

International trade and economic cooperation

Israel has signed extensive agreements with North American, European and Asian countries, including:

- Agreement on free trade, which covers 80% of the Israeli international trade.

- Cooperation on R&D and promotion of industrialization. Financial aids to these programs cover up to 50% of the costs.

- Agreement on avoiding double taxation.

Modern infrastructure

Israel offers modern infrastructure and services to ensure successful and efficient business activities.

- Efficient communication system

- Reliable energy facilities

- Modern, developed, and internationalized transportation system

- Protection for trademark, patent and other intellectual property rights

- Highly-developed and transparent financial system and a legal system that is based on common law system and corporation law.

- Active and mature capital market: companies can be dual-listed in Tel Aviv Stock Exchange and in foreign exchanges.

Israel supports the *OECD Declaration and Decisions on International Investment and Multinational Enterprises*, which builds the frame that facilitates international investment.

Government support

Israel has always been committed to encouraging foreign direct investment through a series of policy changes to achieve free economic development.

- Free management policy on foreign exchange that steadily increases Israeli domestic and overseas capital stock.

- Cut tariff and non-tariff barriers

- Reform legislation on taxation; reduce labor tax, capital revenue tax and global tax; carry out policies encouraging investments in high-tech industry.

- Privatize state-owned enterprises, develop private sectors, and help them to be more competitive.

Israel's legislation encourages capital investment and offers foreign investors sizable investment subsidies, preferential tax exemptions.

Laws that encourage R&D can offer as much as 50% conditional research allowance to authorized program.

Development

Israel's international trade and economic agreement

- Free trade agreement
- Bilateral tariff exemption
- R&D agreement

The Center for Investment Promotion under the Ministry of Industry, Trade and Labor in Israel offers one-stop service to foreign investment firms and individual investors who intend to invest directly in Israel or to set up joint ventures. It offers the potential investors with humanized services and assistants including information services. It also serves as Israel's information source on investment.

I just make a simple introduction to Israeli economy here. Actually, the real blueprint is wider. There is no doubt that China can utilize Israel's advantages in economy so as to benefit both countries in many fields. I wish all the students here can make great contributions to the development of Chinese and Israeli economies after graduation.

Q & A

Audience: What are the main industries of Israel?

Yehoyada Haim: For many years, following the establishment of the State, Israel's most important industries were agriculture, light industry and labor-intensive production. A small country with limited natural resources, Israel has capitalized on its highly skilled, educated and innovative workforce. The results reveal a knowledge-based, technologically advanced market economy with first-class high-tech capabilities in the telecommunications, IT, electronics, and life sciences industries.

Audience: What are Israel's main natural resources?

Yehoyada Haim: Israel's greatest natural resource is its skilled workforce-highly motivated, resourceful and independent-they enable Israel to stay ahead of the competition. The Israeli workforce enjoys the highest ratio in the world of university degrees and academic publications to population and boasts the world's greatest per capita number of engineers, scientists and doctors.

Israel's workforce is particularly competitive because of the informal but effective get-down-to-business culture, exceptional ingenuity and entrepreneurial spirit. The combination of culture, skill and initiative creates a flexible, working system that allows for great adaptability while producing breakthrough technologies and quick time-to-market solutions.

Audience: How the state of Israel support and encourage foreign investment?

Yehoyada Haim: Israel's large concentration of talented and innovative people makes it an ideal place for investment. Characterized by groundbreaking entrepreneurship, Israel yields pioneering technologies, profitable business opportunities and high investment returns.

The State of Israel encourages local and foreign investment by offering grants of up to 24 percent of tangible fixed assets, reduced tax rates, tax exemptions and other tax related benefits through the Law for the Encouragement of Capital Investments. The Law for the Encouragement of Industrial R&D offers conditional grants of up to 50 percent of approved programs.

Israel offers the modern infrastructure and service required to conduct business efficiently and effectively, including: efficient, sophisticated

communications system; reliable energy infrastructure; well-developed transportation system with modern international gateways; protection of trademarks, patents, and other intellectual property; highly developed and transparent financial system and a legal system based on common and corporate law.

Audience: What kind of topographical features a traveler can find in Israel? And what about the flora and fauna?

Yehoyada Haim: Although small in size, Israel encompasses the varied topographical features and climates of a continent. In the north, the forested highlands of Galilee merge with fertile green valleys; sand dunes and farmland mark the coastal plain bordering the Mediterranean shoreline; the rocky peaks of the Samarian and Judean mountain ranges in the center of the country descend sharply to the semi-tropical Jordan Valley and the Dead Sea, the lowest place on earth. Mountainous deserts, stretching southward through the Negev and Arava, end at the Gulf of Eilat, the northernmost tip of the Red Sea.

Regards the second part of your question, The rich variety of Israel's plant and animal life reflects its geographical location as well as its varied topography and climate. Over 500 kinds of birds, some 200 mammal and reptile species, and 2 600 plant types are found within its borders. Over 150 nature reserves and 65 national parks, encompassing almost 1 000 sq. km. have been established throughout the country.

Audience: Ambassador Haim, Could you please expand a little bit about Israel's Population?

Yehoyada Haim: Israel is home to a widely diverse population from many ethnic, religious, cultural and social backgrounds. A new society with ancient roots, it is still coalescing and evolving today. Of its almost 7 million people, 77 percent are Jews, 19 percent are Arabs, mostly Muslim, and the remaining 4 percent comprise Druze, Circassians and others not classified by religion. The society is relatively young and characterized by social and religious commitment, political ideology, economic resourcefulness and cultural creativity, all of which contributes momentum to its continuing development.

Audience: What about culture in Israel?

Yehoyada Haim: Israel is an old-new country, small in size, but with a culturally active, heterogeneous population. Four thousand years of Jewish heritage, over a century of Zionism, , and more than half a century of modern statehood have contributed to a culture which has already created an identity of its own, while preserving the uniqueness of 70 different communities.

A largely immigrant society, Israel's creative expression has absorbed many different cultural and social influences, as it blends tradition and innovation, and strives to steer a course between Israeli particularism and universalism.

The constant search for cultural identity is expressed through creativity in a broad range of art forms, appreciated and enjoyed by a great many people as part of daily life.

后　记

由北京大学经济学院和北京大学国际合作部联合主办的“外国驻华大使眼中的中国经济”系列讲座于2006年5月落下了帷幕。这个系列讲座历时一年，在校内外引起很大的反响。为了让更多的人从大使的讲座中受益，也为了纪念这个系列活动，我们整理出版了这本书，并借此向所有参与到这个活动中的人们表示谢意和敬意。

这个系列活动共举行了八场。美国、德国、瑞典、加拿大、英国、澳大利亚、瑞士、以色列的八位驻华大使先后来到北大，为学子们带来了精彩的演讲。从最初的计划来看，我们本来希望来访的大使在地域分布上更均衡一些，在经济和社会发展的程度上更具代表性一些，但由于各种原因未能完全如愿。大使们作为外国驻华机构的最高行政长官，都是日理万机的大忙人。有一些讲座时间已经安排好了，但由于大使们突然有重要国事活动不能抽身，最后只好“忍痛”取消。但即使这样，作为这个活动的总策划和总主持，我还是颇感欣慰的，因为这个活动基本上达到了预期的目的。对于象牙塔内的师生来说，大使们对中国经济的看法具有一定的权威性和代表性，从他们的演讲中，师生们可以获得许多对研究中国经济有益的信息和视角；对于各外国大使来说，现在的莘莘学子，可能就是一二十年后活跃在各个领域中的领军人物。通过这个系列讲座平台，经过这个最初的接触，可能就为将来不同国家的经济文化交流打下了基础，因此我相信，这是一个“双赢”的结果。

我在这里要衷心感谢北京大学校长许智宏院士。他为每位大使的演讲签发证书，并为本书作序，给予了这项活动以极大的支持；我还要感谢北京大学负责国际合作交流工作的前副校长，现任北京外国语大学校长的郝平教授，他对这个系列活动的高度认可和支持给了我们信心；吴志攀副校长、林建华副校长、经济学院刘伟院长也都在百忙之中会见了大使。我们的合作方北京大学国际合作部的李岩松部长（兼校长助理）、夏红卫副部长、外专办白燕主任、部长助理郑如青博士等对系列活动给予了高度重视和全力支持。此外，借此机会，我还要感谢我的许多同事。“外事无小事”，这是做外事工作的人都知晓的常识。经济学院院长助理章政教授为大使讲座做了很多前期准备工作；外事秘书王蔚菁女士为邀请、联系、协调、组织、安排这个讲座花费了许多心血，她的敬业、认真、细致对大使讲座的成功举办起到了重要的作用；经济学院团委书记王永健，学工办助理詹浩、石拓在讲座的对外宣传和听众的组织工作方面尽心尽力；外事助理陈东博士和经济学院的蔡钡、侯璐同学，承担了讲稿的翻译和整理工作，非常不易；外事秘书张韫之女士为讲稿的确认、修订和出版做了很多工作。在此，我还要对北大出版社对本书出版的支持表示由衷的谢意。由于版面等原因，出版时有所删节。

“外国驻华大使眼中的中国经济”系列讲座虽然落下了帷幕，但我相信，北京大学经济学院的国际交流与合作还将继续开展并深入下去，为创办国际一流的大学、一流的经济学院而作出应有的贡献。

北京大学经济学院副院长

2006年9月15日于经济学院

Postscript

This May, the lecture series, "Chinese Economy in the Eyes of Foreign Ambassadors", jointly sponsored by the School of Economics and the Office of International Relations of Peking University, successfully closed. This lecture series lasted one whole year and had drawn wide attention both within and outside the campus. To allow more people to benefit from the ambassadors' lectures as well as to commemorate this program, we publish this book, and we would like to take this opportunity to express our gratitude and respect to everyone who has taken part in these events.

Eight ambassadors have given brilliant speeches in this lecture series and they are from the following countries: the United States, Germany, Sweden, Canada, United Kingdom, Australia, Switzerland and Israel. Originally we had planned to have a more balanced distribution of countries that the ambassadors came from so that they could represent many different stages of economic and social development. However, this plan was not fully carried out due to various reasons. An ambassador, as the highest administrative officer representing a foreign country in China, has many other obligations and therefore is extremely busy. Because some ambassadors had to handle urgent affairs of state, several speeches were canceled reluctantly after scheduled. Nevertheless, as the coordinator and the host of the ambassador lectures, I feel gratified, since these events have basically achieved their goals. For the faculty and the students inside the ivory tower, lectures by the ambassadors have a certain degree of authority and represent a particular perspective. Both the faculty and the students have gained from the information and views provided by the ambassadors that are related to the study of Chinese economy. For ambassadors, students today will become the future leaders in various fields in one or two decades. The initial contact that was made possible by this lecture series laid the foundation of economic and cultural communications among different countries for the future. Therefore, I believe we've had a "win-win" result.

I sincerely thank Professor Xu Zhihong, President of Peking University and Fellow of Chinese Academy of Sciences. He signed certificates for each ambassador lecture, wrote the preface for this book, and provided generous support for the entire program. I would also like to thank Professor Hao Ping, who is the former Vice President of Peking University and currently President of Beijing Foreign Language University. His great approbation and encouragement of this program gave us confidence. Professor Wu Zhipan and Professor Lin Jianhua, who are both Vice Presidents of Peking University, and Professor Liu Wei, Dean of the School of Economics, made time from their tight schedules to meet the ambassadors. Our cosponsor, the Office of International Relations of Peking University, gave us full recognition and support. Especially I'd like to thank Mr. Li Yansong (Assistant to President of Peking University and Director of the Office of International Relations), Mr. Xia Weihong (Vice Director of the Office of International Relations), Ms. Bai Yan (Director of the Office of Foreign Experts), and Dr. Zheng Ruqing (Assistant to Director of the Office of International Relations). And also, I would like to take this opportunity to thank my colleagues. "There's no bagatelle in foreign affairs"—this saying is well known by people who have worked with foreign affairs. Mr. Zhang Zheng, Assistant to the Dean of the School of Economics, did a lot of preparatory work for the lecture series. Ms. Wang Weijing, our Secretary of International Affairs of the School of Economics, made painstaking efforts to invite, contact, coordinate, and arrange all of the lectures. Her devotion to the job and chariness ensured the success of the lectures. Mr. Wang Yongjian, Secretary of the Youth League of the School of Economics, Mr. Zhan Hao and Mr. Shi Tuo, Assistant of Student Affairs, did their best in promoting the lectures and coordinating the audiences. Dr. Chen Dong, Assistant of International Affairs of the School of Economics, and Ms. Cai Bei and Ms. Hou Lu, who are both students of the School of Economics, did a great job recording and translating the scripts of the lectures. Ms. Zhang Yunzhi, Secretary of International Affairs of the School of Economics, did many works for the confirmation, revision and publication of the scripts. Also, I sincerely thank the staff from the Peking University Press for their support in the publication of this book. Due to layout and other reasons, some parts of the manuscripts have been abridged in the publishing process.

The "Chinese Economy in the Eyes of Foreign Ambassadors" lecture series has ended, but I believe the international cooperation of the School of Economics of Peking University will continue and go further and make its due contribution to the making of a first-class university and a first-class school of economics.

Qixiang Sun
Associate Dean
School of Economics
Peking University
Sept. 15, 2006 in School of Economics, Peking University